Framing Discourse on the Environment

Routledge Critical Studies in Discourse

EDITED BY MICHELLE M. LAZAR, *National University of Singapore*

1. Framing Discourse on the Environment
A Critical Discourse Approach
Richard J. Alexander

Framing Discourse on the Environment

A Critical Discourse Approach

Richard J. Alexander

Routledge
Taylor & Francis Group
New York   London

First published 2009
by Routledge
270 Madison Ave, New York, NY 10016

Simultaneously published in the UK
by Routledge
2 Park Square, Milton Park, Abingdon, Oxfordshire OX14 4RN

Routledge is an imprint of the Taylor & Francis Group, an informa business

First issued in paperback 2010

© 2009 Taylor & Francis

Typeset in Sabon by IBT Global.

Library of Congress Cataloging in Publication Data

Alexander, Richard J., 1945–
Framing discourse on the environment : a critical discourse approach /
Richard J. Alexander. -- 1st ed.
p. cm. -- (Routledge critical studies in discourse ; 1)
Includes bibliographical references and index.
1. Ecolinguistics. 2. Critical discourse analysis. I. Title.

P39.5.A44 2009
306.44--dc22   2008014130

ISBN13: 978-0-415-99123-0 (hbk)
ISBN13: 978-0-415-88835-6 (pbk)

Contents

Tables

Acknowledgements

The author and publisher gratefully acknowledge permission to include revised or expanded versions of articles which previously appeared in edited volumes or journals.

Chapter 2, 'Integrating the Ecological Perspective', first appeared in Alwin Fill (ed.) (1996) *Sprachökologie und Ökolinguistik*, Tübingen: Stauffenburg Verlag, Brigitte Narr, pp. 131–148, and is reprinted with the permission of the publisher and editor.

Chapter 3, 'Ecological Commitment in Business', is reprinted from Jeff Verschueren (ed.) (1999) *Language and Ideology: Selected Papers from the 6th International Pragmatics Conference, Vol. 1*, Antwerp: International Pragmatics Association, pp. 14–24, and appears by permission of the publisher.

Chapter 4, 'The Framing of Ecology', first appeared in Bernhard Ketteman and Hermine Penz (eds.) (2000) *ECOnstructing Language, Nature and Society. The Ecolinguistic Project Revisited. Essays in Honour of Alwin Fill*, Tübingen: Stauffenburg Verlag, Brigitte Narr, pp. 173–190, and is reprinted with the permission of the publisher and editors.

Chapter 5, 'Talking About "Sustainable Development"', was originally published in Alwin Fill, Hermine Penz and Wilhelm Trampe (eds.) (2002) *Colourful Green Ideas*, Bern: Peter Lang Verlag, pp. 239–254, and is reprinted with the permission of the publisher and editors.

Chapter 8, 'Resisting Imposed Metaphors of Value', from *metaphorik.de* 04/2003, appears by permission of the editors, Martin Doering and Wilhelm Trampe.

The author would also like to thank a number of people personally for their inspiration, support and help over the years during which the material in this book has developed. Most of these were also active in helping to put together symposia and panels (at AILA, Pragmatics and GAL Conferences) or in organizing conferences and participating and debating on the subject of language and ecology. These are in particular Frans Verhagen (New York), Jørg Døør and Jørg Christian Bang (Odense), Alwin Fill and Hermine Penz (Graz), Wilhelm Trampe (Diepenau), Bernhard Kettemann (Graz), Ernest Hess-Lüttich (Berne), and Martin Doering (Hamburg), and many others who followed our invitations to discuss their research in the area of ecolinguistics with us. I am extremely grateful to the series editor Michelle Lazar and to Erica Wetter of Taylor & Francis for drawing my attention to ways to enhance the readability of the text and for seeing the project so cheerfully and professionally through the editorial and production process. Naturally, none of the aforementioned persons has any responsibility for the contents of this book, for which I accept full liability.

The book is dedicated to my wife Gerlinde, who has gladly and gracefully kept out of my way when the frustrations and bad moods of the author during the gestation of the book threatened otherwise to make our shared quality of life on this planet unsustainable.

1 Introduction

1 CONCERN WITH THE ENVIRONMENT

Life will probably continue on earth for some millennia. But it is becoming increasingly unlikely that human life will continue for quite so long, given the consequences of ever-rising quantities of man-made CO_2 emissions, among other things.

The current 'preoccupation' with talking about 'global warming' (Stern 2007) appears to have foregrounded an ecological issue at least for a brief span of media attention. The 'startling' pictures of melting icebergs and shrinking glaciers in Africa, Europe and Asia have apparently 'jolted' certain constituencies in the media, government and activist circles into a more serious and urgent consideration of the potential impacts of global warming on the state of humanity. Or perhaps, after all, one might view this as 'simply' one further, more irregular, swing of the pendulum of 'concern for the environment' that periodically has entered public discourse only to be subsequently suppressed. Examples would be Rachel Carson's (1962) pinpointing of the destructive effects of agriculturally applied DDT on bird-life (in the 1950s) and intensified agriculture generally or the consequences of the US Air Force (USAF) dioxin spraying ('Agent Orange') of the forests of Vietnam (in the 1960s). As we know, the effects and spread of such awareness are both narrow and short-lived; while individual historians and the directly affected survivors can retrieve such events and their significance for the biosphere from their personal files, it seems as if a Western memory hole is being maintained which prevents a sense of the past-in-the-present developing. Hence the reports of environmental and ecological disasters, like oil spills at sea or 'famines' linked with desertification processes in Africa, come and go cyclically like the stock market's ups and downs. And clearly, in the world of corporate globalisation, the pronounced priorities of the latter discount the relevance of the former (other than as sensationalized attention-grabbers) in the globally mediatized frame that constitutes the window on the world that is making the running and helping to run the world.

Even severe floods and abnormal storms in Northern and Central Europe are filed away, while the plans for additional runways and new giant airports are rubber-stamped by governments whose allegiances appear more closely aligned with hard-nosed business interests than with apprehension at the increasing propensity for asthma attacks among the children of their electors or constituents (citizens).

Perhaps the appreciation of the sheer complexity of the ways humans interact with and affect the biosphere, upon which they depend for their very existence, cannot be rendered verbally into comprehensible propositions. Maybe it is asking too much to expect people to grasp how the short-term activities they and their forefathers engage (or have engaged) in contribute to long-run and unintended consequences for the globe as a whole. As the Keynesian adage consolingly and individualistically notes: 'in the long-run we are all dead'. But not, of course, all at the same time, he might have added.

That perhaps is the crux of the issue. It seems to be 'just' talk. As long as certain families, tribes, groups, nations of people continue to survive and even to 'prosper', ecological and environmental issues somehow get relegated to the background. Why is this case? Where does anyone's interest in the way people talk or do not talk about the environment originate?

2   EXISTENTIAL AND INTELLECTUAL BACKGROUND

And what could all this concern with ecological issues have to do with language-oriented scholars, we might ask? The answer I attempt to give in this book can perhaps benefit from some biographical background. There are two strands worth briefly disentangling. The first is experiential or, shall we say, existential. The second, as we shall see, is clearly hard to separate from the first. But the spotlight is here on an academic or, perhaps more accurately, an intellectual position which has come over time to shape my professional (and personal) life. Both strands are criss-crossed by, and hard to divorce from, broader societal developments in politics, science and the mass media in the late 20th and early 21st centuries.

Let us start with the fundamentally existential position and how it impinges on language behaviour. Firstly, take the ambiguous term 'environment'. This can be contrasted with 'physical reality'. Human life as part of the broader biosphere, but as one mere element within it, presupposes the constant interaction of human beings with, and as an inseparable part of, their environment (Lakoff 1987: 215). So 'environment' is defined as relative to how human beings interact with 'physical reality'. The former is an anthropocentric notion, while the latter is independent of all animate beings. 'Physical reality', 'ecology', 'biosphere', 'environment', just to list such terms is to underline the difficulty of grasping the location of human existence at the level of individual words or concepts. It is hence perhaps no surprise to see the issue of relating to 'climate change' as humans as being, at least partially, a linguistic or discourse predicament.

Situating the predicament historically can help. There is a socio-political context which has influenced many of us in our everyday lives. The deterioration of the quality of life in the 20th century in post-war Europe is part of the context for ecological foregrounding to develop. Once there was smog and moreover deadly fog in London. Along came acid rain, killing forests in Scandinavia and elsewhere. Chernobyl blew up in 1986. So pollution, nuclear power, as well as nuclear bombs generally disconcerted large numbers of people. 'Something needs to be done' was the watchword of the 1970s and 1980s. The flowering of activist pressure groups, like Greenpeace, was one response in Western countries. Another was the growth of Green political parties in several European countries, sometimes with overlaps between the two.

As linguists and language scholars, many of us hold that language plays a major role in predisposing speakers to perceive or to construct the world in a specific fashion. And certainly, the notion that linguistic processes somehow influence how humans view the world, both natural and social, is hard to completely withstand. The links between language and society clearly exist and have an effect on 'worldviews'. But we need to be cautious here. As some writers argue, the perceptions or non-perceptions of ecological crises or of environmental problems, such as global warming or the destruction of the ozone layer, are not sensorially experienced. It is the many-voiced discourse of scientists that is the source of our knowledge of such issues. These voices are filtered and very often distorted by the media presentations of such happenings. The failure to make explicit 'where people are coming from', that is to say, what real interests underlie writings in both scientific and journalistic genres, as well as in business and politics, is an additional complicating factor in the discourse about environmental issues. There is furthermore the widespread post modernist 'divertissement' that is to be encountered in much intellectual and scholarly life today. I am referring, of course, to the view that all is a question of discourse: 'the real world is simply a discourse construct'. This has to be a bad joke and clearly an untenable position in view of the suffering millions of people continue to experience in our real world.

In academic circles the influence of Foucauldian and other socially grounded discourse notions (see Fairclough 1992) is informing the debate about the relation between discourse, language and ecology. It is increasingly accepted that representations of the 'natural' world are socially constructed: that all representations and presentations of 'facts' involve 'evaluation'.

Also we can adduce work coming from critical media analysts to show how such 'manufactured' manifestations of the socio-political world abound in our contemporary mass media. Critical media analyses, as the investigation of reporting on the Palestinian–Israeli conflict by Philo and Berry (2004) exhaustively demonstrates, can bring out the ways in which the powerful and their media mouthpieces withhold the 'truth' and distort the facts (see Edwards and Cromwell 2006). It is at this point that linguists as intellectuals can usefully remember what Chomsky said (1966: 257): "It is the responsibility of intellectuals to speak the truth and to expose lies." So, if as linguists we find language use and discourse implicated as a tool of misrepresentation of the situation, as thinking and acting and speaking beings, it is our duty to intervene.

The real world is the domain in which we live. And there is (or was) a tendency—let us call it the ostrich-tendency, for the sake of argument—to claim that the academic world is not part of this. It is fair to say that since the Chernobyl explosion (1986) (and not 2001, as some amnesiacs claim) this is a fiction which we can no longer afford to pursue—even if we ever adhered to it! We are not just academics. So how do these two worlds interact? In my own case, the existential and the intellectual planes have coalesced and this book is one of the results of and responses to that process.

The upshot of this 'cascade' of different perspectives and influences on ecological issues means a significant focus of language oriented activities will entail moving beyond what might be conceived as narrow subject boundaries. It is certainly my contention that an interdisciplinary approach is the only way language studies and actions which involve ecology and environmental issues can hope to proceed fruitfully in the future. Understanding of the way language and the investigation of ecology (indeed of science and technological applications in general) are linked requires an interdisciplinary or transdisciplinary approach (see Genske 2006 in this context). Demonstrating the link between language or discourse and the comprehension of ecological issues is a central area for interdisciplinary research to focus on. The need to factor in the social and the political ramifications is likewise paramount. Such an approach is not new for linguists and certainly not for applied linguists. They have long been aware of the need for this orientation. As Halliday says of linguistic analysis:

> Any study of language involves some attention to other disciplines; one cannot draw a boundary round the subject and insulate it from others. (Halliday 1978: 11)

Once we realize that ecological issues are social and political problems, we see it is an exemplary area for interdisciplinary research, in fact. Let me mention the work of Michael Halliday again at this point. He refers to a linguist colleague, Adam Makkai, who "was among the first to think" in ecological terms and goes on to describe his own work: "I was (one could say, perhaps in complementary fashion) trying to adopt a linguistic perspective on the environment" (personal communication). Certainly, Makkai's (1973) work impressed many of us already several decades ago, in its broad ecological sweep. So a call to show how language and thinking about the environment and ecology interact appears to have been a logical development from within certain linguistic circles for many of us. As we then saw, the important keynote speech Halliday (1990) gave at the AILA (International

Association of Applied Linguistics) conference in Greece served as a catalyst for more linguists, who positioned themselves as concerned intellectuals. Together with Halliday, many academics and scholars see this engagement in an area where language and nature come together as proceeding from a specific value stance, although there are a multitude of opinions as to what critical position we need to take up, some of which are discussed in this book.

Furthermore, we should not underestimate the extent and the power of the forces of repression at work in the world. Since the end of the Cold War and the victory of capitalism, it has become fashionable in certain circles to talk of a New World Order and an end to oppression and violence. The role the West plays, however, in earning money from producing military weapons of destruction (mass and otherwise) and selling them to regimes to suppress their minorities or just the political opponents in their countries (whether in Turkey or Indonesia in East Timor) defies credibility. See Chomsky (1994a) for more discussion about this state of affairs.

In view of the way the world is ordered, it is evident that the underlying inequality of access to information about the world—ecology or the environment, in our case—is overlaid by a façade which occasionally represents what goes on in the world as 'natural', as 'harmless' or even as 'inevitable'. It is the dismantling of the language aspects of this façade which I see as the major objective of critical discourse analysis and also one of the major arenas of intervention for students of discourse and ecology. Numerous issues need to be foregrounded in this area. For example, we must stress how 'talk' or discourse is required to appreciate what is happening to the environment. We need to underline how physical seeing alone is inadequate in an industrialized world. This position also necessarily entails looking at what 'science' has to say about environmental issues. And far from being part of the solution to ecological questions, 'science' may well in its 20th and 21st century forms—especially in its linguistic manifestation, in its propensity to 'construe reality'—since Newton onwards, turn out to be an intrinsic part of the problem.

So the dialectics of the Enlightenment force us to question and make clear not only the value stances we take up but also the very scientific methods we employ. Nowhere is this perhaps more obvious than in the treatment and analysis of the environment. We are part of and affect the very object we study. Science and technology go hand in hand. There is no separation possible between subject and object. These are not particularly new ideas of course. But we do well to repeat them in this context, I believe. The socially constructed nature of science is widely accepted by critical and concerned scientists today. When it comes to finding out what the cause of global warming and climate change might be and what actions might be taken to slow it down, we are not faced by a purely 'scientific' matter (Jasanoff 1987). As Ravetz (2006: 77) pointedly notes: "we live in a new age of policy where science is necessary but not sufficient for solutions." The question is, how many politicians are willing to embrace the uncertainty of the post-normal scientific insights (Ravetz 2006) which have become part and parcel of the late 20th century? And how is the layperson's or committed citizen's view of 'scientific' understanding, uncertain and no longer seemingly 'final' as it is, to be integrated as well? The realm of contingency seems to open up before us. Firstly, there was the shift in the epistemological foundations of science in the course of the 20th century, with observers acting as both subjects and objects as mentioned above. Secondly, the insight that chance plays a role in the mechanisms underlying the universe is deeply unsettling. Thirdly, our categories are no longer viewed as 'either-or', but because they have fuzzy edges as 'more-or-less'. Fourthly, the issue of direct human, political and ethical responsibility can no longer be denied. We do not live in conditions and surroundings which humans have not had a hand in making. This means, there is no state of nature from which we are proceeding and to which humanity can return. And to contextualize these abstract considerations and the disillusionment that goes hand in hand with them politically, we need to ask realistic questions.

What do wars about resources have to do with our concerns about the environment and ecology, for example? Very much, I would argue. As long as our political representatives and corporate interests are claiming to be operating in support of human rights and welfare and simultaneously objectively worsening this very situation for reasons of state, or in the name of protection of jobs, national security, free trade, 'shareholder values', democracy or whatever other excuses are given, as language scholars we are being called upon to mediate in this evident mismatch between saying and meaning. I am not suggesting we have a privileged position in this mediation process. Journalists, intellectuals and academics in a variety of disciplines are equally as qualified to intervene. But we surely have a 'professional' responsibility as language scholars *not* to ignore this construction of deceit in which language is massively implicated.

More than three and a half centuries ago Thomas Hobbes (1651: 106), in chapter IV of *Leviathan*, pointed his finger very directly at the problem; and the same dilemma still confronts us today:

> Nature it selfe cannot erre: and as men abound in copiousnesse of language; so they become more wise, or more mad than ordinary.

Hobbes' insight into the prospective profusion of discourse that can be let loose by humans on any subject is telling indeed. But maybe his dichotomous depiction of the potential outcome of such a situation as being either wisdom or madness is somewhat limiting from our modern perspective. It is not sufficient for us to lament. Instead we need a 'more wise' insertion of more questioning and critical language input in the ecological debates being conducted. In this way we can help to map out and pinpoint those areas we know about and those we are still working on and still treading on uncertain ground in. There will thus be a pivotal role for critical language analysis in the sphere of language and ecology. This book aims to highlight certain aspects of discourse in order to discover what the producers of the discourse are really getting at. Its focus is on how speakers and writers position either their listeners or readers, thus getting (bringing) them to understand or see the 'facts' or the events they relate in a particular fashion.

This book consists of a number of previously published and unpublished studies, ordered in a sequentially and logically consistent fashion. In several chapters a critical discourse approach is applied to a variety of different text types and genres—including company websites, advertisements, press articles, speeches and lectures. It is held that critical discourse analysis can be fruitfully supplemented by employing concordancing and corpus linguistic techniques as a heuristic instrument. Using a computer-held corpus of texts with a simple concordancing program, we can automatically ascertain a number of facts. We can know the total number of words (running words) and the total number of different words (word-forms) in a text. On the basis of these two measures we can, among other things, ascertain the degree of *lexical diversity* manifested in the individual texts. This means that in many of the chapters of this book such computer-generated concordances, where texts are electronically available, will be utilized to highlight ideological positions and value stances generally.

3   OUTLINE OF THE BOOK'S STRUCTURE

Here follows a brief outline of the book's structure with a summary of each individual chapter. It is worth noting that the ten later chapters fall loosely into five groups of two each. Chapters 2 and 3 serve as an introduction to the book in a twofold way. They consider, on the one hand, how business and the media have integrated the ecological issue. They also interrogate the nature of ecological commitment on the part of different sorts of businesses. Secondly, in the course of the discussion, a mode of analysis combining critical discourse analysis and computer-generated concordances to empirically locate and tease out the writer's or the speaker's categorizational scheme is developed. Chapter 2 discusses the manner in which politicians, businesses, industry and the media in several European countries have succeeded in ideologically integrating the ecological issue. A number of texts and genres are introduced which deal with the topic in different ways. An issue of *The Economist* is scrutinized and both *The Body Shop Values and Vision 94* mission statement and an advertisement from NIREX, a radioactive waste management firm, are considered. What stance can or should language scholars themselves adopt in view of the assimilation of the ecological issue in numerous discourse genres? Is there a need for critical language studies? Chapter 3 continues this theoretical argument and focuses on the construction of ecological concern by business people. The major, empirical, section contrastively analyzes with the help of concordances a speech given by John Browne, chief executive of BP, in 1997 and the Body Shop Mission Statement for 1994. The use of language can be shown to be a site of contestation on environmental issues.

Chapters 4 and 5 focus on two large oil and energy companies and the way they project their self-images and their orientations to the environment (BP-Amoco and Royal Dutch-Shell, respectively). Chapter 4 argues that the discourse of market economics is colonizing and serving to narrowly frame critical and oppositional discourse on the environment and ecology. The chapter investigates how thoughts and actions on ecological and environmental matters are coming to be linguistically channelled by means of a specific model of market economics. It analyzes the speech given by John Browne mentioned in the previous chapter in more detail. By analyzing features, firstly, of cohesion and arguments, followed by thematic patterns and the structuring of information in Browne's speech, we see how he adroitly employs language to incorporate a particular and partial model of reality and to suggest that BP is operating in a proactive fashion, without being asked to. Chapter 5 uses the same method as the previous one to scrutinize the website presentation of the *Shell Report 1999, People, planet & profits*, in which the company proclaims its commitment to 'sustainable development'. Many observers (Greer and Bruno 1996) have noted the manner in which transnational corporations (TNCs) have been contributing to the definition of environmentalism and of sustainability in recent years. The qualitative textual analysis focuses on the notion of 'sustainable development'. Features of 'over- and under-lexicalization' are highlighted. The prevalence of 'purr-words' is pointed out. The rhetorical techniques designed to contextualize companies in a favourable light are shown to be operating at the lexical-grammatical level.

The next two chapters, 6 and 7, look at a well known British public discourse genre transmitted by radio, namely, the 2000 BBC Reith Lectures on the theme of "Respect for the Earth". The published texts of the six lecturers' talks (downloaded from the BBC website) are subjected to a close quantitative and qualitative textual analysis facilitated by means of language data processing software, as demonstrated in previous chapters. Chapter 6 selectively and critically analyzes the texts and the abstracts of the 2000 BBC Reith Lectures in which Chris Patten talked on governance, Tom Lovejoy on biodiversity, John Browne on business, Gro Harlem Brundtland on health and population, Vandana Shiva on poverty and globalisation and His Royal Highness, The Prince of Wales on sustainable development. Together they constitute a fairly broad mainstream selection of views on this topic, apart from Shiva, that is. Perhaps surprisingly, a consideration of the most frequent lexical items used by each speaker demonstrated a lack of overlap. 'Globalisation' is a term which was used by three speakers and which a close analysis shows to be differently focused on. Chapter 7 reports on further aspects of the 2000 Reith Lectures, supplementing the study in chapter 6. One interesting feature the analysis brings out is how Patten 're-defines' democracy; different lexical collocations of 'democracies' (count-able) and 'democracy' (uncountable) are employed. And omissions can also tell us something about how discourse is shaped. A search for the two items 'climate change' and 'global warming' might tell us something about the orientation of the lecturers. The avoidance of 'global warming' is in itself an interesting observation to be made. A further finding was that the lecturers shared commonalities, for example, an anthropocentric standpoint, at the same time as they took up disparate ideological stances towards the envi-ronmental and ecological degradation confronting us all, and what needs to be done about it.

Chapters 8 and 9 cast light on the impact Western agricultural transna-tional corporations and agribusiness methods are having on the physical and social environment of Third World countries especially. They both take up and analyze the work and writings of one of the 2000 Reith lecturers, Vandana Shiva, in more detail. Seen from the perspective of Third World agricultural workers, environmental and ecological issues take on a com-pletely different appearance in the context of corporate globalisation now sweeping the world. Chapter 8 submits her Reith lecture to a detailed inves-tigation. Shiva's work uncovers the metaphors and the models underlying the so-called 'modernization' of agriculture. This is designed to benefit pre-dominantly the Western corporations which are pursuing it. Her approach can be read on two levels. First we have the factual, objective analysis of how rural traditions in India are being dismantled and the call to resist physically and politically. Then, on the meta-analytical level, Shiva critically delineates how the myths associated with neo-liberal projects and 'solutions' are being formulated. Her contribution highlights the situation of peasant food producers in the Third World in terms of the conflicting metaphors of VALUE or WEALTH CREATION ('market competitiveness and mar-ket efficiency' versus 'sustainability, sharing and survival'). The externally imposed worldviews are shown to be the cause of the ecological disasters which are also social disasters for small farmers in India and elsewhere. Chapter 9, on the other hand, focuses on the self-presentation of two major gene-based agribusiness corporations, Monsanto and Pioneer Hi-Bred, as manifested through their websites. The linguistic features which accompany more extensive discourse processes typical of corporate public relations and advertising materials can be uncovered. For both companies, the use of 'purr-words' or positively sounding words is investigated. Broader corporate rhetorical processes designed to create a specific view of corporate activities come to light. In particular, it is noteworthy how the keyword 'genetic' is carefully employed by Pioneer Hi-Bred. On the other hand, Monsanto pre-fers the term 'biotechnology', only employing 'genetic' three times. The final section contrasts these self-images of the companies with the other-images and practices which opposition activists, such as Vandana Shiva in the Third World and elsewhere, are articulating and condemning.

Finally the last two chapters, 10 and 11, broaden the scope of the book, shifting the focus onto media, political and institutional discourse in the Western world, which is coming to (has already succeeded in) 'control(ling)' how events in the world are 'mis'-represented. The vantage point in chapter 10 shifts to the more general phenomenon of what Noam Chomsky (1986) has referred to as "Orwell's problem". This concerns the situation whereby it transpires that people know so little about the (social and political) world, while being surrounded by so much 'information'. A major contention of this chapter is that part of the explanation for this outcome is relatively simple, namely that, given the configuration of the corporate and governmental set-up in the so-called Western democracies, Edward Herman's (1992) "power laws" operate. Building on the discussion of ideas set in motion in the 20th century by George Orwell (1949), such as the concepts of 'double-think', 'newspeak' and 'duckspeak' and the later derivative 'doublespeak' (not a word Orwell used himself), communicative and discourse strategies employed by governments and political institutions are critically theorized. A selective review and detailed analysis are given of scholarship on Orwell's original insight—that language can be used in some way to control thought, particularly where ideology is concerned. This leads to a discussion of people's variable abilities to see through doublespeak and contest the discourse engineering that they experience in their working and non-working lives in society. Chapter 11 continues this general thrust with its Orwellian ramifications, showing how political and institutional discourse in the Western world has increasingly become militarized. The encroaching militarism, to be observed on the part of activities of the United States in the past few decades, in particular, has spawned a broad range of military euphemisms. The naming practices of the military pertaining to weapons and operations, for example, are discussed in some detail. This final chapter attempts to provide an assessment of the effects such developments are having on political and media discourse and to query in whose interests these linguistic and discourse strategies appear to be. What concerned citizens might be expected to do in open societies in the face of such widespread disinformation and institutional obfuscation is briefly adumbrated by way of a conclusion.

2   Integrating the Ecological Issue

1   INTRODUCTION

I begin with a quotation from C. Wright Mills (1959: 405):

> The first rule for understanding the human condition is that men live in second-hand worlds. They are aware of much more than they have personally experienced; and their own experience is always indirect. The quality of their lives is determined by meanings they have received from others. Everyone lives in a world of such meanings. No man stands alone directly confronting a world of solid fact. No such world is available. [. . .]
>
> [I]n their everyday life they do not experience a world of solid fact; their experience itself is selected by stereotyped meanings and shaped by ready-made interpretations. Their images of the world, and of themselves, are given to them by crowds of witnesses they have never met and shall never meet. Yet for every man these images—provided by strangers and dead men—are the very basis of his life as a human being.

This is clearly a sociological vantage point. Although the word 'language' is not employed, the frequent appeals to 'meanings' clearly presuppose its use. Mills was inspired by George Mead (1934), for whom "significant symbols" were central to the creation of self in society. Sociologically informed linguists in the tradition of Firth (1957) and Halliday similarly see language situated in a social context. Mills' reference brings up the epistemological issue of how we can get to know reality and the world and the role played by social constructs, representations, constructivism, etc. That "images of the world" have power over us and that they are selected, constructed and transmitted to 'us' is practically a truism in many scientific disciplines today.

What implications does this standpoint on 'human' experience, perception and social cognition or 'knowledge of the world' have for the presentation of the environmental facts—such as the reduction of the ozone layer or the increase of greenhouse gases and other examples of ecological shifts taking place? This epistemological aspect will be briefly touched upon in this chapter.

A major task of this chapter is to begin to think through what role language plays in the face of ecological debates, pseudo-debates and distorting campaigns currently under way around the globe. We return to what the response of language and discourse analysts and thinking people to this state of affairs could be in the final section. A basic premise here sees language or texts as only being comprehensible in their contexts. Hence in the framework of their ecology in the broadest possible sense.

With Bolinger (1980) as starting point we envisage abstractly our work as following a trajectory "from the ecology of language to the language of ecology and back to the ecology of language". This might serve as the map for the journey we intend to take combined with a form of "critical linguistics" that informed the work of many people in the 1970s. Halliday's (1978) "social semiotic" contextualized the social ecology of language use and provided a major influence on what has been called "Orwellian linguistics" after George Orwell. Here is how Orwell (1944: 170) viewed political language:

> Political language [. . .] is designed to make lies sound truthful and murder respectable, and to give an appearance of solidity to pure wind.

Practitioners of "Orwellian linguistics" include Fowler (1991), Chilton (1988), Kress and Hodge (1979), Fowler et al. (1979), Fairclough (1989), and people such as Dwight Bolinger (1980).[1] Indeed, the final chapter of Bolinger's book is tellingly entitled "the ecology of language". And already in this chapter we find an explicitly normative metaphorical transfer from the language of ecology to designate through "pollution" the social context via the media, particularly TV, through which language is mediated or amplified. It is worth stressing at this point that the idealistic notion that the major function of language is 'communicative' needs adjusting to reality. Certainly as far as language use in the political and public sphere is concerned, it could be argued that its function has largely become precisely the opposite: namely, a major function of language is that of distortion, obfuscation, deception, if not straight mendacity. Incidentally, the 'common sense' ability to recognize distortion processes of various sorts is surely testified to in the overlexicalized semantic field in English as seen in the list of distortion terms in Appendix 1.

Those of us who are interested in critically focusing on the 'misrepresentations' of ecologically relevant issues which take place via language are, hence, ultimately viewing the ecological issue as *one issue* among many. This is in the spirit of Bolingerian ecology of language. Along with Fowler (1991: 67) we can say that

> [C]ritical linguistics seeks [. . .] to display to consciousness the patterns of belief and value which are encoded in the language, i.e. ideology.[2]

As we will see, I consider that more than critical linguistics is required to uncover and contextualize such issues, alongside the ecological one. Others of interest are civil rights or human rights in general, and freedom of access to information and freedom of expression in particular. I shall frequently be quoting from the work of Chomsky in this context: but not from his work on linguistics. Note that Chomsky too uses the word 'ideology'. His use is invariably a 'negative' one.[3]

We shall be coming back to this as we appeal to Chomsky as a further guide on our journey. As he himself acknowledges, his practice of linguistics has little to do with such issues and their representations. Commenting on his political work on 'ideology', Chomsky (1979: 3) has this to say:

> There is no very direct connection between my political activities, writing and others, and the work bearing on language structure, though in some measure they perhaps derive from certain common assumptions and attitudes with regard to basic aspects of human nature. Critical analysis in the ideological arena seems to me to be a fairly straightforward matter as compared to an approach that requires a degree of conceptual abstraction. For the analysis of ideology, which occupies me very much, a bit of open-mindedness, normal intelligence, and healthy skepticism will generally suffice.[4]

Now let us turn to the ideological integration of the ecological issue.

2 IDEOLOGICAL INTEGRATION OF THE ECOLOGICAL ISSUE

I am using the word 'ideological' and 'ideology' in the non-political sense to refer simply to systems of meaning, value and belief. We can adduce Halliday (1990) and view his discussion of new ways of meaning to be a contribution to an analysis of the linguistic bases of belief systems or ideologies, or as others say, models of the world. Moreover, we can understand Halliday to be calling loudly and clearly for a rapid replacement by alternatives.[5]

Here we are concerned with the channelling of the ecological issue. This proceeds to a great extent via both the print and electronic mass media today. For a major part of the world the mechanism which serves to amplify discourse or wording (to use the Hallidayan term) is the "Cultural Apparatus" as C. Wright Mills (1959) rather quaintly termed it. How specific mass media techniques function has been analyzed by Herman and Chomsky in their book *Manufacturing Consent* (1988), where they have developed a so-called "propaganda model". (See also the film and book of the film, Achbar (1994).) Herman and Chomsky (1988: 1) describe the mass media's function as follows:

The mass media serve as a system for communicating messages and symbols to the general populace. It is their function to amuse, entertain, and inform, and to inculcate individuals with the values, beliefs, and codes of behavior that will integrate them into the institutional structures of the larger society. In a world of concentrated wealth and major conflicts of class interest, to fulfil this role requires systematic propaganda.

3   METHODOLOGICAL EXCURSUS

This chapter does not set out to debate methodological differences in discourse analysis, interesting though they may be. Nor does it engage with the disentangling of 'ideological constructs' which can be said to underlie or even to 'structure' language utterances or discourse in the areas which will be adduced. Neither will the historical contexts for philosophical positions be alluded to.

I am aware of the analytical problems in perhaps not stating 'where one is coming from': whether one assumes the relativism or contingency of one's analysis or whether one states that discourse phenomena can and perhaps should be analytically grounded in historically given contexts. It may be that a shifting between the registers could also be adopted as a median strategy. Be that as it may, the preliminary 'sketch' presented in this chapter is content to 'simply' present data from texts selected for explicit (and doubtlessly implicit) reasons from the broad scope available.

I make no excuses for this selectivity. My contribution does not claim to be from within a specific analytic framework, nor does it expect to be judged from a unique set of criteria. The broad sympathy with a Hallidayan-inspired socio-semiotic starting-point (1978) should not conceal the 'realist' assumptions about language use which hold that humans 'act' in and through language. Moreover, these actions seek to affect others. Whether by threatening, frightening, encouraging, entertaining, persuading or convincing, 'selling' or 'conning' is immaterial. The language user's everyday perception that these actions take place is naturally tempered by the language analyst's desire to comprehend further aspects of such actions and activities, often with a view to channelling such insights into educative processes. Thus the applied linguistic enterprise I am describing—for such it is—is based in the first instance on teasing out a self-reflexive dimension of one's own language use and holding up a mirror to one's own and one's fellow humans' linguistic acts in the areas where ecological issues are articulated and verbalized. We all have a stand on such an issue. Even a neutral position is a stand. In this context, it is well to remember with Bang and Døør (1993: 10) that: "We have no access to a point of view from nowhere." (See also Døør and Bang 1996.)

A few remarks are perhaps in order on the use of the term 'integrate'. It appears as if its connotations or associations may be positive, as contrasted with an opposite like 'isolating', 'marginalizing' or 'keeping out'. Furthermore, a second meaning, that of 'incorporating' or 'taking on board', might be appealed to. Arguably, this is not so positive. In this sense it is used as a rhetorical device, maybe referring to Trojan horse tactics, amalgamating something, as in the phrase: 'We are all environmentalists now!' Or: 'We are in favour of protecting the environment'.[6]

4 EXAMPLES FROM *THE ECONOMIST*

The extent to which the ecological issue has become integrated into the media can be judged by the numbers of weeklies and dailies that have 'Business and Environment' sections, such as the *Financial Times*. As can be expected in a pluralist society, different ideological leanings or biases will lead to different obvious treatments of the ecological issue.

In the realm of the print media I have followed closely the process—in the course of my professional activities of teaching economics in English to students of business administration and commerce—in such publications as *The Economist* and others. I have taken *The Economist* for the purposes of this chapter for a number of reasons: it is readily accessible, it is a widely read or consulted business-oriented magazine with considerable political influence in Britain and the English-speaking world. Moreover, it is also used extensively in English for business purposes and management courses, hence my close familiarity with it. It champions wealthy corporate concerns, carrying its free-marketer and enterprise-oriented banner proudly. This leads it to deal sharply and briefly with events which go against its ideology. As we shall see, it employs put-down techniques, such as sarcastic, even cynical, humour to create in-group and out-group clarity.[7]

Let us take a small selection of articles from *The Economist* in the 1990s. All I intend to do here is to summarize a few of the characteristics of the treatment of environmental topics and ecological issues. I have already mentioned the propensity for humour. Indeed, the leader article 2 needs to be read with a grain of salt in view of the dateline April 1st, perhaps. Then we need to consider the interplay of visuals, photos and graphics together with layout. The titles, headings and subheads are also edited along the 'witty' and 'humorous' lines found in a study by Alexander (1986). One lexicalization technique should be mentioned: 'greenery' (in article 7) is an abstract noun which suggests non-seriousness.[8]

Just listing the titles (see Table 2.1) is enough to see that six of the seven are puns, or contain punning categorizations, e.g. 'Green swingers', jokey allusions, e.g. 'greenery' and 'Stay cool', or else literary allusion, e.g. 'The price of imagining Arden'.

Of article 2 (Stay cool), we could say it is an example of a 'rubbishing' text. It is characterized by specific modality choices, especially the preponderance of conditional clauses and 'would' throughout the text. The use of

Table 2.1 Selective List of Titles from the Economist

---

1 The price of imagining Arden. *The Economist* December 3rd 1994.

2 Stay cool. [Leader] *The Economist* April 1st 1995, pp. 11–12.

3 Global warming and cooling enthusiasm. [International section] *The Economist* April 1st 1995.

4 How to make lots of money, and save the planet, too. [Business Section] *The Economist* June 3rd 1995, pp. 65–6.

5 Ethical shopping: Human rights. *The Economist* June 3rd 1995.

6 Germany: Green swingers. [Europe] *The Economist* May 20th 1995, pp. 37–8.

7 A new case for greenery. [Leader] *The Economist* June 3rd 1995.

---

black humour in the title underpins this orientation. Article 7 (A new case for greenery) contains a belittling, diminutive derivative. This is a fairly patent form of semi-abuse.

Political integration of the ecological issue, which is a further motor of ideological integration, can be illustrated from developments in Austria. As a representative sample of the 'political processing' of the ecological issue I might cite the publication sent by the Austrian government to foreign countries and their representatives abroad: *Austria. Facts and Figures* (published by the Federal Press Service, 1994). In a publication of only 210 pages, including many pages of glossy pictures, the section 'Environmental Protection' takes up six pages. The introduction sets out the stall very clearly: "As a major tourist country and a nation with a proud tradition of social welfare, Austria regards environmental protection as a matter of prime social importance and at the same time as a topic of economic significance." The vital role of the government is documented under the headings: "For a Clean Environment", "Extensive Prevention of Water Pollution", "Forest Conservation", "Reduction of Exhaust Emissions in Road Traffic". This is an obvious instance of showcasing, similar examples of which can be replicated from countless other European government publicity documents.

5   BUSINESS INTEGRATION

Given that the environment and the ecological issue is an item on the agenda for many businesses, as *The Economist's* polemical and reluctant treatment demonstrates, we can inquire how businesses integrate the ecological issue. We can subdivide 'business integration' into two major sectors. The first of these is an alternative strand of business which has been growing apace in the UK and elsewhere. Examples of such ethical business enterprises are The

Body Shop, Tradecraft, Out of this World, Oxfam Trading Company, etc. A newer development is to be found in the financial sector with the growth of ethical investment funds.[9]

6   ETHICAL BUSINESS STRAND

Some comments are perhaps in place on the motivation for this strand. Language actions remain for the most part words unless something is done. Business people claim to act. After all, words about the depredations of the environment change nothing by themselves. Discourse in academia, or symposia, remains academic in the short-term. In the long-term, though, who knows, there may be a trickle-down effect, through education and even training, through students and from them to their future constituencies, once they leave higher education. Values do change. What role does discourse play in this? Discourse accompanies, underlines and encourages special actions. We all hold this to be the case, otherwise those of us in education would not engage in this work!

We do well to recall, also, that the interface where we all meet the real world in our consumer societies is the consumption process—buying and selling. So it is not surprising that this is an area in many countries where we can expect some pressure on attitudinal change to come. How far it will reach is quite another matter.[10]

Some items which were worth considering in 1994 include, firstly, *The Body Shop Values and Vision 94*, with its mission statement. This comes on the inside cover and contains Anita Roddick's comments; a personal, human touch is provided by certain linguistic markers. Secondly, the Out of this World prospectus could be considered.

It is worth stating that, actually, such kinds of organization are not new. As long as people have been aware of the downside of capitalist production, we have had, in the UK certainly, an alternative strand of trading organizations—the cooperative movement. What has changed is the up-front, more prominent self-promotion pursued by this sector.

Taking a brief look at the document, *Values and Vision 94*—including the mission statement of The Body Shop—can give a flavour of this organization's self-image. Through its chief executive, Anita Roddick, this cosmetics company specializing in skin and hair care has developed a very high public and commercial profile. According to its own mission statement it is dedicated "to the pursuit of social and environmental change". There are many examples of how they make their presence felt. Their trucks drive around using, and proclaiming that they are using, natural gas. And they are actively involved against animal testing. Their environmental approach is laid out (p. 6). And, in case anyone might think they are just against animal testing, they emphasize also that they are against the abuse of human and civil rights and that their declared aim is a just and sustainable society.

Out of this World is a trading organization which sets out to open a series of retail shops to sell ethical, environmentally friendly and fairly bought products. Their prospectus is aimed at attracting interested buyers of the company's shares. So the choice of the exclusive use of the pronoun 'we' at the beginning which then gives way after a direct 'you' to an inclusive 'we' in paragraph two attempts to underline the close and informal relationship the organization is trying to imagine with people of like mind and opinion on the issues referred to in their prospectus. In chapter 3 we focus more closely on how personal pronouns contribute in important ways to how writers position their texts in relation to readers.

7   HARD-NOSED BUSINESS STRAND

The second sector is what I call the hard-nosed business strand, who are either bandwagon-jumping or employing the ecological issue as a façade for PR and advertizing purposes. A prime example of the transparently hypocritical nature of this was the Royal Dutch-Shell Nigerian scandal in 1995, involving conflict with the Ogoni people (Greer and Bruno 1996: 54–6). There is more than one corporation which sells the public an ecologically clean image in its corporate advertizing.

Such practices are part of a North American and Europe-wide public relations (PR) wave into which the normal world of advertizing has integrated the ecological issue. Also there is an obligation in the United States on companies to publish some kinds of environmental information and report on their environmental liabilities.[11] As we said above: We are in favour of protecting the environment. After all, who is against clean air and fresh water and a generally unpolluted atmosphere? Nobody. How silly to suggest otherwise?

One example from a fairly sensitive area concerning the atomic energy industry in the UK—the radioactive waste management firm NIREX—will show how significant word choice and lexical patterning is in deflecting attention and downplaying real and potential troubles.

8   NIREX—CORPORATE ADVERTISEMENT

No industry has become more associated with environmental damage and potentially irreparable pollution than the nuclear power industry (Chernobyl is everywhere). This is not surprising, given early scares like Three Mile Island and the horror stories of the Irish Sea being polluted by Calder Hall, Windscale, Seascale and now Sellafield (all different names for practically the same place). Fresh labelling or re-naming is a frequent manoeuvre which aims somehow to limit the damage, by simply distracting attention. Hence it is interesting to see how 'environmental management' is 'sold' to the public as a positive and hopeful activity. The representatives of companies involved in the nuclear industry aim to transmit reassurance and calm. The role discourse plays in 'constructing' this image of comforting and safe reality can be seen by considering part of a NIREX corporate advertisement (published in *New Statesman and Society* 16 June 1995, but permission for its reproduction here unfortunately declined).

This advertisement begins with a simple sentence ("Many people are now questioning the long term safety of Britain's radioactive waste") with the subject "many people" of uncertain reference cataphorically referring ahead, creating tension and hence multiply ambiguous. The following sentence is cohesively linked by means of the pronominal substitution "they", thus prolonging the mystery until the punchline NIREX in the sentence ("They work for Nirex.") disambiguates all! This is a catchy lead-in to the rest of the tightly printed text which accompanies a collage of small photographs portraying NIREX workers pursuing their responsible work.

A textual analysis of this advert can fruitfully continue by considering the cohesive patterns of the text. Here we can note how both lexical repetition, pronominal substitution, choice of semantically related lexical items and the use of sentence connectors such as anaphorically referring adverbials like "just as importantly" can help to bring out the way the argumentation proceeds or how reassurance is arrived at.[12]

In sentences 3 and 4 we have the ascription of radioactive waste to an inclusive first person—"our radioactive waste" (although certainly 59 million or more of Britain's 60 million population will never have produced any such radioactive waste in their life-times). "They" are finding solutions for "us" and by extension "Britain" (in sentence 5). This stealthy substitution chain, which identifies us all with Britain, implicates us all in the production—"Britain has produced".

Temporal expressions like "not just for now" and their usage are of interest also. After all, this is the key 'problem' with nuclear waste, given that the half-life of plutonium is at least 24,000 years! Incidentally, "radioactive waste" is a technical relexicalization which makes it sound more harmless. The word 'nuclear' is studiously unmentioned in the whole text. Instead, having recourse to technical and scientific terms, like "radioactive wastes" sometimes in the plural or "isotopes", serves to distance the real matter and to transform it into an abstract, merely technical problem. The friendly and homely resort to invoking a football pitch to indicate how minimal the amount can 'really' be seen to be is a further index of the copy-writer's care in dowsing any possible second thoughts we might have concerning the potential dangers involved. A brief analysis, starting with "safety" in the title, brings out lexical patterning created by the six occurrences of "safe", "safety" or "safely" throughout the text. These items collocate mostly with "disposal" or "dispose".

There are further aspects that can be shown to underpin the 'matter-of-fact' and controlled environment the NIREX technicians have under construction. The text suggests that safety requirements somehow operate of their own accord. The deletion of agents is a by now well known device for distracting attention away from the human actors who have to carry out the disposal process. But, in short, the NIREX slogan that is used to round off the text says it all: "Responsible environmental management". So that is all right then! There is no need to think about human agency.

Our economic and political systems and the industrial system depend on a specific framework of ideas for their functioning and survival, the outlines of a set of "necessary beliefs" (Edwards 1995: 42–3), for example, that we all freely and voluntarily participate in their goals. These are in opposition to such values and beliefs as were outlined above in the section on ethical business enterprises (6). As the NIREX advert makes clear, core assumptions or presuppositions about the 'naturalness' of nuclear power go unquestioned.

The pooh-poohing of the *Economist* leaders discussed above is a feature of the overt strategy to talk down the importance of the ecological issue. Preventing an alternative space from developing is part of the not so subtle method of such organs. As David Edwards succinctly notes (1995: 44): "corporate consumerism will tend to discourage the capacity of people to imagine alternative ways of living." Which brings us to the question of critically integrating the ecological issue.

9   CRITICAL INTEGRATION

We have begun to interpret the discourse surrounding the ecological issue. We have seen how (easily) it has been 'integrated' in the two senses of the word I referred to. Firstly, this has happened in the sense that the issue(s) have entered common political, commercial and media discourse. But secondly they have become 'watered down' and 'displaced' via the well-known strategies of the 'brainwashers'—the advertizers, the public relations people, the spin doctors. As Gerbig (1996) demonstrates in her insightful and convincing analysis using quantitative computer-based methods, there is much evidence for a language-constructing role in the Australian debate about the causes of ozone deletion. In any case it has become a minor subject within the overall set of ongoing discourses, one form of psychobabble alongside the others. How? Well, we have seen the talking down and ridiculing techniques used by *The Economist*.[13]

So how is the language-oriented scholar or the responsible citizen supposed to respond to these developments? What do we do when especially faced with the evidence of the assimilation of the ecological issue in various discourse types—media discourse, advertizing, political discourse and business talk, for example under the heading 'environmental technology'? This will entail adopting a critical and decisive stance.

In the first place, discussions and actions about ecological problems need to be contextualized. The work of Susan George on, for example, food resources or debt can help give direction. As she states unequivocally (1990: 225):

> There *are* no ecological problems, only the social and political problems that invariably underlie and cause ecological damage.

For our purposes this is a central insight that needs to be and will need to be frequently underlined. But it is precisely the representations of these "social and political problems" in themselves which pose difficulties to understanding. This is where Noam Chomsky's political writings can inform and help. He writes (1985: 1):

> We live entangled in webs of deceit, often self-deceit, but with a little honest effort, it is possible to extricate ourselves from them. If we do, we will see a world that is rather different from the one presented to us by a remarkably effective ideological system, a world that is much uglier, often horrifying. We will also learn that our own actions, or passive acquiescence, contribute quite substantially to misery and oppression, and perhaps eventual global destruction.

Language is—by metaphorical extension—a sophisticated sort of tool used for shaping or coping with, managing or manipulating natural and social reality, via a dialogic and dialectical form of communication (Døør and Bang 1996) that gives rise to a socio-cognitive framing system. The ontological and epistemological relation between reality (the 'world') and language ('wording') need not delay us here. Later, in particular, the nature of the relation between the economy, ecology and language is discussed in more detail in chapter 5. For a different but complementary approach to this relation see Mühlhäusler (1996).

In short, we must endeavour to counteract 'linguistic engineering'.[14]

10   LINGUISTIC ENGINEERING, LINGUISTIC CO-OPTING OR DISCOURSE ENGINEERING

Arguably, it is reasonable to include what we are here calling 'linguistic engineering' as a branch of "engineering current history" (Chomsky 1994a: 94–5), when events are being politically constructed, as they are retrospectively reconstructed. Such tactics are also to be observed in business discourse, advertizing, TV and radio news, media commentaries etc.[15] Much proceeds unconsciously. But where it is overt we can speak of manipulation and seeming acquiescence. Herman and Chomsky have revived Walter

Lippmann's phrase "manufacturing consent" for this phenomenon. Language, after all, provides the form for thought. So thought control and formation is at stake.[16]

Chomsky has demonstrated to the full his ability to dissect texts and to expose their ideological presuppositions, hypocrisy and duplicity. His writings on politics and current affairs are crammed with what others call text analysis, even discourse analysis, and language criticism. A concrete example is when Chomsky has been discussing the way "national interest" is used when the special interests of US industrial leaders are really meant (1988a: 663). He comments:

> This is a typical case of the way the framework of thought is consciously manipulated by an effective choice and reshaping of terminology so as to make it difficult to understand what's happening in the world.[17]

Chomsky refers to Hume's First Principles of Government to demonstrate how long this technique has been used. As Chomsky notes (1994a: 86), "the governors must control thought" in a "democracy".

Let us return to the term "linguistic engineering". Although it is in common parlance, it is inexact. It is an open question how much language or the language system can be engineered. It would be going too far to argue that this is at stake when talking about terminological manipulation. Halliday (1990) refers to the lexico-grammatical spectrum. The 'lexis' end is like the visible tip of an iceberg. What Halliday calls cryptogrammar, which interlocks with the meaning system, also changes over time, but imperceptibly, he argues. He gives examples like the increase in usage of nominalizations or the use of what he terms grammatical metaphors. Strictly speaking, Halliday's perspective shows you can only 'co-opt' lexis or language (perhaps terminology, as stated), but you cannot 'engineer' it. At least this is not possible where it interfaces with the inner layers of grammar. It is thus perhaps misleading to talk of linguistic engineering when texts are employed to present a specific 'spin' or 'slant' on an event or process. A more suitable term would be 'discourse engineering'.

Language analysts can do little in the face of the integration we have referred to, other than draw attention to it. It proceeds through texts produced by dominant groups of people in society. The process is amplified by the mass media. We find that such discourse shaping and text moulding attempts to mould thinking of others. This process will continue apace (see *The Economist* articles discussed above in section 4 and in following chapters). Terms and phrases will stick. The new buzzword of 'sustainable development', has, as we see, quickly made inroads internationally into many languages (Germany 'nachhaltige Entwicklung' or Spanish 'desarrollo sostenido') and into South American, for example, Ecuadorian discourse, where the outreach of the TNCs is especially great.

But we can engage in pinprick-like educational activities.[18]

11 THE ROLE OF CRITICAL LANGUAGE STUDIES

Critical applied language studies can be used as one 'tool', alongside others, perhaps, to enhance 'doubt' in the necessary illusions which the propaganda systems of corporate consumerism are both generating and bolstering up.

One example is to demonstrate what 'economic growth' means from the perspective of the emerging nations. It is meaningless as an economic metaphor! Growthism is an element of economic, especially media-talk oriented, discourse of the type used by politicians. Since Dennis Meadows and the *Limits to Growth* models of the 1960s and the 1970s, externalities have started to influence, slowly, the economists' models of the economy. 'Economic growth' in point of fact entails for many 'social, economic and environmental collapse'. For, as can be convincingly demonstrated, economic growth and expansion of certain activities are dependent on social dislocation and ruin. For example, in the Western world, social collapse gives rise to the growth of counsellor therapy. Alienation and loneliness which go along with it lead to more work for psychoanalysts, therapists, help-lines etc. The increase in crime results in greater sales of locks, alarms, car-security systems, chains, infra-red checking systems, computer systems. We need more guards, prisons, judges etc. This is not specifically new to human history, as the words of the old proverb remind us: "It's an ill wind that blows no one any good."[19]

One modest aim critical language studies might have is the extraction from the entanglement in webs of deceit, often self-deceit, people are involved in. However, whether merely 'a little honest effort' will make it possible is perhaps debatable.[20] The use of critical language studies can help to provide a 'different understanding' or to illuminate problems that are 'misunderstood' or 'misinterpreted'—namely, the 'causes' of environmental and ecological degradation.

12 DISSEMINATION OF THE INSIGHTS OF CRITICAL LANGUAGE STUDIES

In the immediate context this consists in demonstrating that the environment and the ecological issue represent a case of how disarmingly the status quo works via its agents. This may entail uncovering the processes of so-called 'common sense' or of 'naturalization' (see Fairclough 1989: 91ff.). When this is questioned, people in higher education—they could be students—respond by saying 'that's the way things are'. But we must counter by stressing that there is no need for that to mean that is how 'they have to stay'.[21]

We must build into our linguistic and language study a self-reflexive component. This will include bringing students at all levels into contact with critical thinking models. The work undertaken by Fill (1993) in his text for German university students and Mühlhäusler (2003) are good examples of the kind of concrete work at one level to be employed. As too would be the work under the heading of language awareness studies (see Fairclough and related work) or the background work included in Fill and Mühlhäusler (2001) on language and ecology.[22]

A university education needs to contain not just the affirmative presentation of facts and theories—irrespective of the field we specialize in. We need, for instance, to work against the reification of market processes that besets the mainstream economic and social sciences. We need to demonstrate that these are constructs of academia and mostly a very interested academia to boot.

13 WHAT CAN BE DONE?

In view of the extent, as we have seen in previous sections, to which the ecological 'problems' (which, as George (1992: 225) says, are political and social problems) have been integrated—in the sense of pacified—by the media and propaganda systems, we might be forgiven for wondering what the role of linguists *qua* linguists might be.

Of course, the linguist *qua* socially responsible citizen or thinking person (intellectual) following Chomsky's injunction to expose mendacity (1966) remains no less forceful. Whether the 'techniques' of linguists are required—and arguably it depends which linguistics you mean—is a debatable point not pursued further here.

If we see discourse engineering, say, in the form of terminological 'shaping' as a part of the greater, more amplified process of historical engineering—of indoctrination—which goes on, today employing the full range of mass media images, sounds and discourse, then a multi-disciplinary or interdisciplinary approach must be employed. In another context Chomsky (1988a: 623) talks of the need to acquire the means or "the tools of intellectual self-defence". I would agree with Chomsky (1987: 81) that it is "useful to [. . .] provide information and analysis and, I hope, understanding that is different from what is readily available."[23]

Chomsky has said (1988a: 623) that schools and colleges are failing to provide this. If they were doing their job, "[t]hey would be devoting themselves with great energy and application to precisely the kinds of things we're talking about so that people growing up in a democratic society would have the means of intellectual self-defense against the system."

But it will mean co-operating with others in our workplaces, commitments and participation networks of relationships. We all in our individual ways may endeavour to apply these tools. However, this may not be enough.

In the sphere of environmental activities, aimed at combating the destruction of the ecological balance, we need to get together. As Chomsky says in the film *Manufacturing Consent*, there is no choice. The alternatives are painfully clear: either the corporate consumerist predatory system continues (in George's (1992) graphic description) to destroy the biosphere, or democracy and freedom will win through and prevent this happening. For, only when actually existing communities control the fates of their immediate environments and decide to produce for life and not death, will the biosphere be retained.

14 BEWARE OF FALSE FRIENDS

At the same time we need to be extremely wary and watchful for 'false friends'. See what happened in the USA, with the 'disarming' of the environmentalist lobbies by the logging companies and President Clinton.[24] This bodes ill—but is typical of 'false friends' who may begin to 'accompany' us everywhere. And this does not just mean NIREX! We need to beware of 'false friends' in ecologically oriented business activities. As Edwards (1995: 37) writes, the emphasis "on green consumerism, corporate responsibility and sustainable growth in the late 1980s and early 1990s can be seen [. . .] to be corporate-friendly surrogates for a true analysis of the causes of, and solution to, environmental problems."[25]

15 CONCLUSION

Bateson (1972) picked up early on what he isolated as "the dynamics of the ecological crisis". He uses a diagram (1972: 467) to illustrate the interconnections between what he saw as three fundamental factors which were the necessary conditions for the destruction of our world. The factors interact. The increase of population (factor one) spurs technological progress and creates that anxiety which sets us against our environment as an enemy. Technology (factor two) both facilitates increase of population and reinforces our arrogance, or 'hubris' (factor three), vis-à-vis the natural environment. The simple solution for him was to introduce some anti-clockwise processes into this system. Time moves on and we seem no further along the road to this anti-clockwise motion. One reason may be that failure to 'see' the ecological issue prevents activity on a global scale. The pinpricks of David (Greenpeace) on Goliath (Royal Dutch-Shell or the French Government) do not yet constitute this.

I build into Bateson's model a further element. An absence in his scheme is evident, in view of how closely human 'seeing' is implicated with 'language'. If we add language, there are four fundamental factors. We can also modify hubris to focus on science, hitherto taken to be the antidote to all our ills. By many people it is said to be the solution to the problem. As we see, however, it is part of the problem itself. The role that distortion via language plays in obfuscating the real issues is now what becomes our focus. The outcome of the subsystem in the model which leads to ecological imbalance or homeo-static disturbance where language is involved I have entitled 'distortion'.[26]

By using the spiral representation of Bateson we can note that 'language' (or 'language-in-text'), the 'resource' (to use Hymes' and Halliday's help-ful metaphor) contains or sustains this dynamic and indirectly supports or underpins the other elements that make up the 'ecological crisis', see Appendix 2. This is essentially the thesis this chapter has been making indirectly by referring to integration. The use of language in this process is preventing analysis and resolution of the ecological issue (and others) by distorting what is going on and thus dispersing energy and activities away from these issues.

At several points in this chapter specific aspects of linguistic form have been picked out as contributing to what I termed 'discourse engineering'. Throughout the following chapters I shall be focussing on and employing analytical notions around which discourse engineering can be demonstrated to proceed. At this juncture it may be helpful to indicate briefly some lin-guistic or lexicogrammatical categories that are likely to be involved. The procedure of lexicalization or re-lexicalization is one such; this may entail either morphological changes (often leading to neologisms) or conscious word preferences or euphemistic re-naming on the part of writers or speak-ers. The propensity for nominalization (especially forming nouns from pro-cess verbs) is a feature that will be taken up in several chapters, as too will be the extremely significant role played by metaphoricization processes and metaphor selection generally. More narrowly conceived 'grammatical' fea-tures like modality choices, pronoun usage and the role of different clause types will also figure centre stage in the qualitative and quantitative textual analyses which are undertaken in this book.

We might finally ask, whose 'language' is at stake? The inequality of access to resources is a key factor; amplification of images of the world, we started with, of 'constructions' and 'shapings' by specific corporate and gov-ernment 'interests', via propaganda (media)-transmitters *does* make a differ-ence.[27] 'Loudness' drowns out 'alternative' softer voices. This is an analogy we might use from the physical sphere. Except that in media access terms it is ridiculous. 'Anyone' is free to buy a radio or TV station if they have several million dollars![28]

3 Ecological Commitment in Business

1 BUSINESS AFFECTS ECOLOGY: THE CONSTRUCTION OF ECOLOGICAL CONCERN BY BUSINESS PEOPLE IN THE CONTEXT OF "GREENWASH"

This chapter reports on the interim findings of computer-assisted analyses of texts by business people dealing with ecological concern. Together with the work reported on in chapters 2, 4 and 5 the study was part of a project which focuses on the dialectical relationship between language and ecology. (See Alexander 1993 and 1996 and Fill 1993 and 1996.) It is argued that environmental discourse and ecological thinking are severely constrained within the frame of economic discourse and thinking. We are dealing here with a specific model of economics with a firmly established institutional base. The rich and powerful business corporations, in particular, but also their acolytes in politics and the media, employ discourse to channel tolerance for further environmental degradation. But all is not lost. Fair trading and more considerate commercial relationships between ethically motivated companies of the North and the peoples of the South do exist. Consumers as thinking citizens are able to make an impact by buying products of such businesses.

2 ENVIRONMENTALLY COMMITTED BUSINESSES CLAIM TO BE ACTING IN AN 'ALTERNATIVE' WAY

The publicity material provides a statement of the approaches of such firms. The Body Shop, as one such company, is discussed in this chapter. If, as critical linguists such as Fowler (1991: 67) claim, there are "certain areas of language particularly implicated in coding social values", how far are the examples of discourse such as that initiated by Body Shop-like organizations capable of counteracting the trends we are discussing? Does hard-nosed business deal differently in discourse terms with environmental issues? We briefly address this by summarizing the analysis of a speech by John Browne, chief executive of BP (for a full analysis see chapter 4), and contrasting it with a textual analysis of the Body Shop Mission Statement 1994.

3   USING COMPUTER-GENERATED CONCORDANCES TO ANALYZE TEXTS: METHOD

Areas worth investigating from a critical discourse perspective (Fairclough 1989) can be illuminated by concordancing and corpus linguistic techniques. As mentioned in chapter 1, the analyses undertaken in this and other chapters will be facilitated by using computer-generated concordances. They allow us to automatically ascertain a number of facts.[1] One of the most basic techniques of language data-processing is the production of alphabetical frequency lists.

The term overwording can be given a material basis using computers. They can aid us to automatically access items, displaying how frequently they are used, for instance, and their collocational co-texts, which a cursory reading may well have overlooked. We thus receive additional evidence to support our qualitative analysis of argumentation structures.

4   ANALYSIS FROM A CRITICAL DISCOURSE PERSPECTIVE

Hence critical discourse analysis can be significantly enhanced by using concordancing and corpus linguistic techniques (see Mautner 1997 and 2000). From a critical discourse perspective 'experiential' values of words may be worth investigating. How often a word is used in a text, perhaps in proportion to other, say, lexical words, may have something to do with points the writer wishes to stress. The role of lexical repetition should not be underestimated.

5   ANALYSIS OF BP CHIEF EXECUTIVE'S SPEECH 'OUR COMMON JOURNEY' AT STANFORD UNIVERSITY, CALIFORNIA, 19 MAY 1997: THE EMPIRICAL STUDY SUMMARIZED

I chose Browne's speech for two reasons: relevance and accessibility. It is relevant because BP claims to be making the running on green strategy. It is an edited version of a speech given by John Browne (1997), the chief executive of BP, at Stanford University, California, 19 May 1997. The text, "Our common journey", appeared as one of a trio of texts in *New Statesman* 20 June 1997. The analysis of the text was facilitated by computer-generated concordances.[2]

6   NOMINALIZATIONS IN BROWNE'S SPEECH

Grammar may aid us in unravelling the ascription of causality. How are processes realized? Are nominalizations used? Following Gerbig (1993) and Schleppegrell (1996) one can look at features rendering abstraction and agency or lack of it. Nominalization is a feature which allows the agent to be omitted, for example, "extinctions of the rainforest" leaves unstated who is responsible for the extinction. If we compare the concordance for the uses of 'solutions' in Browne's speech (Table 3.1), we see that it may well be used in a positive sense.[3] It is remarkable for its lack of specification of who is doing the solving, however.

The collocate 'right' is of interest. The evaluative element in the adjective in this collocation is prominent. The stress on 'market-based' shows up as a collocation of 'solutions'. This is a major theme of Browne's speech.

The use of nominalizations like 'solutions' reminds us of questions which critical discourse analysts pose. For Fairclough (1992: 236) one objective is to see "how significant is the nominalization of processes. A major concern is agency, the expression of causality and the attribution of responsibility". Recall some of the questions Fairclough proposes as a heuristic device: What experiential value do grammatical features have? How is causality ascribed? What types of process and participant predominate? Is agency unclear? Applied to example (1) we see that Browne employs the full gamut.

> (1) Those market-based solutions need to be as wide-ranging in scope as possible, because this is a global problem, which has to be resolved without discrimination and without denying the peoples of the developing world the right to improve their living standards.

The following features can be isolated:

  a. nominalization: 'Those market-based solutions'
  b. generalized agency responsible for the problems: 'a global problem'
  c. passivization: 'which has to be resolved'
  d. nominalization: 'without discrimination'
  e. nominalization: 'without denying'
  f. generalized agent: 'the peoples of the developing world'

Table 3.1 'Solutions' Concordance of Browne's Speech

25	need for action and	**solutions.**	But what sort of action? I
50	Can produce the right	**solutions**	for the long-term common
61	agreed market-based	**solutions**	are more likely to produce
65	Those market-based	**solutions**	need to be as wide-ranging

Table 3.2 'We' Concordance of Browne's Speech

24	by society.	**We**	in BP have reached that point. It
35	disequilibrium.	**We**	've looked carefully at the precise
45	But that does not mean	**we**	should do nothing. We have to
45	we should do nothing.	**We**	have to look both at the way we
46	We have to look both at the way	**we**	use energy and at how our products are used.
54	responsibility to act.	**We**	're therefore taking specific steps:
60	is not proprietary and	**we**	will share our expertise openly
73	movement who say	**we**	have to abandon the use of oil and
75	But that disagreement doesn't	**we**	can ignore the mounting evidence
	mean		
77	are concerned,	**we**	'd better take notice. To be
82	and mobility which	**we**	take for granted and which the
86	must work together if	**we**	are to match and master the
86	master the challenges	**we**	all face. We share a common,
86	we all face.	**We**	share a common, vital interest in
88	goals. All the actions	**we**	're taking and will take are

The suggestive nature of the sentence becomes evident when we analyze the means employed to obfuscate who is responsible for the processes or verbs (nominalized as they are). If the question "Who is doing what to whom?" is posed with regard to the six listed points, what are the possible answers? The reader will have to draw his or her own conclusions. But perhaps the following answers are possible:

a. BP?
b. the whole world
c. somebody other than BP
d. members of the environmental movement
e. members of the environmental movement
f. everybody other than members of the environmental movement

The point to be made here is that a list of such features might serve as an initial crude index. In the case of Browne's speech, however, the issue of causality is precisely one of the items under contestation. Hence a closer look at the occurrences of 'cause' might well provide a further avenue to pursue. But space does not allow it.

7   PERSONAL PRONOUNS AND THEIR SIGNIFICANCE IN BROWNE'S SPEECH

The use of the pronoun 'we' is worthy of attention. Sometimes it is used exclusively, as in 24, 'We in BP'. But often Browne slips into the 'we' of consensus. See lines 45, 45(2), 46, 73, 77, 86, 86(2) and 86(3). This is a way of fudging the issue of causality referred to above.

Table 3.2 displays the 'we' concordance in the order of occurrence of 'we' in the text (15 occurrences in all).

A complementary concordance (Table 3.3) which might bring out either differences or a related patterning is that for 'our'. We can note that of the eleven instances, perhaps only one, line 60(2), is the consensus use.

It is evident that a business must pursue self-representation in a positive light—see 'Our own house is in order'. The semantic prosody which the brief span of left and right collocates hints at is certainly designed to be positive. While the environmentalists and BP disagree on the influence of oil and gas on the environment, both groups share an interest in preventing

Table 3.3 'Our' Concordance of Browne's Speech

1		**Our**	common Journey JOHN BROWNE
35	the precise impact of	**our**	own activities. Our operations,
36	of our own activities.	**Our**	operations, in exploration and
37	is produced by	**our**	chemical operations. If you add
39	by the consumption of	**our**	products, the total goes up to
44	is small, and	**our**	actions alone could not resolve
46	use energy and at how	**our**	products are used. That means
47	That means ensuring	**our**	own house is in order. It also
53	monitor and control	**our**	own emissions; to support
60	and we will share	**our**	expertise openly and freely. Our
60	Openly and freely.	**Our**	instinct is that once clear
76	business people, when	**our**	customers are concerned, we'd

further emissions that could contribute to possible climate change. There is no contradiction perceived by Browne in this. Analysis of the pronominal usage of 'we' and modality (which is left out here) can help us to see how this state of affairs is packaged linguistically.

8   THE BODY SHOP MISSION STATEMENT: "VALUES AND VISION 1994"

Turning now to the Body Shop text, this can be seen as part of wider trends in the past few decades. The rise of the 'green' movements, or environmental campaigning groups, political parties in some countries and opposition to ecologically harmful social and commercial practices has led business and economically powerful groups to go, first, on the defensive, and then, to begin to counter-attack. As the Greer and Bruno (1996) book, *Greenwash*, demonstrates, a response on the part of large business corporations which were responsible for environmental degradation was to "adopt" the surface language and claims of the environmentalists.

Other, usually smaller and mostly retail- or trade-oriented groups and firms were to be found embracing 'Third-Worldism' and certain high-profile issues. The Body Shop is such an organization. One can learn much about its orientation by reading its Mission Statement and following its 'business fortune' over the past years.

A concordance programme can help the corpus-oriented critical discourse analyst who wishes to follow up hunches. The crudely quantifiable data may well serve to highlight some of the preoccupations of such a firm. At the same time, we need not overlook the fact that as a commercially operating firm the self-serving advertizing is also ever-present. As Fairclough (1992: 92) writes: "Hegemony is a focus of constant struggle around points of greatest instability between classes and blocs, to construct or sustain or fracture alliances and relations of domination/subordination, which takes economic, political and ideological forms." "The Body Shop is, after all, a cosmetics company." Thus writes the mission statement author.

9   WHERE THE COMPANY STANDS: 'AGAINST', 'AIMS', 'EFFORTS'

Certainly the stand of the company on certain principles is worth investigating. What are the salient items? What is the semantic focus of the text(s)? Possibly also, what collocations are prominent? Which words collocate with salient items? As we may find, this could be an important feature distinguishing different texts—and hence writer perspectives—from one another. What might count as keywords in order to start to uncover these? This section looks at three such words.

Table 3.4 'Against' Concordance of the Body Shop Mission Statement

18	and civil rights, and	**against**	animal testing within the
81	activities. We are	**against**	animal testing in the
544	mounted a campaign	**against**	domestic violence in March
548	human and civil rights	**against**	the oppressive Nigerian
366	Level of awareness of	**Against**	Animal Testing Issues
543	Day of Protest	**Against**	Violence Against Women.
544	Against Violence	**Against**	Women. The Body Shop in
308	change. up till now	**AGAINST**	ANIMAL TESTING Our
337	testing. We will	**AGAINST**	ANIMAL TESTING continue

The nine occurrences of the preposition 'against' (in Table 3.4) give some idea of where the company stands. The left and right collocates bring out what Body Shop opposes. Five of the nine instances collocate with 'animal testing', two with 'violence' ('domestic' or 'against women') and one with 'oppressive Nigeria'.

An example of the broader co-text of item 18 (example 2) shows it is one of the campaigning positions of the Body Shop. The positive campaigning 'for' certain issues is also to be seen here.

(2) To passionately campaign for the protection of the environment and human and civil rights, and against animal testing within the cosmetics and toiletries industry.

A further obvious keyword to access where the company stands is 'aim' or 'aims'. The thirteen instances (verb, noun, past participle) (in Table 3.5) all serve to underline where the company is directing its efforts as both right and left highlighted collocates indicate.

The broader co-textual usage of line 822 is illustrated in (3).

(3) After meeting local demand, the co-operative offers The Body Shop their excess stock. The Body Shop aims to work towards sourcing more of our sesame oil from the cooperative as and when the producers can produce the quantities which we need.

The term 'effort' is itself a further item which, when concordanced automatically (Table 3.6), helps to uncover Body Shop's concerns. The highlighted items have positive associations.

Table 3.5 'Aim**' Concordance of the Body Shop Mission Statement

52	with principles We	aim	to achieve commercial success
63	our core values we	aim	to ensure that human and civil
564	decisions. The	aim	of these procedures and
567	or our suppliers. The	aim	is simple, but translating all
599	decisions. The	aim	of these procedures and
602	or our suppliers. The	aim	is simple, but translating all
1017	Could be used. The	aim	of the proposed campaign would
453	bear soaps. Though	aimed	primarily at children, the
532	with Shelter	aimed	to raise awareness among
470	Convention which	aims	to review and amend the
633	Itself to these	aims,	The Body Shop believes that
822	Stock. The Body Shop	aims	to work towards sourcing more
1068	to traditional and	aims	to avoid dependency

Table 3.6 'Effort*' Concordance of the Body Shop Mission Statement

760	markets in an	effort	to make the trading
252	devote increasing	efforts	to establishing
289	business. We want our	efforts	to set a precedent for others.
373	To increase our	efforts	on contact building, and
509	maintained by the	efforts	of hundreds of The Body
577	our fair trading	efforts	and for eventually making
583	rights work and our	efforts	to develop our Human
612	our fair trading	efforts	and for eventually making
618	rights work and our	efforts	to develop our Human

10   THE USE OF PERSONAL PRONOUNS BY THE BODY SHOP

The occurrence of four out of nine instances of 'efforts' preceded by 'our' can serve as the transition to a discussion of personal pronouns. How they are used can show their significance in the scheme of things, as we saw in the case of Browne's speech. An extract from the 'we' concordance (total = 140) demonstrates the preoccupation with self-presentation which the mission statement genre clearly dictates. The positively connoted collocates (highlighted in Table 3.7) both before and after the pronoun underscore by close juxtaposition the total commitment of Body Shop.

It is striking to note how all uses of 'we' are exclusive, that is, self-referential.

11   ANALYSIS OF KEYWORDS IN THE BODY SHOP'S SCHEME OF THINGS

There are a number of words that appear to stand out. Concordances for them can bring out patterns arising in their use. This may help us to underline some of the hunches which our qualitative and interpretative analysis is unearthing. Just picking out some of the keywords will prompt further investigation.

Let us take 'staff', 'volunteer' and 'involve'. If we count the word forms of the lemma 'involve', we get twelve instances, plus two of 'involvement' (Table 3.8). Even with the small span of collocates, which the program automatically generates, we see that 'staff' is a collocate, either left or right in seven cases.

If we now look at the concordance for the twenty-seven occurrences of 'staff' (Table 3.9), what do we find?

Right collocates include 'volunteer(s)' (4 instances), 'initiative' (2) and 'commitment' (1). Left collocates include positively connoted items: 'dedicated'. Word forms of the lemma 'involve' are found as both left (4) and right (3) collocates. What of the 'volunteer' concordance (Table 3.10)?

Of the ten related instances, four and possibly five have 'staff' as a left collocate. The impression which the text itself creates about Body Shop's commitment to charities, campaigns on human rights and animal welfare is borne out by frequency counts and concordances. Indeed the following co-text (4) for 'involve' demonstrates clearly the positive semantic prosody which the juxtaposition of some of the words discussed is intended to generate.

(4) And the key to The Body Shop's approach to giving is staff involvement. We're always looking for new ways to get staff involved, new ways to raise funds. It is easy for the Company to give money, but it is

Table 3.7 'We' Concordance of the Body Shop Mission Statement

13	communities in which	**we**	trade, by adopting a code of
29	wait for the day when	**we**	replace the value of money-with
35	The ways that	**we**	put our principles into practice
43	Make no mistake—	**we**	are not bystanders. We stand out,
43	We stand out,	**we**	stand up and we shout. We're
44	out, we stand up and	**we**	shout. We're passionate and
44	and driven. And	**we**	care. Never forget that care, like
50	charter The way	**we**	trade creates profits with
63	our core values	**we**	aim to ensure that human and
82	On animals, nor will	**we**	commission others to do so on
93	are the qualities	**we**	enshrine for our products in The
97	' and cosmetics if	**we**	didn't offer them value, no
100	Of a product-just as	**we**	want to ensure quality
100	quality ingredients,	**we**	want to guarantee that in the
101	Of these ingredients,	**we**	improve, wherever possible, the
107	the shop shelf,	**we**	underline its value with simple,
151	Company. In America,	**we**	have a stand-alone environmental
155	In mid-1993,	**we**	have developed policies and
171	During 1993/94	**we**	updated our policies and
174	practice worldwide,	**we**	now have a comprehensive
186	Wherever possible,	**we**	try to close the loop and use the
232	been done before, and	**we**	want to include our staff,
237	around the world,	**we**	will set ourselves clear targets
243	around the world—	**we**	will try to use renewable
244	feasible, and	**we**	will conserve natural resources
259	replacing what	**we**	must use with renewable
262	responsible business	**we**	adopt a four-tier approach: first,

Table 3.8 'Involve**' Concordance of the Body Shop Mission Statement

952	but it is not easy to	**involve**	staff in an exciting and
1114	They may prefer to	**involve**	staff rather than donate
162	have also been	**involved.**	in the autumn of 1992,
566	business processes	**involved,**	either ours or our
601	business processes	**involved,**	either ours or our
750	of the Indians	**involved**	in the programme. Our
950	New ways to get staff	**involved,**	new ways to raise funds. It
953	That staff can become	**involved.**	Money is the means but
959	shops in the UK are	**involved**	in community projects. At
900	the process of	**involvement**	across the company by
950	to giving is staff	**involvement.**	We're always looking
269	than exploitation, it	**involves**	degradation and
982	in Bristol. This	**involves**	dedicated staff time and
989	term commitment,	**involving**	input from staff in several

not easy to involve staff in an exciting and engaging way. The Body Shop uses money as a resource so that staff can become involved. Money is the means but staff are the most important vehicle for our charitable activities.

12 CONCLUSION: LANGUAGE AS A SITE OF CONTESTATION ON ENVIRONMENTAL ISSUES

This brief exposition of some of the preoccupations of the Body Shop has served to demonstrate how concordances can readily supply the linguist with evidence for interpretative analysis. We are arguing that critical discourse analysis can benefit from employing such methods. The quantitative counts give us explicit data about the writer's categorial scheme. Hence the ideological or principled position which an environmentally committed organization adopts can be shown to have clear counterparts in language. While we need have no illusions about how swiftly or slowly values can

Table 3.9 'Staff' Concordance of the Body Shop Mission Statement

232	want to include our	**staff,**	franchisees, subsidiaries and
274	rests on safety-for	**staff,**	for customers and for the
290	education for our	**staff**	on environmental issues. We
320	By increasing	**staff**	and public awareness of the
367	Issues amongst both	**staff**	and customers through
403	283 members of our	**staff**	volunteered for 12 different
877	Shop's head office. All	**staff**	had an opportunity to discuss
882	what is important to	**staff:**	a sense of family, caring,
949	approach to giving is	**staff**	involvement. We're always
950	for new ways to get	**staff**	involved, new ways to raise
952	is not easy to involve	**staff**	in an exciting and engaging
953	as a resource so that	**staff**	can become involved. Money is
954	is the means but	**staff**	are the most important vehicle
960	Littlehampton, 15% of	**staff**	spend half a day a month on
962	The Body Shop's	**staff**	to interact with communities
965	In order to help	**staff**	find ways to volunteer, the
967	their causes to	**staff**	and recruit new volunteers.
973	Shop, working with	**staff**	and other organisations will be
982	involves dedicated	**staff**	time and commitment from
989	involving input from	**staff**	in several areas of the
1049	to support this	**staff**	initiative with matching
1056	to support this	**staff**	initiative with matching
1079	Giving Scheme for	**staff**	has been introduced and the
1099	projects, with which	**staff**	are quite familiar: The Eastern
1107	group, comprising	**staff**	volunteers, meets every month
1109	written off stock to	**staff.**	Over £20,000 was raised and
1114	may prefer to involve	**staff**	rather than donate money or

Table 3.10 'Volunteer**' Concordance of the Body Shop Mission Statement

965	staff find ways to	**volunteer,**	the Company has set up
403	members of our staff	**volunteered**	for 12 different tests
404	outside the company	**volunteered**	in 7 different tests.
961	on company time	**volunteering**	in local projects. This
978	in community	**volunteering.**	• The Foundation is
346	We also use human	**volunteers**	to evaluate products prior
506	a relief drive to fund	**volunteers**	to renovate orphanages in
968	staff and recruit new	**volunteers.**	the future For The Body
1107	comprising staff	**volunteers,**	meets every month to
977	Community Service	**Volunteers**	(CSV) to encourage

change, it seems evident the value shifts organizations engage in are in part reflected in specific discourse strategies and lexical choices they employ. While not being impossible, it is debatable how much these can influence the wider community.

And, as we can see in Beder (1997), the struggle and contestation for dominance in the sphere of ecological and environmental discourse has not been left to the greens or environmentalists! The backlash has become vigorous and sustained. As Beder (1997: 122–3) indicates, the American Right, in the person of Newt Gingrich, appreciates that "Language, A Key Mechanism of Control" is central to the art of propaganda and to influencing people. In this document Gingrich points out which are "positive, governing words" and which are "name-calling words". (Chapter 11 refers to the work of Frank Luntz, on whose work Gingrich was dependent.) The role of the media in all this has been trenchantly analyzed by Herman and Chomsky (1988).

The contradictions inherent in a "trade not aid" policy are clear when we realize how the World Trade Organization (WTO) and most major trade and "aid" operations are constructed within the narrowly defined "Washington Consensus". Corporate free-market policies are paramount! See Beder (1997) on the response to environmental protection legislation, among other things. Roddick's (1998) "alliance" with, among others, BP and Unipart in a "New Vision for Business" also serves to highlight more than adequately the contradiction. In this connection it is worth quoting Alex Carey (1995:

133–4), where he refers to "widespread social and political indoctrination, an indoctrination which promotes business interests as *everyone's* interests" (emphasis added, RJA). The neo-conservative and neo-liberal swing in Western democracies since the 1990s has been pursuing and underlining this process. The "market" and business are the solution to all our problems and the key to our futures: this is the message the advertizers, the media and the politicians are transmitting loud and clear to us.

4   The Framing of Ecology

1   INTRODUCTION

This chapter argues that the discourse of market economics colonizes and serves to narrowly frame critical and oppositional discourse on the environment and ecology. In particular, we consider a speech, already discussed in chapter 3, by John Browne (1997), the chief executive officer (CEO) of BP, a major multinational corporation, whose operations do not normally associate them with the cleaning up of the globe. The framing of ecology in this fashion is proceeding rapidly within our prevailing capitalist economic system. Moreover, this is no recent development. In the seventies O'Neill (1972: 20) drew attention to the issue I wish to discuss: "Political imagination is shackled by the corporate organization of modern society." It is difficult for governments to limit the ability of multinational corporations "to shape *the national ecology* and *psychic economy of individuals*" (emphasis added, RJA). O'Neill continues (1972: 20):

> The corporate economy stands between the state and the individual. Its power to determine the life-style of modern society must be recognized as the principal subject of political economy.

About the same time, an American (and British) fiction audience was reading passages such as the following:

> 'There's a river in Cleveland which is so polluted that it catches fire about once a year. That used to make me sick, but I laugh about it now. When some tanker accidentally dumps its load in the ocean, and kills millions of birds and billions of fish, I say, "More power to Standard Oil," or whoever it was that dumped it.' Trout raised his arms in celebration. "Up your ass with Mobil gas," he said. (Vonnegut 1973: 84)

The ecological movement of the past thirty odd years (of which Vonnegut's black humour formed part) represented an optimistic and once popular counter-current that mobilized critics of the depredation of the environment

by industrial corporations. Government threats to limit the anti-environmental activities of capitalist corporations have resulted in them fighting
back. Numerous publications in recent years document the tactics which
"corporate environmentalism" has adopted to undermine the ecological
movement. This chapter focuses on the way language, in this case the public
discourse of a transnational corporation like BP, fits into this pattern.

Facts about the environment or ecological problems scarcely ever get presented without a 'spin'. One of the functions of this discourse is not to be
informative but persuasive, not to 'tell it like it is' but to 'tell it like you want
people to believe it to be' or 'like they want to hear it'. Ask no questions and
you will be told no lies: this is the essence of so-called polite behaviour or
acting as people expect one (you) to act. Linguists have called this "phatic
communion". One of its functions is that of creating bonds between people—
what Fill (1993: 55) discusses as "bandstiftendes Sprechen" ("bond-creating
talk"). We all know how thin the line is between phatic communion, being
diplomatic and polite, and lying. The speech task in hand overrides truth
values. The interactional function displaces the informative function.

2   DISCOURSE ANALYSIS OF BP CHIEF EXECUTIVE'S SPEECH

This study again combines concordancing and corpus linguistic techniques
with qualitative critical discourse analysis. It sets out to see how specific
linguistic features are associated with or serve to uphold larger discourse
processes, such as evaluation, argumentative strategies and discourse tactics.
Critical linguists such as Fowler (1991: 67) claim there are "certain areas of
language particularly implicated in coding social values".

This approach is applied to the analysis of an edited version of a speech
given by John Browne, the chief executive of BP at Stanford University,
California, 19 May 1997. Browne's speech is of interest for two reasons:
appropriacy and intelligibility. It is appropriate because BP claims to be proactive in environmental issues. Browne made his speech before a 'friendly'
audience—at a large private US university, Stanford. Yet at the same time he
designated it for wider, public broadcast. The fact that a 'left-leaning' British
weekly magazine, the *New Statesman*, 20 June 1997, published it is evidence
for this. On 4 July 1997 the *New Statesman* also published an interview
with John Browne (Ghazi and Hargreaves 1997), subheaded: "BP's chief
executive is making the running on green strategy. But how does that square
with controversy in Colombia and the Atlantic Ocean?"

3   BROWNE'S SPEECH AS SEMANTIC NEGOTIATION

A close reading aided by a computer-assisted analysis of the relatively brief
speech (826 words) makes clear the public relations (PR) or 'massaging'

function of the speech. Whether we have a clear case of "corporate environmentalism" (Beder 1997) at work here, I leave the reader to conclude. A study of the frequency list and the concordances of individual lexical items in the text makes it obvious that the speech deals largely with semantics. That is to say, John Browne, as the chief executive of BP, presents, debates and negotiates a series of propositional truths and meaning values for the issue he has chosen to discuss.

4   *A PRÉCIS* OF BROWNE'S SPEECH

The following is an attempt to summarize the speech. We know that a problem exists—climate change may or not be happening. Whatever the case, we all need to pull together. BP can bring its (superior) knowledge to bear on providing a solution (involving the market, not regulation). A problem facing the whole world needs a co-ordinated response. We all need to face the challenge together.

On the surface BP appears to be facing the issue directly and indeed altruistically. Common problems require solutions to come about from the co-operation of all. What could be less matter-of-fact? We see how such modes of discourse can powerfully appeal to the normal. They engage in the process of "naturalization" (Fairclough 1995a: 13), which critical linguists wish to uncover. During a speech or conversation people may aim to transmit certain views of the world, as if they have entirely unquestioned validity. Fowler (1991: 57) has also commented on this process: "[T]he ideological function of conversation is to naturalize the terms in which reality is presented."

Having made a preliminary sketch of the overall intent of the speech, we might expect that the use of a concordance program could serve to provide an objective answer to the question of what the text is about. Hence we might anticipate a clustering of lexical items, with the salient items repeated. Consider the concordance for 'climate' and 'climate change' (Table 4.1).

Here we receive little assistance from the computer. Although the word 'climate' occurs five times, with 'change' four times as its right collocate, it

Table 4.1 'Climate and Climate Change' Concordance of Browne's Speech

12	by the debate around	**climate change.**	Yet there is now
14	influence on the	**climate,**	and a link between the
19	policy dimensions of	**climate change**	is not when the link
20	greenhouse gases and	**climate change**	is conclusively
76	concern about	**climate change.**	As business people,

turns out to be far more revealing to engage in a qualitative analysis of the text. For it transpires that BP's chief executive engages in a brief, and yet detailed, semantic analysis of the very bases of and the ramifications of the putative 'climate change'. This may not be the place to develop the analysis, but a glance at the concordance line numbers shows that four uses of the term occur within a relatively short section of the speech—the three introductory paragraphs. Paragraph 13 is the next occurrence of the phrase.

From a critical discourse perspective several areas are worth investigating: lexical features, grammar and the text-forming component of grammar. The latter comprises cohesion and theme-rheme structures (Halliday and Hasan 1976: 27).

5   COHESION AND ARGUMENTS IN THE SPEECH

Taking the features in reverse order, we can say that cohesion may constitute a significant element of the ideological work going on in a text. A listing of the lexical cohesion elements and the related semantic coherence through synonyms and equivalent expressions (which lack of space does not allow) would give a glimpse of the way Browne structures the discourse and the rhetorical arguments. Notice how Browne 'slips' very swiftly from the journey metaphor introduced in paragraph 4, by way of 'involvement' (paragraph 5) to 'activity' and back to 'actions' (paragraph 9) by way of 'problems' and 'caused' (paragraph 8).

What does a study of the most frequent items in the text tell us about the inter-relation between the textual function and the logical argument? Two noteworthy features are the third and the seventh most frequent items— 'and' and 'that', with thirty-one and eighteen occurrences, respectively.

If we consider the 'that' concordance first, we can isolate the anaphoric demonstratives—twelve instances. Whether a stand-alone pronoun or a demonstrative adjective modifying a noun, the demonstrative 'that' contributes cohesion and thus focuses or even systematically weights argument elements. If we sort the twelve demonstrative items regarding their collocates and the structural patterns they appear in, we obtain four groups of 'that' (Tables 4.2–4.5).

We can make a number of observations about the use of the demonstratives in the speech. Firstly, they are clearly important features of spoken English and contribute a major part to the comprehensibility of the speech. The line numbers generated automatically by the concordance program show the even distribution through the text. Secondly, they can be interpreted in terms of theme-rheme and information structures. In the cases where the form initiates a clause (group B) it is clearly focusing the argument consciously on elements which Browne wishes to be 'taken for granted' as common-sense knowledge. In the context of spoken language we might note how important such a command over the means for directing attention are for the

Table 4.2 Group A 'That' Concordance of Browne's Speech

38	If you add to	that	the carbon produced by the
33	of carbon, but it is	that	part which could cause
10	What he meant by	that	was that all science is open to

Table 4.3 Group B 'That' Concordance of Browne's Speech

47	our products are used.	That	Means ensuring our own house
79	a sustainable world.	That	Means a world where the
45	the problem. But	that	does not mean we should do
74	positive action. But	that	disagreement doesn't mean we
39	about 95 megatonnes.	That	is 1 per cent of total carbon

Table 4.4 Group C 'That' Concordance of Browne's Speech

73	of oil and gas. I think	that	view underestimates the
11	and to development.	That	view is certainly confirmed by

Table 4.5 Group D 'That' Concordance of Browne's Speech

24	We in BP have reached	that	point. It is an important moment
27	have started on	that	journey. The Rio conference

speaker. Both the conjunction 'and' (see below) and the anaphoric demonstrative 'that', together with their collocates and grammatical environments, play a central role in organizing the focus on or emphasis of items Browne is presenting. See lines 10, 33, 45, 73, 74, 11, 39, 47, and 79. We might add that 10 has 'that' in a pseudo-cleft, while line 33 has it in a cleft sentence. These structures are commonly employed in spoken English to explicitly emphasize items. Another position in which the concordance shows 'that' appearing (in lines 24, 27 (group D) and 33) is at the end of clauses or sentences, directly preceding the full stop, thus giving them end-weight. This is a further device which serves to mark priorities and emphases in the exposition of the theses Browne is presenting.

We may note that groups A, B and C have the demonstrative in theme position or at least focused initially. Five concordance lines have one form of the lemma 'mean' either as a left or right collocate. If we add line 39 containing forms of the verb 'to be' to this, we see that, quite literally, at least six instances of Browne's engaging in 'negotiating meaning' are to be found in the speech. Actually the computer concordance shows us a sixth instance of the lemma 'mean'.

50　is in order. It also **means** contributing to the wider

If we add this to group B (Table 4.3) we have further evidence of the ideological work Browne is engaged in. 'Also' as a left collocate of 'means' is an indication of meaning enlargement which Browne engages in at this point. In fact in paragraph 9 where the 'also' occurs we see Browne employing several re-definitions. He is positioning BP as a major player in the scientific research and technology required to solve the problem, having first acknowledged that, in actual fact, BP has little to do with the problem.

6　THEME AND THE STRUCTURING OF INFORMATION IN BROWNE'S SPEECH

Theme is the speaker or writer's point of departure. By investigating thematic structures, light can be thrown on the way Browne shapes information. The initial items of a clause serve to position what the writer considers to be "common-sense assumptions" about the world and the social order. Furthermore rhetorical strategies or moves which Browne makes are marked thematically. A marked theme, like "Let us be clear" in paragraph 6, has the function of pointedly focusing or 'naturalizing' what is to follow. If we look at thematic structures we can trace and lay bare assumptions and strategies which are not made explicit.

A significant example in Browne's speech occurs in paragraph 13. The nominal group "real sustainability" starts the sentence, thus being introduced as a 'matter of fact' entity. The sentence goes on to analyze the term semantically and to define what Browne wishes it to mean.

The thematic structure of the speech is also related to coherence, on which Fairclough (1995a: 122) comments, "local coherence relations are very significant indeed in the ways in which texts position people as subjects and cumulatively shape identities [. . .], and how texts work ideologically." An important role in this is played by the expansion techniques for clauses and hence arguments, which Halliday (1985: 202–27) terms "elaboration, extension and enhancement". If we look at these, we will gain a first approximation of how Browne employs coherence to structure his arguments. A preliminary step is to ascertain automatically by computer analysis how frequent certain lexical items are. The conjunction 'and' (together with other items such as 'but' (thirteenth most frequent item with eight occurrences), 'because' (paragraph 12), 'so' (paragraph 12), 'yet' (paragraph 2), 'therefore' (paragraph 10) and 'if' (paragraph 7)) is an item which may well play a role in expansion processes. We will focus on a selected 'and' concordance (Table 4.6).

Table 4.6 Selected 'And' Concordance of Browne's Speech

11	to amendment	**and**	to development. That view is
14	on the climate,	**and**	a link between the concentration
16	about cause	**and**	Effect and, even more
16	cause and effect	**and**,	even more importantly, about
21	cannot be discounted,	**and**	is taken seriously by society.
36	in exploration	**and**	refining, produce about eight
44	contribution is small,	**and**	our actions alone could not
46	way we use energy	**and**	at how our products are used.
48	research, technology	**and**	engaging in the search for the
53	steps: to monitor	**and**	control our own emissions; to
54	scientific work	**and**	to encourage new research; to
56	for the long term;	**and**	to contribute to the public policy
60	is not proprietary	**and**	we will share our expertise
62	to produce innovative	and	creative responses than an
67	discrimination	**and**	without denying the peoples of
70	being profitable	**and**	responding to the reality and
82	we take for granted	**and**	Which the oil industry helps to
84	actions were taking	**and**	will take are directed to
86	if we are to match	**and**	master the challenges we all

A preliminary analysis of the 'and' concordance shows that the high-lighted items are markers of elaboration or extension. Arguments are developed in linguistic terms by the addition (marked by 'and') of a finite "**and** at how our products are used" (line 46), or infinite clause, "research, technology **and** engaging in the search for the" (line 48) which extends the meaning by linking something further or 'new' or by describing or making the preceding clause more specific. A similar case could be made for the other items, namely where nouns or nominal groups appear to be grammatical metaphors for processes ("to amendment **and** to development. That view is" (line 11), "to produce innovative **and** creative responses than an" (line 62) or even seemingly 'fixed expressions' like the irreversible binomial in (line 16) "about cause **and** effect and, even more").

7   PROCESSES AND AGENCY IN THE SPEECH

As Fairclough says (1992: 179), a multitude of linguistic means can represent a real process in the world. This depends (will depend) on the observer's perspective. In systemic grammar this grammatical element is called "transitivity". Voice (whether active or passive) is one of the grammatical choices that can create perspective. Hence the 'goal' can become grammatical subject or the agent is either a 'passive agent' or omitted altogether. There are various motivations for choosing the 'passive'. Firstly, passives may serve to obfuscate agency; hence causality and responsibility associated with processes is unclear. Secondly, a passive construction shifts the goal into initial or 'theme' position, which means presenting it as given or already known information.

Like the passive, nominalization shares the option of leaving out the agent in representing processes. Various motivations may underlie this choice of what Halliday terms (1985: 321) "grammatical metaphor". Writers can suggest anonymous or invariant, even universal, processes by means of nominalization. They may omit all participants, besides agents. They thus create an impersonal style. Nominalization thus turns processes into states and objects; concrete factors into abstract elements. Writers seem to construct 'objectivity'.

Agent deletion is widespread in Browne's speech. 'Karl Popper' is the only specific participant mentioned in the first three paragraphs of the speech. 'There' in paragraphs 2 and 3 are clear instances of depersonalization. We find the processes thus introduced lack any ascription to specific participants of the views, opinions and knowledge of climate change which are mentioned.

8   BROWNE'S EXPOSITION BECOMES HORTATORY

Martin (1984: 23) makes a relevant point for our purposes in a discussion of impersonal writing. He says: "Exposition which tries to persuade people to do something is more like spoken language—a number of feelings and attitudes are expressed." He coins the phrase "hortatory exposition" to characterize this phenomenon. The Browne speech contains traces of this hortatory element. Note the five instances of the first person pronoun 'I' (Table 4.7). They all have mental process verbs (Halliday 1985: 111) as collocates. These in themselves are either perception or cognition processes.

Use of the first person pronoun is itself a marker of subjectivity, which contrasts with the otherwise impersonal and objective discourse. In analytical exposition feelings and attitudes hardly occur at all. Nouns or nominalizations are a way of avoiding them. Take the noun 'concern' in Browne's speech. Turning attitudes into abstract qualities is one way of sounding objective while still presenting a point of view (and thus expressing an attitude).

Table 4.7 'I' Concordance of Browne's Speech

26	what sort of action?	I think the right metaphor for the
58	steps on the journey.	I hope to be able to announce further
72	in which you operate.	I disagree with some members of the
73	the use of oil and gas.	I think that view underestimates the
82	helps to provide.	I don't believe those are incompatible

Browne's use of the first person pronoun plays a role in one of his pivotal arguments. This is the tenet that market-based solutions are preferable to regulation, introduced in paragraph 11. The mental process and first person pronoun deliberately personalize the 'human' dimension. The willingness to be open and to share scientific knowledge and expertise is presented as self-explanatory. The modal adverb 'more likely' together with the appeal to common sense in the phrase 'our instinct' serve to soften the claim that the market is to be preferred over governmental regulation.

The three subsequent paragraphs broaden and support this argument. In addition to the insistence on "wide-ranging" solutions, "because this is a global problem" in paragraph 12, paragraphs 13 and 14 contain an almost surreal discussion of the notion of 'sustainability' from the vantage point of an oil company.

Paragraph 13 is a good example of how hortatory exposition instrumentalizes and downplays attitudes and beliefs of others.

"Real sustainability is about simultaneously being profitable and responding to the reality and concerns of the world in which you operate. I disagree with some members of the environmental movement who say we have to abandon the use of oil and gas. I think that view underestimates the potential for creative and positive action. But that disagreement doesn't mean we can ignore the mounting evidence and growing concern about climate change. As business people, when our customers are concerned, we'd better take notice."

At least three linguistic features are involved in the highlighted items. Firstly, we have nominalization and thus inexplicit agency. Who is concerned in "concerns of the world in which you operate"? Who is disagreeing in "that disagreement"? Here we have an ambivalent potential anaphoric reference to the previous sentence as well as back to the verb "I disagree", two sentences back. Secondly, in the collocation "that view underestimates", we see the role the negative semantic prosody plays in criticizing "some members of the environmental movement". Thirdly, the subjective use of the personal pronoun followed by the modalizing "think" seemingly weakens the force of the criticism Browne is expressing. A final point has to do with the lexical cohesion created by "concern" and "concerned" in the final two sentences of the paragraph. Here again the ambivalent nominalization "growing concern" suggests a distinction between valid concern—that shared by "our customers"—and invalid concern—that of "some members of the environmental movement".

The final four paragraphs (12–15) try to round up and deliver the convincing message that BP's way is the way the 'world' is going and will continue to follow. From the market (paragraph 12) Browne proceeds without transition to "sustainability". The latter, "real sustainability" (paragraph 13), he defines idiosyncratically and yet in keeping with what his Stanford audience will expect to hear. Being sustainable is attributed by elaboration, again without transition, to "companies" and associated with "a sustainable world" (paragraph 14). Browne concedes that "environmental equilibrium" is desirable but that the oil industry's activities can continue as well. Thus an implicit inconsistency is proposed, immediately to be rhetorically gainsaid by the next sentence: "I don't believe those are incompatible goals". This clinching personal view has had the way for it prepared by a series of first person mental process verbs of cognition as indicated above. Until now this 'personal' touch has been avoided. Paragraph 14 uses an exclusive 'we', only for a series of inclusive 'we' to provide the common 'we are all together in this' appeal or final flourish in paragraph 15.

9   MORE NOMINALIZATIONS IN BROWNE'S SPEECH

One consequence of the widespread use of nominalizations and grammatical metaphors is that written exposition is 'less explicit' than speech. A further feature, which allows the expression of objectivity or represents the covert way exposition interprets the world, is writers' use of metaphors.

By explicitly appealing to the metaphor of a "common journey" in paragraph 5 Browne adopts a clear ideological position. As the speech continues, it sets out to "naturalize" this position. The presupposition that everyone shares the same goals as Browne continues. This is first rather vaguely introduced (paragraph 1) "the debate around climate change" and then developed (paragraph 2) "effective consensus", (paragraph 3) "the policy dimension" through "journey" (paragraph 5). In paragraph 9 "the best public policy mechanisms" are being sought. This development culminates in the final paragraph (15) in "the challenge we all face" and the claim that "we share a common, vital interest". The highly evaluative epithet 'vital' seems to allow of no exceptions. The common-sense understanding here being appealed to excludes any alternative interpretation! We here see how Browne presupposes harmony that in a circular fashion provides the basis for the construction of a presumed consensus.

Browne shifts us into an area of discourse we recognize from political and church-based religious 'arguments'. The implied universality of the problems we face with climate change is taken for granted. We are all party to a kingdom of harmonizing ends in which human wills unite. The presupposition that human ends in the real world harmonize is clearly empirically false. In sociological terms, class interests, or the North and the South in the global economy, or even consumers and producers most certainly do *not* share the same purposes in relation to pollution and emissions control. Corporate responses to ecological and social damage are clearly and demonstrably not the same as those of injured, killed and uprooted inhabitants of Bhopal where and when Union Carbide's pesticide plant blew up in 1989 (Greer and Bruno 1996).

10   CHOICE OF WORDING OR LEXICALIZATION IN THE SPEECH

Identifying the processes of wording the world, 'lexicalization', can give insight into how the speaker operates. For alternative wordings can carry political and ideological significance in their application. Particular structurings of the meanings of a word are forms of hegemony. The lemma 'mean' in the Browne text (see the section on the demonstrative 'that' above) can serve to bring out how Browne actually engages in this re-working or re-signifying process as an element of his argument or exposition. The co-text of 'sustainability' is a good case in point.

A further focus is upon metaphor. The sub-text of the speech clearly hinges on 'science' as a metaphor for how BP approaches the issue of climate change. Browne takes great trouble to underline this orientation. We know the role of scientific discourse is becoming hegemonic and taking over other orders of discourse. In Fairclough's (1989: passim) phrase, we can see how rapidly the "colonization" of much public discourse by science is proceeding. Browne utilizes this trend to encourage BP's almost detached, distant and yet qualified view of the circumstances under discussion. It is certainly a less explicit metaphor than that of 'journey' introduced in paragraph 4 as a rallying cry.

It is almost as if Browne is saying "we are simply faced with a scientific conundrum when it comes to climate change. BP is proposing to participate in the scientific and disinterested debate in as objective and creative a fashion as possible. If we all co-operate in this, sharing our knowledge, as we are prepared to do (paragraph 11), things can be achieved, but only if regulation is not resorted to!" If we go through the text paragraph by paragraph we can mark the science-coloured lexis and the syntax (impersonal, grammatical metaphors, i.e. nominalization) which contribute to this. Consider the terms "confirmed" (paragraph 1), "discernible" (paragraph 2), "large elements of uncertainty", "cause and effect", "consequences", "unwise", "ignore", "consider the policy dimensions", "conclusively proven" (paragraph 3), etc. This is evidence of the web woven by the inexplicit metaphor of science that envelops the speech. Paragraph 1, with the scene-setting allusion to Karl Popper's falsification hypothesis, is an explicit beginning. The rest of the speech is an exposition (despite being a speech, with its clearly identifiable spoken markers). A look at the 'that' concordance, as we have seen (Tables 4.2–4.5), provides solid evidence for this. The anaphoric tying of the foregoing points to the elaboration or enhancement of the clauses to follow (in real time in the speech) is a device of spoken language. Further related devices are 'this' (three times), 'these' (once) and 'those' (twice).

Marketization is the true message behind the speech. Yet apart from two paragraphs (11 and 12), Browne does not make this explicit. Instead, as we have seen, the appeal to science and the use of scientific language aim to present a sober and convincing exposition of the problem and to propose a balanced, reasoned and logical set of solutions. This is presumably exactly what a university audience expects!

11   CONCLUSION

The suggestion Browne is making is that BP is operating in a proactive fashion, without being asked to. This is a gambit Athanasiou (1996) refers to. The green PR operations of large corporations are part of a strategy to lay claim to having been the prime movers in the fight against preventing emissions which 'might' contribute to climate change. It is part of the economic logic that sees increased environmental protection arising from growing prosperity in the North and the accompanying 'trickle down' to the South. Such features are not so easy to grasp automatically through computer analysis. Yet as Athanasiou (1996: 171) writes: "There is a fundamental conflict between the logic of social and environmental protection and the demands of deregulated international trade". For Athanasiou (1996: 183) there are moral and ecological limits to economics.

Despite many writers making this point, the fact remains, as Greer and Bruno (1996: 11) comment, that transnational corporations (TNCs) "help set the agenda for global negotiations on the crises of environment and development". This is precisely what we have seen John Browne engage in during his Stanford speech.

In chapters 2 and 3 we argued that part of the problem of changing people's behaviour regarding environmental and ecological issues is appreciating that differing social, economic and political forces employ language and discourse in persuasive terms in different ways. The language employed to represent reality, to present arguments, to develop proposals, incorporates a model of reality. We all meet discourse pre-patterned by choices that speakers and writers who have gone before us have made. Education has as one of its central functions the sensitization of young generations to those patterns of discourse deemed to be suitable for survival in the social formations for which they are being educated and socialized. Where people are employing this discourse to systematically prevent perception of certain facts, the critical linguist and the critical reader need to help students, readers and media recipients to recognize how this proceeds.

5   Talking About
'Sustainable Development'

1   INTRODUCTION

The earlier analyses of the BP CEO's speech, in chapter 4, and other corporate analyses in chapters 2 and 3 have already prepared us for the 'greenwash' they manifest. The Greenpeace activists Greer and Bruno (1996: 11) characterize this process thus:

> A corporate leader in ozone destruction takes credit for being a leader in ozone protection. A giant oil transnational embraces the "precautionary approach" to global warming. A major agrochemical manufacturer trades in a pesticide so hazardous it has been banned in many countries, while implying that it is helping to feed the hungry. A petrochemical firm uses the waste from one polluting process as raw material for another, and boasts that this is an important recycling initiative. A logging company cuts timber from natural rainforest, replaces it with plantations of a single exotic species, and calls the project 'sustainable forest development.'

Greer and Bruno continue (1996: 12): "Through a sophisticated greenwash strategy, TNCs are working to manipulate the definition of environmentalism and of sustainable development, and to ensure that trade and environment agreements are shaped, if not dictated, by the corporate agenda."

The study of the *Shell Reports 1999* and *2000* which follows is a further investigation of 'greenwash'. Linguists (such as Harré, Brockmeier and Mühlhäusler 1999 and Mühlhäusler 2003) have analyzed the language companies use to talk about the environment in order to distract attention from environmental problems. My study falls under the heading of the critical analysis of what Alwin Fill (1998: 12) has called "surface ecologization" of discourse. It focuses on one giant corporation, Shell, which is clearly engaged in 'greenwashing'. The chapter investigates the textual usage and the 'content' of 'sustainable development'. Why? Because if everyone is talking about sustainable development, there is no guarantee that they are talking about the same thing.

2 METHOD

Once again a computer-held, machine-readable set of data—in this case the electronically available *Shell Report 2000*—is searched by means of a software programme. After the by now routine quantitative analyses, a qualitative analysis of certain lexical items in selected concordances was undertaken. The results allow us to see how micro-level or textual level linguistic features are linked to broader argumentative processes, including standard persuasive, rhetorical techniques from PR and advertising.

3 DESCRIPTION OF THE MATERIAL

What is the nature of the text? Although it can be printed out on paper, it was designed to be read on the website of Shell. Hypertext links to other sections and multi-coloured graphics and illustrations cover the webpages. In the written text format it reads like a self-explanatory, matter-of-fact report of how Shell has voluntarily taken sustainability on board. My analysis does not address the impact that such a modality has on internet users. It still assumes that language and discourse can be analyzed in isolation from other modi and habitual patterns of internet usage. This is clearly an oversimplification.

At various points the skilfully produced text makes the usual appeals to authority, firstly, in the section entitled "What is Sustainable Development?", to the Brundtland Report and its definition of sustainable development and secondly, by quoting from "one of the world's leading environmental economists, David Pearce". The constituent businesses of Shell, Exploration and Production, Oil Products, Chemicals, Gas and Power, and Renewables, are all said to be adhering to "The Sustainable Development Management Framework". The latter is Shell's company-internal way of building 'sustainable development' into its planning process. A section called "Sustainable development—an independent view" appeals to autonomous authorities from outside the company—in this case the CEOs of customers and strategic partners. In the sections summarizing Shell's "approach to Sustainable Development" there is one which highlights the ethical dimension. It is entitled "As an expression of values". It is not intended as a pun that the next section is called "As a creator of business value." But the dual recourse for support to both the modern capitalist realm of investor relations as well as to the outside public as a whole is evident!

Two factors probably influenced this greenwash tactic: first came the Royal Dutch-Shell Brent Spar oil-container scandal and the ensuing boycotts. Perhaps this 'bad publicity' provoked by Greenpeace's actions 'compelled' Shell to engage in greenwash. Livesey (2001) has analyzed in some detail how Shell attempted subsequently to construct an ecological identity.

Secondly, there was competitive pressure on the public relations front, in particular in the form of the high profile position of BP and its CEO, John Browne (see chapter 4). BP's takeover of Amoco is clear evidence that selling the public an ecologically clean image in its corporate advertising has not reduced the bottom line. Indeed quite the opposite seems to have happened. Shell was perhaps being forced to jump on the ecological bandwagon, we might conclude. Yet Shell's 'interpretation of sustainable development' by appealing so late to the authority of the Brundtland Report makes this sudden revelation appear rather hollow, not to mention hypocritical!

4   QUANTITATIVE ANALYSIS: VITAL STATISTICS OF THE MATERIAL

The text contains a total of 4,896 running words, with a total of 1,461 different words. This gives it a type-token-ratio (TTR) of 0.298. The degree of lexical diversity might reflect the values coded in the texts. There may well be a relationship between repetitiveness and accustoming readers or listeners to certain notions. This text has either much in-built redundancy or much repetitiveness. In view of the fact that the text consists of the separate frames downloaded from a website, and hence the components of a hypertext, it may well be that we are dealing with an artefact of such a genre. However, in the absence of comparative data this argument cannot be pursued further.

Frequency and 'over- and under-lexicalization' are features that the computer can help us rapidly to access nowadays. Focuses of semantic interest may well be reflected in lexical repetition, if we ignore the function words and count content words. So the 27 occurrences of 'Shell('s)' need not surprise us. Taking 10 occurrences as an arbitrary cut-off point the most frequent item is 'sustainable' (72 times) followed by 'development' (64). Then come 'business' (52), 'way(s)' (27), 'need(s)' (19), 'environmental' (17), 'management' (17), 'society' (17), 'principle(s)' (16), 'social' (16), 'gas' (14), 'performance' (14), 'product(s)' (13), 'chemical(s)' (13), 'sustainability' (12), 'environment' (11), 'market(s)' (11), 'people' (11), 'progress' (11), and 'value(s)' (11). 'Sustainability' occurs 12 times, 'sustainable' 72 (= 1.47%) (14.7 per 1,000). Looking at the seven immediately right collocates of 'sustainable' we find this picture: it is followed by 'development' 64 times, 'foundation' once, 'growth' once, 'management' once, 'world' twice, 'way' once and 'mobility' twice. The two related words 'sustained' and 'sustaining' occur once each. In all, the string 'sustain**' occurs 86 times out of 4,896 running words. This is a ratio of 17.5 per 1,000 (1.75%). The frequency of 'sustainable development' is clearly an artefact of the text form, since seven occurrences are in subheading titles.

5 TEXTUAL ANALYSIS OF THE SHELL REPORTS

The Shell Report 1999 cover bore the title *People, planet & profits an act of commitment* over a sepia coloured photograph of a male acrobat flying through the air towards the 'catcher' acrobat on a trapeze. The metaphor is thus pictorially underscored. "The global debate continues" is printed in the bottom left-hand corner. *The Shell Report 2000* devotes a major portion of its website to the 'issue' of sustainable development.

To continue the pictorial metaphor, words like 'commitment' and 'issue', and in the body of the report 'value' and 'principle', are used like the paints from an artist's palette. In addition to the choice of positively associated words (purr-words), including 'sustainable development' itself, the well-known rhetorical figure of the appeal to authority, in particular to the Brundtland Report, has already been mentioned.

A preliminary look at a selection from the concordance for 'sustainable development' (Table 5.1) shows that the semantic prosody surrounding it, in the concrete case of left collocates, contains (highlighted) positively loaded or associated items, sometimes known as 'purr-words' among non-linguists.

The left collocates are mostly process words, either verbs, reified processes or nominalizations: 'definition of', 'on how to achieve', 'planned to

Table 5.1 Selected 'Sustainable Development' Concordance of Shell Report

64	definition of	sustainable development	still has an
105	—on how to achieve	sustainable development.	The
114	planned to integrate	sustainable development	thinking
129	planned to integrate	sustainable development	into the
206	been contributing to	sustainable development	as a normal
210	and contribution to	sustainable development	reflecting
310	The concept of	sustainable development	helped us to
316	drive to integrate	sustainable development	throughout
335	dedicated solely to	sustainable development	is being
337	the contributions of	sustainable development	'champions'
366	"The concept of	sustainable development	helped us to
592	to contribute to	sustainable development	

integrate', 'planned to integrate', 'been contributing to', 'and contribution to', 'the contributions of', 'The concept of', 'to contribute to'. Positive-sounding items include 'technology focused on', 'The concept of', 'drive to integrate', 'dedicated solely to'. The verbs 'achieve' and 'integrate', with their accompanying terms, 'drive' or 'planned', reflect either performance or rational orientation. In any case they are affirmative. Here we can see the almost standard corporate principle at work: "accentuate the positive, decentuate the negative".

6 ANALYSIS OF SELECTED ASPECTS OF THE SHELL REPORTS 1999 AND 2000

A *prima facie* argument can be made that PR material serves to confuse and distract from the issues by looking at a simple passage from the 1999 report. This extract is enough to demonstrate that 'sustainable development', the buzzword or significant symbol of the moment seemingly, is viewed instrumentally by the drafters of the report. The last two sentences contain purr-words (highlighted in extract 1).

> (1) We aspire to be a leader in the economic, environmental and social aspects of everything we do; first choice for our shareholders, our customers, our employees, those with whom we do business, society and future generations. We believe that our commitment to contribute to sustainable development holds the key to our long-term business success. The values that underpin sustainable development are embodied in our Business Principles that provide the foundation for everything we are and everything we do.

Also at this point the text seems to take off into the realm of a kind of pseudo-religious, ethical-moralistic discourse. The co-textual words are moral or altruistic, e.g. "our commitment to contribute to". The use of words like 'values' which are supposedly "embodied in" the "Business Principles" of the company and providing "the foundation for everything we are and do" appears to position the activities of a business organization as if it were a human agent. This is the kind of discourse which we may not expect from annual reports but which seems to be engulfing the realm of so-called "investor relations" over the past decade (Jameson 2000). Nor should we overlook the fact that the author of the report has already systematically prepared the way (extract 2) for this possible pseudo-religious interpretation, by quoting from "one of the world's leading environmental economists, David Pearce."

> (2) Brundtland's definition of sustainable development still has an enormous following, perhaps because most people want to believe in it. One

of the world's leading environmental economists, David Pearce, thinks it survives because it appears to build bridges between the demands of environmentalists and developers: "It is an article of faith, and in that sense almost a religious idea, similar to justice, equality and freedom". It is also wide in scope and loosely defined. So almost everyone can identify with it, even though it will not teach them about any practical changes which they need to make.

Nausea, although likely, is not an adequate response to this kind of discourse. As detached academic analysts we need to ask to what extent discourse engineering is at work here. It may help in this connection to look closely (Table 5.2) at the eight uses of other nouns that collocate with 'sustainable' in the *Shell 2000 Report*.

Significantly perhaps, as the high numbers generated by the program indicate, these uses come in the sections of the report dealing with individual Shell companies and company-internal operations. Below I have collated the broader co-texts of these eight items. Apart from the somewhat specialized jargon that occurs in 3, 4 and 5, the prevalence of (highlighted) 'purr-words' is very obvious.

(3) One of its goals is to develop, in dialogue with customers and with the help of wide-ranging alliances, a new generation of enhanced products, services and technology focused on sustainable mobility and energy. In 1999 it launched new fuels such as Shell Pura TM, Shell Optimax TM and Shell V-Power TM, which offer significantly enhanced consumer benefits, including reduced emissions and more efficient engine performance.

Table 5.2 Selected 'Sustainable' Concordance of Shell Report

268	technology focused on	**sustainable**	mobility and energy. In
275	a working group on	**sustainable**	mobility, which Shell
279	personal mobility in a	**sustainable**	way. OP is contributing
358	in Indonesia and a	**sustainable**	management project for
381	true and will provide	**sustainable**	growth opportunities for
463	contributes to a more	**sustainable**	world through the very
571	you are to build on a	**sustainable**	foundation. The truly
624	who want a more	**sustainable**	World, and evolving

The extracts (4) and (5) coincidentally contain "wider" or "broader arena" in the co-text of 'sustainable', thus positioning Shell in the world in general.

(4) In the wider arena, OP will be actively supporting a working group on sustainable mobility, which Shell will co-chair with Toyota and General Motors, set-up under the auspices of the World Business Council for Sustainable Development (WBCSD). Amongst other things, this working group will seek to identify strategic options for enabling future personal mobility in a sustainable way.

In (5) purr-words again accompany 'sustainable'. Also 'reputable'-sounding organizations are tied in with Shell's experience—Project Better World and Earthwatch. Self-enhancement by association, we might call this technique.

(5) Shell Chemicals will also continue to participate in Project Better World. This allows staff to gain experience in a broader arena and gain valuable two-way exchange of competencies and learning. In 1999 staff worked with Earthwatch in construction of solar ovens in Indonesia and a sustainable management project for Lake Naivasha in Kenya.

Co-text (6) illustrates a wider tendency to use 'sustainable' to qualify companies. Here we see that 'sustainable' followed by whatever noun, in this case 'growth', presents commercial opportunities for enterprises to seize.

(6) The key is to work with others in the supply chain and to create whole systems solutions for the benefit of people and the environment. The conventional wisdom that trade-offs are required between development and the environment no longer limits our thinking. The reverse can be true and will provide sustainable growth opportunities for enterprises that can innovate.

Extract (7) contains three instances of 'sustainable' in the space of two sentences. PR-speak is often visibly repetitive. But, as we see, repetition is no guarantee of 'clarity'. No further explanation is required, since "through the very nature of its business" Shell Renewables is doing the 'right thing'.

(7) Shell Renewables, which supplies energy and wood from renewable sources, contributes to a more sustainable world through the very nature of its business. It has adopted six sustainable development principles like those used by Exploration and Production in line with the sustainable development management framework SDMF and is applying this thinking to all its business decisions, no matter how small.

In extract (8) the trend to 'justification by proclamation' is continued with the metaphor of the three legs of a stool serving as a sustainable foundation.

This rhetorical figure shows the lengths the speech-writers go to in order to infiltrate sustainability into every sphere of corporate communication.

> (8) Our chairman Mark Moody-Stuart expressed it in a recent speech: 'As you seek to build your business, standing—as it were—on the stool, each leg must be in place if you are to build on a sustainable foundation. The truly sustainable development of a society depends on three inseparable factors: the three-legged stool.'

Extract (9) illustrates a feature foreshadowed also by BP (see chapter 4). This is the appeal to serving customers who want sustainability.

> (9) Other elements ensure that we can derive value through four key levers:
> Reducing costs—in the short-term by becoming more eco-efficient (doing more with less) and in the long-term working with others to ensure that nothing is wasted
> Creating options—anticipating new markets driven by people who want a more sustainable world, and evolving business portfolios and supply chain relationships to match

7 SITUATING SHELL IN THE WIDER DISCUSSION OF 'SUSTAINABLE DEVELOPMENT'

We can see how 'sustainable' and 'sustainability' are 'slipping' or 'drifting' into or even 'colonizing' other areas of social and business life. Everyday experience shows that 'sustainable development' is used, on the one hand, by business people to refer to their industrial and business operations. On the other hand, environmentalists attempting to prevent further ecological devastation of global resources, such as air, water, forests and land, also use it. Against this background it is difficult not to agree with the British historian Eric Hobsbawm's comment on the term as being "conveniently meaningless". In discussing the rise of so-called ecological policies, Hobsbawm makes clear (1994: 570) how important the concept is:

> Yet, rich or not, the supporters of ecological policies were right. The rate of development must be reduced to what was 'sustainable' in the medium run—the term was conveniently meaningless—and, in the long run, a balance would have to be struck between humanity, the (renewable) resources it consumed and the effect of its activities on the environment.

As we have just seen, this view is echoed in the Shell Report, "wide in scope and loosely defined. So almost everyone can identify with it". Such comments lead one to ask what, if any, reality exists behind such notions. Is it simply a term for a concept which is largely socially constructed? It certainly appears to refer to no observable entity. In linguistic terms we are clearly dealing with a nominalized process. But even this is obscure and raises all manner of questions. Who is developing what? What is 'sustainable' about a process of 'development'? Is 'sustainable development', as the British economist Joan Robinson (1962: 29) notably stated of the economist's term 'value', "[l]ike all metaphysical concepts, when you try to pin it down it turns out to be just a word"? Except that it turns out to be just two words when one attempts to ascertain 'sustainable development's' meaning!

So, when faced with this broad lack of consensus, why not bring in a dictionary definition? (From *Encarta World English Dictionary* 1999):

> *Sustainable development*: economic development maintained within acceptable levels of global resource depletion and environmental pollution.

The evaluative weasel word 'acceptable' stands out. This immediately invites a debate. Agreement on denotation is hardly likely to be achievable. We can draw a parallel with how the expression 'political correctness' or 'politically correct' (p.c.) has come to be used in the English-speaking world (and beyond). As Robin Lakoff writes (2000: 94) of 'p.c.': "For a term on everyone's lips, p.c. remains remarkably elusive." For instance, Lakoff suspects that writers "are using definition-making politically." One suspects the same in the case of 'sustainable development'. Lakoff's (2000: 86) discussion of presumed 'neutrality' can serve to underscore how rhetorical processes like 'defining' work:

> Neutrality is advantageous only if it can be exploited and extended into an effective means of persuasion. Language both creates a message, through devices like framing and presupposition, and uses that message, winning the uncommitted over by assuming the 'normality' and 'neutrality' of the speaker's position, as transmitted through arguments that (because they rely on neutrality) need not be overtly stated and therefore need not be exposed to the rigors of examination.

Lakoff goes on to ask who has power to define, refers to dictionary making and thus makes the explicit link to our current concern (2000: 88):

> Definition, then, may not be as neutral an act as it appears to be, but may be used with the explicit motive of giving more power and legitimacy to those who already have enough of it to control the connection between word and definition.

8   PR AND DEPARTMENTS OF APPLIED SEMANTIC OR DISCOURSE ENGINEERING

'Sustainable development' finds itself in good (bad?) company in the Media or Information Age that surrounds us. Discourse engineering is the very stuff of party and governmental politics of course. But it is a feature of media-speak, business-speak, manager-speak and academy-speak too. 'Sustainable development' has much in common with other 'zeitgeist' phenomena and their linguistic realization and discourse shaping. Examples would be 'peace process', 'new economy' and 'Leitkultur' in Germany. Humpty-Dumpty (H.D.) semantics may well be how such phrases come to be denoted. You may remember that in response to Alice's pondering, "whether you can make words mean so many different things", H.D. said: "The question is which is to be the master—that's all" (Carroll 1970: 269).

Can powerful groupings, Humpty-Dumpty-like, make their words mean whatever they choose them to mean? The question today is who is the master of the world. Chomsky (1994a) has commented often enough on "the lords of human kind". The guardians of the New World Order are keen to define the meanings of words if it suits them. I would claim that discourse engineering via media control by oligopolistic capitalist corporations allied with state bodies is becoming ever more potent—as we saw during the Kosovo War, which was officially not a war, you may remember. Chomsky refers to Hume's First Principles of Government to demonstrate how long this technique has been used. As he notes (1994a: 86), "the governors must control thought", especially in a 'democracy'.

Where and how is the raw material of discourse operated on? Is it, as some commentators say, the fact that advertising and marketing is essentially the process of creating 'meaninglessness'? The Australian social psychologist Alex Carey, who pioneered the study of corporate PR, always claimed (1995) that the spin-meisters strive for a public reaction that is at once 'intense and shallow'. This is doubly true in times of war and national emergency. The main enemy of the propaganda machine will always be those who reject emotive invitations and continue to think for themselves. To put things in everyday language: as critical citizens, we must learn how to decipher the bullshit. Carey (1995: 12) quotes from a 1953 book by Harold Lasswell, the American propaganda analyst:

> Propaganda is the management of collective attitudes by the manipulating of significant symbols . . . Collective attitudes are amenable to many modes of alteration . . . intimidation . . . economic coercion . . . drill. But their arrangement and rearrangement occurs principally under the impetus of significant symbols; and the technique of using significant symbols for this purpose is propaganda.

But are we living in times of war and national emergency? Nonetheless the concept of 'sustainable development' has rapidly acquired the status of such a "significant symbol", since it was first introduced in Britain in modern discourse by *The Ecologist* in 1972 in *A Blueprint for Survival*.

9   CONCLUSION

I have argued that "Everyone is talking about sustainable development." I have tried to show that the *Shell Reports* appear to over-lexicalize and to over-state their commitment to sustainable development. It is fairly self-explanatory to anyone who only cursorily looks at the public relations work of megacorporations, what its function is. The genres of the website report, even the hard copy report, together with so-called video news releases specially produced to be sent out to TV stations all around the world are all part of the massive campaign to control the agenda and to crowd out critical voices. We can demonstrate that the arguments for "a new, environmentally sustainable economy and society" are being reformulated and re-semanticized by PR departments and marketing agencies to remove the potentially radical demands which citizens would otherwise be making of business and government. We need to focus a critically discourse-based analysis of language and discourse directly at these processes being employed by both business lobbies and politicians.

Other chapters analyze at the lexical-grammatical level the techniques that are employed to use language to persuade people of the 'benign intents' of companies. One sees how companies combine in other operations to consciously prevent or attack environmentalists who draw attention to their pollution activities (see Beder 1997 for more on this). One need have, however, very little expectation that my analyses will serve to slow down the expansion of the corporate domination of what we are able to hear, see, know and think. Herman and Chomsky's (1988) book called *Manufacturing Consent* is perhaps still even more potent today in its essential claim that the media are preventing freedom of information. It is by now a truism that company CEOs and reports tend to distance themselves from the bad news by using impersonal expressions and simultaneously ascribing bad news to external circumstances, thus effectively denying agency and responsibility.

I am aware that students' education prepares them to exist in the world that surrounds them and not a world that does not yet exist. Our students will be expected to participate in and to actively construct such discourse patterns as I have been analyzing. But critical scholars and critical linguists should not despair. They should continue to tell the other story. This says that the world our students are being prepared for may not exist for very long. If we do not learn to limit the power of corporations to overexploit our resources before it is too late, the world around us will be gone.

6   Wording the World

1   INTRODUCTION

It is sometimes said that we are nearly all 'constructivists' of one form or another, today, in post-modern times. Yet clearly the physical, sociological, institutional and organizational surroundings, even though mediated and filtered by language, will also affect what we see and hold sacred or valuable in the world. In societies where 'money makes the world go round' young children will be brought up differently from those where 'the spirits of their forefathers' speak to them through the trees and rivers and mountains.

In a paper at the Jyväskylä AILA symposium on 'Language and Ecology' Alexander (1996) wrote:

> As linguists and language scholars many of us hold that language plays a major role in predisposing speakers to perceive or to construct the world in a specific fashion. So we need to be cautious here. As some of our colleagues will be arguing, the perceptions or non-perceptions of ecological crises or of environmental problems, such as global warming or the destruction of the ozone layer are not sensorially experienced. It is the many-voiced discourse of scientists that is the source of our knowledge of such issues. These are filtered and very often distorted by the media presentations of such happenings. Hence we might well hear the question being posed: how far is the 'real world' really endangered, after all?

In addition, the voices of politicians, influential corporations and business people contribute their 'spin' or interpretations to the ways of viewing or perceiving such issues as 'global warming' and related environmental and ecological phenomena. Consider, for example, how in the words of Kofi Annan, onetime Secretary General of the United Nations (UN), corporations, once the major opponents of UN initiatives against corporate power, are now 'valued partners' of the United Nations. Such Orwellian language usage is an index of how successfully corporate power, together with its allies in the political parties and media world (see Herman and Chomsky

1988), has undermined what little opposition once faced them (see New Internationalist 2002).

How have people shaped discourse which obfuscates, distracts and denies that there are any problems in the world that are in urgent need of solution? What discourse on the environment now predominates in academia, science, business and the media to serve this purpose? Fairclough (1992: 122) has referred to processes of 'semantic engineering' to characterize this activity. An approach that uncovers this is critical and differs from "non-critical approaches" in as far as discourse is not just described but the attempt is made to show how "discourse is shaped by relations of power and ideologies" (1992: 12). And what role does the BBC play in all of this?

2   WHAT ARE THE REITH LECTURES?

In 2000 the BBC devoted its élite Reith Lectures to a series in which prominent scholars, practitioners, politicians and activists debated from their separate and individual perspectives different aspects of the umbrella topic "Respect for the Earth". This is an interesting departure from the normal scheme, where one lecturer usually gives the whole series.

This constellation offered the ecologically interested critical discourse analyst the opportunity to observe in a microcosm a fairly representative selection of 'differing' English-speaking (there were only two non-native speakers) views on this topic. But more importantly it highlighted their media representation via both radio and the Internet backup the BBC now offers.

3   WHY ANALYZE THE MILLENNIUM REITH LECTURES?

These lectures also gave us the opportunity to see whether we can document any progress in slowing down the environmental degradation of the earth. They may, more correctly, be a partial index of how far regression on this topic and the acceleration of degradation have proceeded.

The occasion of the millennium Reith Lectures may also serve as a turning point. It allows us to observe and summarize the academic debate on the role of discourse or semantic engineering (see Fairclough 1992: 132, and Herman and Chomsky 1988: passim) to be observed in media discourse. This consists of cosmetic and manipulated political messages from the leaders of opinion designed to distract and divert attention away from the destruction of the biosphere. It proceeds today via mediatized discourse and images or through industrial and business marketing and PR and is supported by governments such as the USA.

The constant re-branding tactics of telecom companies today was practised by the big polluters in the early 1990s, as Greer and Bruno (1996) have documented in the case of numerous companies such as the Dow Chemical Company. And as Athanasiou (1996) shows, the greening of corporations has reached near surreal lengths. This is reflected in the words of the then CEO of DuPont, Ed Woolard, who, just after the *Exxon Valdez* spill in Alaska, claimed "the environmental groups cannot solve any of these problems. Governments can't do it. Corporations have to do it."

The re-positioning of multinational corporations as promoters of 'sustainable development' has proceeded so rapidly and with so much PR flak and smoke screening that today no one really knows, nor do they care, what the concept means. We have also analyzed this in chapter 5.

4   A DIALECTICAL 'FRAME OF RESEARCH'

If we adopt a critical and analytical approach, a questioning perspective will see us attempting to get behind the text, to read between the lines. Employing rational thinking in these enlightened days does not permit us to take things at purely face value. Among other things, it entails discussing and disputing the substance and truth of opinions or propositions.

I have found myself employing the term 'dialectical reading' as a label for work on language and ecology. Alwin Fill (1996) and others (Fill and Mühlhäusler 2001, Harré et al. 1999 and Mühlhäusler 2003) have developed a similar variety of the approach I have referred to. My work is inspired by 'critical linguistics' and 'critical discourse analysis' (Fairclough 1989 and 1992, Fowler 1991 and Halliday 1990).

5   A CRITICAL DISCOURSE PERSPECTIVE
ON LEXIS AND GRAMMAR

Throughout this book I am arguing that critical discourse analysis can benefit from employing concordancing and corpus linguistic methods. The quantitative counts give us explicit data about the writer's categorial scheme. Hence the ideological or principled position which speakers adopt can be shown to have clear counterparts in language. This is perhaps an instance of the 'container' metaphor we often employ (see Lakoff and Johnson 1980).

The language employed to represent reality or to present arguments incorporates a model of reality. As Halliday has said,

> I think that if we recognize that the grammar of everyone's mother tongue is (or embodies, since it is other things besides) a theory of human experience, then it will follow that this must affect the way we interact with our environment; and—just as with so many of our material practices—what is beneficial at one moment in history may be lethal and suicidal at another. (Personal communication)

While we need have no illusions about how swiftly values can change, it seems evident that specific discourse strategies and, at the level of wording we look at in this chapter, lexical choices can contribute in some way to potential value shifts. These need be by no means advantageous, either!

Chapter 2 showed how environmentally invasive industries have integrated the ecological issue into their PR. Such practices are part of a North American and Europe-wide PR wave of 'corporate environmentalism' into which the normal world of advertizing has integrated the ecological issue, as we saw in chapter 3. Chapter 4 presented evidence that the discourse of market economics colonizes and serves to narrowly frame critical and oppositional discourse on the environment and ecology.

6   SO WHO WERE THE REITH LECTURERS?

Our approach entails going beyond the information given. We need to contextualize the Reith Lectures. Knowing about the situation they arise in is necessary in order to critically analyze what texts are actually trying to say. The importance of contextualizing the uttered is self-evident. This means knowing who the utterers are, of course. This background knowledge is central to our interpretation. For as Halliday (1978: 125) says:

> A text is the product of infinitely many simultaneous and successive choices in meaning, and is realized as lexicogrammatical structure, or 'wording'. The environment of the text is the context of situation, which is an instance of social context, or *situation type*.

As part of the context of situation we need to know "where people are coming from" when we try to understand or interpret their wording. Table 6.1 summarizes who was giving the lectures.

7   STATISTICS OF THE 2000 BBC REITH LECTURES

We selectively and critically analyze the texts of the 2000 BBC Reith Lectures, which were downloaded electronically from the BBC website. As in previous chapters, we employ concordancing and corpus linguistic techniques of language data processing to show how linguistic features are linked with argumentative positions in the presentations of the various speakers. There are three steps to be taken.

The first step calculates totals of words (i.e. groups of characters between spaces) and different word forms, which gives rise to type-token-ratios (TTRs). The next step looks at the frequency lists generated by the concordancing program used. The third step compares the concordances of selected items that occur in more than one of the lectures. The idea is to see

Table 6.1 The 2000 BBC Reith Lecturers

Name	Position	Topic
Chris Patten	*British Tory politician*, European Commissioner, former Overseas Development Minister and last Governor of Hong Kong.	governance
Tom Lovejoy	American tropical and conservation *biologist*. *Advisor to the World Bank*. Coined the term *biological diversity* in 1980. Made the first projection of global extinction rates in the Global 2000 Report to the President.	biodiversity
John Browne	British businessman. *Chief Executive Officer (CEO) BP-Amoco*.	business
Gro Harlem Brundtland	Former Prime Minister of Norway, Chairperson of Commission on Sustainable Development, now *Director General of WHO* (the World Health Organisation).	health and population
Vandana Shiva	Indian *scientist*, *physicist*, *activist* in the movement "Navdanya" trying to conserve biodiversity. Recipient of the Alternative Nobel Prize.	poverty and globalisation
His Royal Highness, The Prince of Wales	*Heir to British throne*, owner of an organic farm. Winner of "Euronatur-Umwelt-Preis 2002" from the Stiftung Europäisches Naturerbe "für sein umweltpolitisches Engagement".	sustainable development

what light the concordances can throw on collocational patterns. We then ask whether these correlate in any way with centres of interest, evaluation and ideological positions of the various speakers.

Table 6.2 shows the totals of words in the individual lectures. The Conc. programme ran on a Power Macintosh and was used to calculate the type-token-ratio of each lecture. This is computed by dividing the total number of different words (word-forms or 'lemmata') by the total number of words (i.e. of running words). Maximum diversity, i.e. every other word being different, equals unity (1). The more repetitive the text, the closer to zero (0) the ratio will be.

We can generally say that the more lexically diverse the discourse or text is, the higher the ratio will be. There may be situations in which comparisons of texts with regard to lexical diversity might tell us something about the values coded in the texts. For instance, there may well be a relationship between repetitiveness and accustoming readers or listeners to certain notions. Such lists may be helpful; but they tell us little by themselves. As Sinclair notes: "A frequency list of word-forms is never more than a set of hints or clues to the nature of a text" (Sinclair 1991: 31).

Table 6.2 Totals of Words in the Individual Reith Lectures

Speaker and Topic	Total Words	Total Lemmata	Type-Token-Ratio
1 Patten on governance	4721	1709	0.361
2 Lovejoy on biodiversity	3275	1210	0.369
3 Browne on business	3308	1085	0.328
4 Brundtland on health and population	3536	1259	0.356
5 Shiva on poverty and globalisation	3663	1234	0.337
6 Prince of Wales on sustainable development	2355	883	0.375
Total all six lectures and averages	21028	3504	0.354

Since we are dealing here with relatively time-constrained lectures, the differences are minimal. Little, if anything, can be read into the differences I have discovered.

But do the frequency lists generated by the concordancing program tell us anything useful? Are any of the most frequent lexical items shared, for instance? Taking the most frequent items in each of the six lectures it is interesting, if not surprising, to note the lack of overlap. As we can see in Table 6.3 only seven items are common to two or more of the lectures: 'believe' (Browne and Prince of Wales), 'change' (Browne and Brundtland), 'development' (Browne, Brundtland, Prince of Wales, Lovejoy and Patten), 'environmental' (Browne, Lovejoy, Patten), 'people' (Browne, Brundtland, Patten and Shiva), 'world' (Browne, Brundtland, Prince of Wales, Lovejoy and Shiva), 'more' (Brundtland, Prince of Wales, Patten).

Table 6.3 shows that Shiva has 'farmer(s)', 'women', and 'biodiversity', 'rice', 'seed(s)', 'feed' and 'food'. Given her interests, the terms relating to agriculture come as no surprise (see Shiva 2001b), nor does the health-related lexis in Brundtland. Brundtland has 'children', 'health', 'disease(s)', 'population', 'poverty' and 'poor'. Browne, predictably, has business-related lexis, Patten a preponderance of items related to politics and Lovejoy many ecologically oriented items. One might also note items used by one or more speaker, but not used by others. For example 'optimist' and 'optimism': Browne uses these six times, Lovejoy once, the others not at all.

There are a number of items which occur in all lectures and which can thus be compared. This may give us evidence of the differential values the speakers ascribe to seemingly similar notions. This feature may underline how the differential coding about the earth or the world proceeds. The remaining sections of the chapter will examine the selected lexical terms 'globalisation', 'sustainability', 'company' and 'connected economy'.

Table 6.3 The Most Frequent Items in Each Lecture

Patten	government/s (27) more (25) good (23) country/ies (16) political (16) development (15) environmental (15) public (15) sustainable (14) democratic (14) most (13) democracy/ies (12) even (12) between (11) little (10) organisations (10) NGO/s (10) people (9) environment (9) better (8) national (8) own (7) global (7)
Lovejoy	ecosystem/s (31) biological (23) diversity (20) species (20) live/lives/ living (13) water/s (12) natural (11) Florida (11) California (11) problem/s (10) world (9) Amazon (9) make/s/ing (9) just (9) conservation (8) environmental (8) river (7) like (7) sustainability (7) sustainable (7) example (7) even (7) development (7) forest/s (7) biologically (6) environment (6) flow/s (6) life (6) case/s (6) decision/s (6) year/s (6)
Browne	world/'s (20) company/ies (19) businesses (16) change (16) development/s (13) believe (12) people (12) connected (12) way/s (11) progress (11) technology (10) economy (9) work working works (9) climate (8) make/s (8) fuel/s (8) environmental (8) power (7) emissions (7) concern/s (6) issues (6) knowledge (6) society/ies (6) sustainability (6) sustainable (6) technical (6) years (6)
Brundtland	health (43) people (28) country/ies (22) year/s (19) poverty (18) more (18) poor (17) development (16) world (15) about (14) population (14) economic (12) increase (12) disease/s (11) new (10) children (10) global (9) change (8) become (8) need/ed/s (8) growth (7)
Shiva	food (40) farmer/s (26) being/s (23) world (22) production (20) women (19) globalisation (16) feed/ing/s (15) small (14) people (14) global 14) seed/s (14) rice (12) million (12) nature (12) biodiversity (12) economy/ies (12) species (12) other (12) crop/s (11) because (11) diversity (10) sustainability (10) all (10) work/ing (9) based (9) become/s/ing (9) agriculture (8) creation (8) corporation/s (8) local (8) property (7) create (6)
Prince of Wales	all (19) world (16) development (15) sustainable (15) about (13) nature (13) wisdom (11) natural (10) more (10) understand (10) know/ing/n (7) believe (7) need/s (7) scientific (7) heart (7) approach (6) life (6) balance (6) creation (5) Creator (5)

8   THE CONCORDANCES FOR 'GLOBALISATION'

'Globalisation' is a term which has influenced the discourse of economics and politics considerably in the past decade. In view of its broad usage it is to be expected that different value associations accompany its usage. This section discusses and compares three lectures.

John Browne uses 'globalisation' only once, but its positive semantic prosody is evident from the concordance entry.

the great benefits of **globalisation.** One way of seeing

Brundtland's three instances reflect her view of health and the link with increased international contacts. Not surprisingly, by contrast with Browne, her associations are not all purely business oriented nor positive, as the three instances and the related verb *globalise* in Table 6.4 show. It is clear from these three instances that Brundtland engages in a variety of semantic negotiation, as observations of the broader text (1) and (2) show.

(1) In the modern world, bacteria and viruses travel almost as fast as money. With globalisation, a single microbial sea washes all of humankind. There are no health sanctuaries.

(2) Interestingly enough, not only infectious diseases that spread with globalisation. Changes in lifestyle and diet prompt an increase in heart disease, diabetes and cancer. More than anything, tobacco is sweeping the globe as it is criss-crossed by market forces. Only weeks after the old socialist economies in Europe and Asia opened up to Western goods and capital, camels and cowboys began to appear on buildings and billboards.

In one usage (3) Brundtland argues for an important and (social democratic?) extension of the meaning of 'globalisation'. We see her engaged in meaning negotiation and meaning potential extension.

(3) Think about it. Globalisation is about much more than trade. It is about communicating with an infinity of new people, about relating to them—and therefore also getting involved in their lives.

The related verb 'globalise' is used (4) by Brundtland. It appears in what would be by Browne's standards a seemingly critical passage on labour standards and health. It echoes a traditionally social democratic or trade union position, we could almost claim! Brundtland does not forget her political roots, even though she is now running part of the UN.

(4) A company that deals with developing countries has to confront the challenge of poverty and ill-health. A company's stock price can fall on

Table 6.4 'Globalisation' Concordance in Brundtland's Lecture

175	Fast as money. With	**globalisation,**	a single microbial sea
197	That spread with	**globalisation.**	Changes in lifestyle
298	Think about it.	**Globalisation**	is about much more
321	Activism become	**globalised,**	large companies find that

Wall Street because workers in a subsidiary's plant in Malaysia are not provided with health insurance. As communication and social activism become globalised, large companies find that labour standards are important. Ignoring them can be costly both to public image and stock price.

It would certainly be welcome if such were really the case. Brundtland's hedge-like use of the modal 'can' twice indicates that she may well not believe her own wishful thinking!

Turning now to Vandana Shiva we see that she uses the term 'globalisation' the most. It is clear that a major portion of her lecture is devoted to re-directing attention to significant aspects of the topic which have been omitted by the previous speakers, as she politely but pointedly states. Her lecture was the fifth in sequence, so she makes some inter-textual references to what the previous speakers have said.

Just consulting the concordance of the sixteen instances in Shiva's lectures in Table 6.5 makes the negative or critical semantic prosodies evident.

Table 6.5 'Globalisation' Concordance in Shiva's Lecture

39	about the impact of	globalisation	on the lives of ordinary
44	development taking	globalisation	for granted. For me it
46	doing in the name of	globalisation	to the poor is brutal
48	unfolding disasters of	globalisation,	especially in food and
104	engineering and	globalisation	of agriculture the
135	This is how	globalisation	destroys local
152	. . . ineering of food and	globalisation	of trade in agriculture
159	countries. Economic	globalisation	is leading to a
164	introduced through	globalisation,	higher costs are
166	to survive. The	globalisation	of non-sustainable
209	under the pressure of	globalisation,	things are changing.
223	tonnes of waste. The	globalisation	of the food system is
368	poor. But the rules of	globalisation	are not god-given.
374	The rules of	globalisation	are undermining the
367	people. Economic	globalisation	has become a war
371	a rule based system.	Globalisation	is the rule of

The highlighted right and left collocates in Table 6.5 refer to negative and harmful items.

The broader co-texts below of 'globalisation' make clear Shiva is using the prominence of the occasion to take a stand in favour those who suffer from globalisation. Shiva lays out determinedly and uncompromisingly her arguments against the orthodoxy on globalisation. She wishes in (5) to look at "the impact of globalisation on the lives of ordinary people".

> (5) It is experiences such as these which tell me that we are so wrong to be smug about the new global economy. I will argue in this lecture that it is time to stop and think about the impact of globalisation on the lives of ordinary people. This is vital to achieve sustainability.

Particularly in instances (6), (7) and (8) Shiva engages in meaning contestation which is signalled explicitly by "re-evaluate" and in "the name of globalisation". She goes on to make strong judgements and forceful evaluations. She does not hesitate to 'put her cards on the table'.

> (6) (7) (8) Throughout this lecture series people have referred to different aspects of sustainable development taking globalisation for granted. For me it is now time radically to re-evaluate what we are doing. For what we are doing in the name of globalisation to the poor is brutal and unforgivable. This is specially evident in India as we witness the unfolding disasters of globalisation, especially in food and agriculture.

In the next instance (9) the right collocates of 'agriculture' are developed in a critical fashion to question the orthodox claims of genetic engineering.

> (9) While women and small peasants feed the world through biodiversity we are repeatedly told that without genetic engineering and globalisation of agriculture the world will starve. In spite of all empirical evidence showing that genetic engineering does not produce more food and in fact often leads to a yield decline, it is constantly promoted as the only alternative available for feeding the hungry.

Shiva's critical argument in (10) links 'patriarchy' to globalisation. Despite the current political situation in India, this is an aspect that receives little coverage in the Western media.

> (10) The devaluation of women's work, and of work done in sustainable economies, is the natural outcome of a system constructed by capitalist patriarchy. This is how globalisation destroys local economies and destruction itself is counted as growth.

In (11) Shiva turns seemingly 'progressive' concepts dialectically on their heads, calling them "recipes for creating hunger, not for feeding the poor".

(11) However, industrialisation and genetic engineering of food and globalisation of trade in agriculture are recipes for creating hunger, not for feeding the poor.

She stresses the corporatization of agriculture, which the WTO is furthering in Third World countries like India, in (12) and (13). The collocates "increased debt" and "higher costs" leave this in no doubt.

(12) (13) Economic globalisation is leading to a concentration of the seed industry, increased use of pesticides, and, finally, increased debt. Capital-intensive, corporate controlled agriculture is being spread into regions where peasants are poor but, until now, have been self-sufficient in food. In the regions where industrial agriculture has been introduced through globalisation, higher costs are making it virtually impossible for small farmers to survive.

She has no illusions in (14) about the effects of non-sustainable capitalist modes of production on the Third World.

(14) The globalisation of non-sustainable industrial agriculture is literally evaporating the incomes of Third World farmers through a combination of devaluation of currencies, increase in costs of production and a collapse in commodity prices.

The finer points of WTO 'rules' are not highlighted in the West. Their consequences in (15) for the people of the Third World are even less so.

(15) Now, under the pressure of globalisation, things are changing. Pseudo hygiene laws are being used to shut down local economies and small scale processing.

Shiva's negative correlation of globalisation and diversity (16) is in marked contrast to Lovejoy's 'troubled' yet complacent treatment which makes no reference to the real sources of the extinction of biodiversity!

(16) The globalisation of the food system is destroying the diversity of local food cultures and local food economies. A global monoculture is being forced on people by defining everything that is fresh, local and handmade as a health hazard.

Shiva activates in (17) the metaphor GLOBALISATION IS WAR AGAINST NATURE to dramatize the situation. She sustains this metaphor for several sentences (18)

(17) (18) other species and other people. Economic globalisation has become a war against nature and the poor. But the rules of globalisation

are not god-given. They can be changed. They must be changed. We must bring this war to an end.

Shiva also equates globalisation with 'the rule of commerce' (19). In the ensuing discussion it is interesting to note that Anthony Giddens, Director of the London School of Economics (LSE) and Tony Blair's 'guru', criticizes Shiva for her arguments. She employs the legal metaphor of rules to deftly turn the legalistic arguments on their heads in (20).

> (19) (20) Globalisation is the rule of commerce and it has elevated Wall Street to be the only source of value. As a result things that should have high worth—nature, culture, the future are being devalued and destroyed. The rules of globalisation are undermining the rules of justice and sustainability, of compassion and sharing. We have to move from market totalitarianism to an earth democracy.

It would indeed be interesting to look in more detail at the various metaphorical concepts that Shiva activates, some unconsciously (perhaps) like 'worth' and 'value', others more explicitly like 'earth democracy' (20). In the discussion after her lecture there are twelve further occurrences of the term 'rule'. The concordance programme thus gives us an index of what Shiva's lecture focused attention on. By looking at the highlighted items we can see that Shiva's arguments and evidence point their finger firmly at the fact that globalisation is creating more inequality. She demonstrates how sustainability cannot be maintained amidst such one-sided exploitative relationships on the part of multinational companies.

9   SUSTAINABILITY IN VANDANA SHIVA'S LECTURE

In this section, rather than comparing the usage of the expression 'sustainable development', which we might expect all the lecturers to use in some form or other, we concentrate on Shiva's treatment of the topic of 'sustainability'. Shiva has five occurrences of 'sustainable', one of which precedes development. More interestingly, however, is the fact that she uses 'sustainability' ten times and 'sustainably' once. Like Lovejoy, Shiva makes more use of 'sustainability'. As was the case with 'globalisation' Shiva's usage suggests that she is trying to extend the potential of the term, sometimes alluding to the negative aspects.

The variation of right collocates of 'sustainable' hint at this: 'economies', 'systems of food', 'regenerative production', 'industrial agriculture', 'development'. But more important are the collocates both right and left of 'sustainability', in Table 6.6, which by themselves suggest a new orientation towards justice and related concepts. As with 'globalisation', Shiva is attempting to extend the understanding of what true 'sustainability' for her signifies.

Table 6.6 'Sustainability' Concordance in Shiva's Lecture

40	is vital to achieve	**sustainability.** Seattle and the World
314	down the road to non-	**sustainability,** they become
342	become a threat to	**sustainability** and the very survival
359	is the real basis of	**sustainability.** The sustainability
360	of sustainability. The	**sustainability** challenge for the new
375	rules of justice and	**sustainability,** of compassion and
379	the limits set by	**sustainability** and justice. As Gandhi
308	creation but plunder.	**Sustainability** requires the
346	fundamental level.	**Sustainability,** sharing and survival
365	dignity for all beings.	**Sustainability** demands that we move

10 JOHN BROWNE'S LECTURE AND DISCUSSION

As a stark contrast I would like to look at certain aspects of John Browne's lecture. I have already analyzed the 'corporate environmentalism' of the CEO of BP-Amoco (see chapter 4). In his Reith lecture and especially in the discussion section after his lecture Browne employs similar discourse strategies. Below I have extracted excerpts from the lecture in which the word 'company' occurs. When talking about his company's business in (21) and (22) John Browne takes trouble, as always, to emphasize the benevolent nature of its operation towards the environment.

(21) Let me give a few examples from the experience of the company I work for. [BP Amoco]

(22) My company's aim is now to eliminate this practice during the next three years, except on the rare occasions when safety is in question.

The positive semantic prosody is evident in this extract (23).

(23) Steps like these are significant contributions to the goal of our company—which is to reduce the emissions of greenhouse gases from all our operations by at least 10 per cent from a 1990 baseline by 2010 . . .

Then there is an interesting example (24) of self-positioning:

(24) The enlightened company increasingly recognises that there are good commercial reasons for being ahead of the pack when it comes to issues to do with the environment.

Here (25) is a case of redefining (re-wording) in answer to a questioner:

(25) I think it's an interesting misnomer that we in every introduction are called an oil company. We're not an oil company—we're a gas company with oil, with lots of other associated energies. Renewable energy is one of those things. Technology is very much improving and we are improving the photo-voltaic section of renewable energies—so-called solar energy.

In the discussion following his lecture a questioner asks about profit distribution. This (26) is Browne's answer:

(26) Well I think the distribution of profits to different parts of the economy is something which is changing the whole time. For us yes we do this. We don't do it with profits directly but we do it with distribution of the underlying ownership of the company—that is to say shares and options. It has to make sense to people of course, and it has to be something which is adopted and adapted on a global basis depending on the particular culture of the place and many people still in the world, it may surprise you, do not agree that employees should own parts of a company, and indeed many employees in some parts of the world don't want to do that. They simply want to be paid and go home and rest easy. The distribution of profits is definitely changing but I think reflected better by a distribution of ownership which is continuously changing and will continue to change again in the future.

This certainly demonstrates Browne's deft ability to argue proactively and forcefully in favour of capitalism and against co-determination and profit sharing! The next extract (27) demonstrates how Browne can even make light of the dark side of apartheid in South Africa. He shows the positive side of BP staying in South Africa during its existence!

(27) I believe our role is to engage wherever we can and to demonstrate that we're actually doing something that makes a difference—that makes a difference and a positive difference—however small. BP of course stayed in South Africa during a very tough time during Apartheid bringing our own employees to a different level of educational qualification, maximizing the number of black people working inside our company.

11 BROWNE ON THE 'CONNECTED ECONOMY'

Finally, let us look at the way Browne expands the semantic potential of *economy* by calling it the 'connected economy'. This puts us in familiar territory (see chapter 5). Browne is engaged, in his public speaking, as so often, in semantic engineering. The choice of the adjective 'connected' is clearly a conscious attempt to integrate with ecological thinking. As we see in Table 6.7 however, the fact that the term is almost exclusively used as a collocate of *economy* shows that the tactic is very limited.

I have extracted the broader co-texts of the twelve instances of this expression. After a brief introduction come five closely following uses (28), (29), (30), (31) and (32) of the word 'connected'.

(28) (29) (30) (31) (32) I think of it as a "connected economy" but connected in ways we have never known before. Connected not just from one person or company to another, from one buyer to one seller—but connected as the brain is connected—as a network of multiple and simultaneous linkages.

In particular the superficial analogy drawn with the brain and its neuronal networks is one which was being used in 2000 even in scholarly circles. But the metaphorical linkage is especially favoured in advertizing too. The

Table 6.7 'Connected' Concordance in Browne's Lecture

185	I think of it as a "	connected	economy" but connected in
185	economy" but	connected	in ways we have never
187	to one seller—but	connected	as the brain is connected—
188	as the brain is	connected	—as a network of multiple
192	linkages. The	connected	economy is beginning to
229	the second point, the	connected	economy isn't just about
389	I believe it is the	connected	nature of four crucial
441	great gains from the	connected	economy is transparency—
462	true than ever in a	connected	economy—where every
490	available. In this	connected	economy companies and
526	behaviour of the	connected,	knowledge driven economy

next usage (33) brings us down to earth with a pragmatic, business and utilitarian bump, however!

> (33) The connected economy is beginning to give us the ability to create new marketplaces and to integrate and manage complex systems at a distance and with great precision and speed. It is also giving us the ability to spread and share knowledge instantly.

The buzzwords of manager-speak are all there in the next instance (34), along with the positive spin put on globalisation.

> (34) But, and this is the second point, the connected economy isn't just about productivity—it is also about learning and the way in which knowledge and best practice can be developed, disseminated and applied on a global basis. This, after all, is one of the great benefits of globalisation.

The hard-nosed businessman is never far away from his true vocation, as the 'semantic slippage' in the next extract (35) brings out.

> (35) The question to the accused is whether business can be trusted to do all this, or to put it another way—what keeps us honest? I believe it is the connected nature of four crucial relationships in which we are involved—with our employees, with our customers, with our shareholders and the public, and with governments.

Purr-words such as "the great gains", "transparency" and "key to confidence and trust" persist in the semantic prosody of the next instance (36).

> (36) I believe this new approach to corporate reporting is also entirely consistent with the economic revolution which is now upon us. One of the great gains from the connected economy is transparency—because that is the key to confidence and trust, and to the granting of permission by society for companies to pursue their activities and to continue to make progress.

As always, Browne strengthens his scholarly credentials and credibility by appealing (37) to an intellectual authority, no less a person than Bertrand Russell himself.

> (37) It is said, and I think has even been said in this series of lectures, that the power of companies has increased while the power of Governments has declined. I don't think it is quite so simple. As Bertrand Russell once said, "from any single perspective power always seems to be elsewhere"

and that is more true than ever in a connected economy—where every decision is dependent on the decisions of others.

A rather empty rhetorical gesture accompanies the next occurrence (38) in the semantically void cliché "honour their responsibilities".

(38) In this connected economy companies and governments both need to honour their responsibilities.

Browne makes a gesture in the direction of dealing with his potential opponents and critics in (39), but this again is done by means of nominals, agentless passives and unspecified generic others. For example 'who' is concerned in "valid concerns", 'who' is dismissed as being unenlightened, 'whose' "technical progress" is meant, 'who' knows 'what' in the "knowledge driven economy" and 'whose' "judgement" and 'whose' "optimism" is meant? The slippery or weaselly use of the adjective "universal" suggests subliminally that we are all in the same position and share the values that Browne selflessly is protecting and expanding for us all in his business activities.

(39) Of course there are valid concerns which exist over the role of business. The track record is mixed and enlightenment is not universal. But if you look objectively at both the technical progress which is being made, and at the impact on business behaviour of the connected, knowledge driven economy the judgement must come down in favour of optimism.

12 CONCLUSION

Browne is constantly suggesting and indeed bluntly stating that BP is operating in a proactive fashion, without being asked to. This is a gambit Athanasiou (1996) refers to. The 'greening' PR operations of large corporations are part of a strategy to lay claim to having been the prime movers in the fight against preventing emissions which 'might' contribute to climate change. BP-Amoco positions itself as slightly apart from the main pack, to be sure. But not as far as Browne would like us to believe.

It is part of the economic logic that sees increased environmental protection arising from growing prosperity in the North and the accompanying 'trickle down' to the South. Such features are not so easy to grasp automatically through computer analysis. Yet as Athanasiou (1996: 171) writes: "There is a fundamental conflict between the logic of social and environmental protection and the demands of deregulated international trade". For Athanasiou (1996: 183) there are moral and ecological limits to economics, whereas for Browne there is no alternative to the market solutions which so conveniently supply his company with massive profits and make it one of the three or four leading 'sisters' in the oil business!

Given what we know of the corporate control, financial support of, and close cooperation with, neo-liberally oriented political élites in all major Western nations, this need come as no surprise. The fact that the media conglomerates and even the public broadcasters such as the BBC in Britain give their CEOs airspace in the Reith Lectures to underpin and to diffuse their messages, even if countered in part by Vandana Shiva's alternative voice, need likewise not surprise us. After all, Shiva's voice will scarcely get heard in the media mainstream after the Reith Lectures, whereas the media conglomerates and the political and business channels will continue to broadcast loudly the message: the Market is the only way forward! (See New Internationalist (No. 347) July 2002, for a thematic issue entitled 'Inside business. How corporations make the rules' with a critical and dialectical reading of corporate power's role in the world today.)

7 Shaping Environmental Discourse

1 INTRODUCTION

This chapter considers further aspects of the 2000 BBC Reith Lectures "Respect for the Earth" as a sort of stocktaking exercise also using computer-generated concordances and frequency counts. How much has ecological and environmental awareness developed in the past thirty years? The Reith Lectures can serve as a kind of index of ecological progress or regression. Areas worth investigating from a critical discourse perspective (Fairclough 1989) can be assisted by the computer.

Fairclough shows (1992: 188ff) how different elements of the meaning potential of 'enterprise' are used by a British politician in different types of discourse to restructure the notion. We can note that this is what can be seen to be going on as John Browne uses the expression 'sustainable development' (in chapter 5). More particularly and more sadly we can see how the UN has been undermined and taken over by the anti-environmental lobby, in the form of the giant corporations who rule our world. They have taken over the agenda of the 'Earth Summit', which long after Rio appears to have 'pacified' the world for corporate power and profit and practically 'buried' any attempts to stop climate change, prevent toxic waste from polluting the seas and air, or even work against apartheid-like régimes in the interests of human justice.

How has this happened? Who has contributed to the turn-around, which has resulted in one-time pacifists and environmentalists waging war (see the Greens in Germany) on innocent civilian populations (Serbia, Afghanistan) in the name of humanitarian interventionism? What channels of communication have so successfully brainwashed or dead-brained the Western world to the extent that increased exploitation of natural and human resources in so-called Third World countries is welcomed as civilizing the world? When did it become possible for Manichaean and simple notions of 'wars on terrorism' to become self-evident responses to complex histories of depredation and destruction? What role do the media play in this? And, more ironically, what role do Western notions of liberal and free discussion of central issues affecting the Fate of Mankind, like the question of Respect for the Earth, play in integrating, neutralizing and pacifying potentially alternative visions and strategies on how to liberate the oppressed of the human and natural world? How has discourse been shaped and how does it now succeed in pre-dominating in academia, science, business, the media, to obfuscate, distract and deny that there are any problems in the world that are in urgent need of solution before the planet sizzles out in a solar storm in a few hundred years?

What role does the BBC play in all of this, we can reiterate? This is also an occasion on which we can ask how politics and democracy might or can contribute to shaping environmental discourse. Certainly to listen to Chris Patten is to receive an indication of how the issues can be watered down and distracted from. I shall briefly look at Patten's lecture 'Governance' and ask how the ecological issues are framed and shaped by such interventions.

In view of the situation characterized pointedly and controversially by the Cambridge professor of political science John Dunn (2000), we might expect it to be high time for such an ecological stocktaking. In his book Dunn sees accurately the modern democratic state as being a major con-tributory factor to environmental destruction or what he calls ecological degradation. Faced by this assessment one might be forgiven for thinking that the situation has reached the point of no return! There is a section of his book entitled: 'The Modern Republic as Bearer of Ecological Degradation'. In it Dunn (2000: 226) argues:

> Viewed as a system of rights, the modern democratic republic is an empty political form, designed by humans for humans for quite mod-est purposes [. . .]. But, when encountered in the historical world, the economic, social and ecological content which inevitably fills it reveals it instead to be as deadly as it is arrogant, an irresistible machine for destroying the human world.

The occasion of the millennium Reith Lectures could also serve as a vantage point to observe and summarize the academic debate on the role played by semantic or discourse engineering, whether via mediatized discourse and images or through industrial and business marketing and PR, supported by cosmetic and manipulated political messages from the leaders of opinion, in distracting and diverting attention away from the destruction of the bio-sphere. If Europe is a yardstick of the level of awareness and concern with environmental issues, we can say that the counter-attack against environ-mentalism has been very successful. The Green Party in Germany became sucked up into the 'Power Machine' and practically cut itself off from not only its early pacifist roots but also its once strong ecological supporters. The latter appear to have left few traces of the environmental movement in the following generations. The non-existence of any substantial student activism in all fields of political life, but especially in the area of green issues, shows how successful the integration of the ecological issue has become (see chapter 2). Environmentalism has been reduced to 'glossy images' in corporate advertisements.

2   ADOPTING A QUESTIONING PERSPECTIVE

And, so what? Nobody cares, do they? How many students or readers are capable of, or willing to engage in, looking "beyond the information given"? A 'dialectical' reading, thinking, investigating 'frame of research' is needed! In the first place this entails discussing and disputing the substance and truth of an opinion or a proposition. Basically it helps to adopt a questioning perspective. In chapter 6 I have situated this approach primarily in an eco-linguistic context.

In a secondary, and equally as important, respect, Fill (1998 and 2002) underlines how "the 'ecological' concepts of *interaction, interplay and networking*" (my emphasis) come to be used in many applied linguistic fields, such as conflict study and language and gender issues. My own work was inspired originally by 'critical linguistics' and 'critical discourse analysis' (Kress and Hodge 1979, Fairclough 1995b, and Halliday 1978). But it soon became clear how important it is to enlarge and enhance this approach by integrating an 'ecological' vantage point, if not methodology (Halliday 1990 and Fill and Mühlhäusler 2001).

Work over the past few decades has heightened our awareness of the role played by language in conditioning our responses to the deterioration of the natural, physical and social environment. Unless a disaster happens in one's immediate vicinity, such as the torrential rain and floods experienced in southern and eastern Germany, Austria and the Czech Republic in the month of August 2002, one of the few resources available to apprehend or to note the effects of climate change has been language. This means people talking and writing about the results of everyday or scientific observations and investigations. (We can go back to Rachel Carson 1962 or Gregory Bateson 1972.) The perception that discourse, 'talking' or the shaping of messages, can cause people to perceive reality in different ways is practically a platitude of applied linguistics and even journalism and media reception studies (see Bolinger 1980).

The very 'staging' of the 2000 Reith Lectures certainly did very little to counteract the trends of our one-dimensional Age of Information in this observer's view. Consider, for example, the fact that the final lecture was a brief one given by the Prince of Wales, heir to the British throne. It was entitled 'A Royal view [. . .]'. I would assume this was intended to be totally without irony and entirely sincere I quote the beginning of his lecture because he summarizes the previous five lectures concerning a major point that united them all.

Like millions of other people around the world I've been fascinated to hear five eminent speakers share with us their thoughts, hopes and fears about sustainable development based on their own experience. All five of those contributions have been immensely thoughtful and challenging. *There have been clear differences of opinion and of emphasis between the speakers but there have also been some important common themes, both implicit and explicit.* One of those themes has been the suggestion that sustainable development is a matter of enlightened self-interest. Two of the speakers used this phrase and I don't believe that the other three would dissent from it, and nor would I. (Emphasis added, RJA)

For reasons of courtly tact he emphasizes the common features. But what is of significance for this chapter is the phrase "clear differences of opinion and of emphasis between the speakers". This is to euphemize and to take the sting out of the critical contribution of Vandana Shiva, who spoke last but one, just before the Prince. Such 'levellings' are typical for the one-dimensional thought that our Age of Information is coloured by (see Fill 1993 and Marcuse 1964).

This is the crux of my argument. The most powerful figures in the world can put forward their viewpoints, whereas the minority points of view—in the case of the Reith Lectures this is Vandana Shiva—can gain a brief airing, as the BBC demonstrates, once every ten years or so, or at the turn of the millennium (Shiva 2001a). But otherwise, it is 'business as usual.' Euphemizing the true threats and problems, playing down the issues, and contributing to the hegemonic views of what is really good for the planet. Namely, in the Washington Consensus view, leave it to good governance, the United Nations, the World Bank and business interests and all will be well.

While we need have no illusions about how swiftly or slowly values can change, it seems evident that specific discourse strategies and, at the level of lexis we look at in this chapter, lexical choices can contribute in some way to potential value shifts, on the surface at least. After all, there is an obligation in the United States on companies to publish some kinds of environmental information and report on their environmental liabilities. Everyone is in favour of protecting the environment. No one is against clean air and fresh water and a generally unpolluted atmosphere? Perhaps only political freaks, as his opponents view him, like Noam Chomsky can suggest that "[t]he basic principle is that hegemony is more important than survival", for the rich and powerful (Chomsky 2003: 231). To suggest otherwise would be to appear insane. Yet, on closer observation the reality of capitalist industrial (and state capitalist, communist) activities might provide hard counter-evidence.

The re-positioning of multinational corporations as promoters of 'sustainable development' has proceeded so rapidly and with so much PR flak and smoke-screening that today no one appears to really know, nor do they seem to care what the concept means. This was also analyzed in chapter 5.

3   "RESPECT FOR THE EARTH": CONCORDANCES FOR 'EARTH'

For the purposes of this chapter I shall begin with a general comparison of some of the most frequent lexical items used by the speakers. By focusing on this feature I can underline how the differential coding about the earth or the world can be indicated. Using concordances can serve to make concrete what is otherwise only to be extracted with difficulty by means of an 'explication de texte'-mode of analysis. Let us start with the word 'earth' itself, since, after all, the umbrella topic of the Reith Lectures was "Respect for the Earth". Strangely, the actual word 'earth' only occurs in five of the six lectures.

Patten has two occurrences. One is a quotation attributed to a friend. The second is a sarcastic wordplay, if you know the subject is "dictators"!

```
96      should live here on   earth",  he says, "as though we were
304     rarely friends of the   earth.   But even those democratic
```

Lovejoy's one use of 'earth' is as a qualifier of 'variety of life' referring to the physical environment, as the wider co-text and context (1) shows. It is clear that Lovejoy is appealing emotionally to his audience or at least attempting to transmit to a wider audience the pleasure he experiences as a biologist of biodiversity.

(1) The natural world in which we live is nothing short of entrancing—wondrous really. Personally, I take great joy in sharing a world with the shimmering variety of life on earth. Nor can I believe any of us really want a planet which is a lonely wasteland.

Brundtland's single occurrence (highlighted in 2) is of little or no relevance for this chapter. She uses it as a modifier of 'population'.

(2) Over the past twenty-five years or so, population growth in many countries has slowed rather faster than demographers had first expected—especially in east Asia. Thanks to this slowing down, the experts now believe the earth's population will stabilise around 9 billion—rather than 12 to 15 billion as some feared.

Shiva has three instances in her lecture, plus one of 'earthworms'.

```
357     as members of the       earth      family. This awareness that in
376     totalitarianism to an   earth      democracy. We can survive as
380     had reminded us: "The   earth      has enough for everyone's
353     security. In feeding    earthworms we feed ourselves. In
```

Two of these uses have 'unusual' right collocates: 'family' and 'democracy'. In view of the critical and radical positions she develops in her lecture, the metaphor of 'family' plays an important role in her argument. This can be seen in the wider co-text (3), where all animals and creatures of the world are part of a family. Accordingly, by nourishing them we contribute to our own nourishment. One is reminded of Lakoff's 'Nurturant Parent Morality' conceptual system rather than that of 'Strict Father Morality' (Lakoff 1996).

> (3) In feeding earthworms we feed ourselves. In feeding cows, we feed the soil, and in providing food for the soil, we provide food for humans. This worldview of abundance is based on sharing and on a deep awareness of humans as members of the earth family. This awareness that in impoverishing other beings, we impoverish ourselves and in nourishing other beings, we nourish ourselves is the real basis of sustainability.

Two of the Prince of Wales' occurrences are physical and one with the collocate 'stewardship' has an ecological component.

34	stewardship for the	**earth,**	has been an important feature
173	to remind us that the	**Earth**	is unique and that we have a
60	dioxide into the	**earth's**	atmosphere. Yet the actions

A perusal of the frequency lists shows that the synonym 'world' and the adjective 'global' occur more frequently. (See Table 6.3.)

4   PATTEN ON 'GOOD GOVERNANCE'

At the beginning of Patten's lecture more than one page is filled with anecdotes about his time as a minister for Overseas Development, to certify his credentials, one assumes. An intertextual reference to sustainable development and the Brundtland commission brings him back to the theme of the lecture series. Then comes a paragraph in which the major theme and thesis of the lectures is laid out:

> I think that we understand today that sustainable development is about much more than environment policy defined in terms of departments, ministers and white papers. It requires a mosaic of institutions, policies and values. Mosaic may even be too static a word for what is required; *it is really a political eco-system that is needed to save the real one.* (Emphasis added, RJA)

Given that Patten was a VIP (very important person) politician, a European Commissioner at the time, this need not surprise us, of course.

On the whole, Patten's lecture on 'Good governance' is a somewhat paternalistic hymn to the British-style political class, with rather negative comments on African countries, complete with Burke and Lao Tzu quotations. He warns against minority groups, which he suggests may be undemocratic. He refers explicitly to NGOs (nongovernmental organizations) in this context and seems to suggest that they are a threat to 'sustainable development'. His use of 'good governance' echoes closely its usage in Washington Consensus circles. As Aziz Choudry comments (2002) on the phrase:

> 'Good governance' is a serious contender for a prize for the best example of Orwellian doublespeak. It has nothing to do with democratisation, humanitarianism or support for peoples' rights. It is a euphemism for a limited state designed to service the market and undermine popular mandates. The term is explicitly linked to the kinds of structural adjustment measures promoted by the ADB [Asian Development Bank]—measures for which there is little popular support and which are rapidly increasing economic inequalities.

And indeed Patten's discussion of and re-definition of democracy in the final three paragraphs of his lecture is an autocratic, Mandarin, top-down view par excellence. Consider this passage:

> Behind these organisational and political shifts is a reaffirmation of the democratic spirit, the understanding that democracy is an adventure in dialogue, the attempt to persuade and secure consent, the belief in Adlai Stevenson's memorable phrase that average men and women are a great deal better than the average.

'Government by the people' is a far cry indeed from "the attempt to persuade and secure consent". But those who know Patten and his role as European Commissioner will realize that the notion of democracy being best left in 'good hands' is part of a long tradition of what Chomsky (1991) has called "Deterring Democracy". I shall take up Patten's treatment of the developing world further below.

In view of the coupling of the concepts of good governance or democracy in the course of the lecture, consider the collocations and broader co-texts for these items in Table 7.1.

The lexical collocations of 'democracies' (countable) and 'democracy' (uncountable) are similarly (as compared with the 'good governance' ones, as we shall see) vague. They point to an abstract notion, where they are not referring to concrete state forms or are sarcastic as in: 'so-called people's'. Others are 'liberal, pluralist', 'Pluralist developed' for 'democracies'. Then 'liberal', 'fabric of a liberal', 'struggle bravely for' and 'thereby revitalize', 'understanding that' and 'is by revitalizing'. It is clear from just listing these left collocates that Patten's view of democracy is by no means idealistic.

Table 7.1 'Democra*****' Concordance in Patten's Lecture

214	so-called people's	democracies.	And note that
216	of liberal, pluralist	democracies.	Concepts of good
514	Pluralist developed	democracies	need to understand that
265	laws all being flat?"	Democracies	are not corruption-free
219	of good governance or	democracy	were arguably implicit in
294	. . . strophe. No hymn to	democracy	can be without its
313	Some concede that	democracy	may be the most
330	From time to time for	democracy	to turn into illiberal
333	the mechanism of	democracy.	A liberal democracy
334	democracy. A liberal	democracy	requires more than
338	fabric of a liberal	democracy	is what we today call
442	struggle bravely for	democracy	itself. But that is not the
492	and thereby revitalise	democracy,	then they have to lead the
521	understanding that	democracy	is an adventure in
561	is by revitalising	democracy	to save our world, with
296	in practice.	Democracy	is not the only ingredient
299	care and attention.	Democracy	is more likely to produce
223	be helped to promote	Democratization,	civil society and

If we consider the verb forms accompanying 'democracy' as right collocates, we find a preponderance of copulas ('is') with modals in two instances, realizing relational processes of identity. The clause structure is equative in Halliday's (1976) model. By equating democracy with certain entities, Patten is semantically shaping what he holds to be a democratic way of governing. This is continued in the appeal to the 'fashionable' buzzword 'governance' which has entered both élite business and political circles in recent decades. As the concordances document, an establishment politician like Patten views democracy or 'democratisation', as an agentless nominalization. Note particularly how in this passage he details a top down approach to 'democracy'.

Concepts of good governance or democracy were arguably implicit in the earliest definitions of sustainable development. In recent years, the references have been explicit. The richer countries' club, the OECD, is today, for example, seeking ways in which developing countries can be helped to promote democratisation, civil society and the rule of law and to conform to internationally accepted human rights norms.

A brief look at the concordance (Table 7.2) for the abstract noun 'governance' shows that the collocates are also concerned with negotiating the meaning of the concept. For 'who' governs 'whom' or 'what' remains unspoken.

Arguably, Patten implicitly presses for a top-down view of democracy for the 'developing countries'. Without analyzing the whole of his speech, his top-down view of democracy is evident. This is especially so when it comes to what he euphemistically calls the 'developing countries' in a passage on page 3 of the printed version of the lecture. A consideration of the lexico-syntactic patterns is enough to show that things just seem to have 'happened' to these countries. No actors appear to have had any influence. The suggestion, in view of the absence of any agents, is that 'the President' was responsible for everything. Some comments on the syntax and lexis of one paragraph will serve to underline this point. (Each sentence is numbered for ease of reference.)

(4) Then the president began to stir uneasily under the restraints of constitutionalism, or maybe he <u>was replaced</u> by a Sandhurst socialist who had not himself read Jennings on the British Constitution but knew someone who claimed to have read Tawney.

(5) Political opposition <u>was curtailed</u>.

(6) The press <u>was muzzled</u>.

(7) Unchecked, political leaders **ceased** to make any distinction between the state's reserves and their own bank accounts.

Table 7.2 'Governance' Concordance in Patten's Lecture

182	development and	good	**governance?**	Simple. The Land Rover
207	Concepts of	good	**governance**	or democracy were
280	ingredient of	good	**governance,**	nor a guarantee that
332	notions of	good	**governance**	must take far greater
455	. . . ll-intentioned.	Good	**governance**	does not mean that the
489	they have lessons of		**governance**	to learn as well. Good
489	to learn as well.	Good	**governance**	is not simply a subject on

(8) Family values **came to mean** the President's family skimming the nation's G.D.P.

(9) **The first victim was** usually the independence of the courts, and with that gone the integrity of the public services disappeared too.

(10) In order to hold onto power the army <u>was cosseted</u>, but spending money on the military **meant** there was less for educating children or agricultural extension or primary health care.

(11) Soldiers <u>were paid</u>; teachers and nurses were not.

(12) Taxes on the honestly entrepreneurial <u>were hiked</u>.

(13) Ethnic minorities <u>were dispossessed</u>.

(14) Industries <u>were nationalised</u>, which **often resulted in** their assets <u>being slipped</u> into back pockets.

(15) To retain popularity or at least acquiescence in urban areas, food prices <u>were held down</u> which discouraged farmers, already <u>often discriminated against</u> by global trading rules, from growing as much as they could have done.

(16) Increasing rural poverty **led to** deforestation and the collapse of rural infrastructure, for example irrigation systems.

(17) As the mountains <u>were stripped</u> of their trees, so the rain gouged the soil from the rock, silted the rivers and flooded the plains.

(18) **It was** an awful cycle of political repression, war, corruption, woeful economic management, environmental calamity, starvation and debt.

- Note the passives (underlined) in nearly every sentence (4, 5, 6, 10, 11, 12, 13, 14, 15, 17). These serve to delete the agents of the actions mentioned.
- See also how the copula and similar verbs like 'mean' (in bold in 8, 9, 10, 16, 18) are used to transform events and actions into relational processes. The use of nominals complements this.
- The nominals and nominalizations (highlighted), together with the above mentioned features, emphasize the process of simplification of complex relations to a single entity. They contribute markedly to the general and unspecific nature of the text. Such nominals become more opaque. Used as Subjects (Actors or Experiencers) they make the listener or reader less likely or able to interpret them! Note the complexity of the final one (18)! Sentences (16) and (17) contain an

attribution of cause for the cutting down of trees to the abstract agent-less entity 'increasing rural poverty'. This contrasts markedly with the treatment of the concept of poverty and the explicit reference to the participants to be found in both Brundtland and Shiva's lectures—notably described as 'the poor' in Shiva's case! Sentence (7) contains an inherent negative term 'ceased'. This is a subtle way of avoiding using an explicit 'not' or negative marker.

Patten seems to be suggesting that the situation in these post-colonial countries is solely of their own making. The section is sometimes sarcastic, as in sentence (4) with the Jennings versus Tawney contrast! This did not remain unnoticed by his listeners. Actually, in the following question session one of the discussants does challenge Patten on this:

> Raj Thamotheram, corporate social responsibility consultant: I think we've got an incomplete picture here. *Partly what's missing is the industrialised world's role in the post colonial failures which I think we need to remember as we deal with the sensitive debates of today*, otherwise we could be a bit complacent. (Emphasis added, RJA)

5 THE CONCORDANCES FOR 'WORLD'

There are a number of relevant lexical items which are used by all lecturers. 'Globalisation' was already considered in chapter 6. A comparison of these may give us evidence of the different modes of reasoning or differential values the speakers ascribe to seemingly similar experiential or ideational notions. Further candidates for a comparative analysis are 'world' and 'sustainable development'. We can see how the lecturers conceptualize or even construct their view of "Respect for the Earth" by looking at the concordances of each individual speaker for the item 'world'. Table 7.3 displays some quantitative data.

The electronically generated concordances give a span of about nineteen characters (four words) to the left of the item and twenty-three characters (five words) to the right of the node word. But even this limited span can provide some evidence of semantic prosodies of lexical items and thus can give us a glimpse of the underlying values of the discourse patterns. This is in addition to noticing the more frequent use of 'world' by Shiva and the Prince of Wales, as compared with the other lecturers. Here we ignore wider co-texts and just consider the concordance lines.

What is interesting are the collocates both left and right of the node word. Let us consider Browne's uses in Table 7.4.

Three out of thirteen of Browne's occurrences have 'around the' as left collocates. This makes up the 'fixed expression' or fixed collocation 'around the world'.

Table 7.3 Number of Occurrences of 'World' in All Lectures

	Occurrences of	
Speaker	*World (%)*	*World's*
Patten	11 (0.23)	(1)
Lovejoy	7 (0.21)	(2)
Browne	13 (0.39)	(2 's)
Brundtland	9 (0.25)	(6)
Shiva	22 (0.60)	(4 worldview)
Prince of Wales	16 (0.68)	

Table 7.4 'World' Concordance in Browne's Lecture

. . . erating. We are in a	**world**	without certainty—except for
certainty of change. A	**world**	where national cultures and
the needs of today's	**world**	without depriving future
ends. In the real	**world**	we have to act on the balance
recognise that in a	**world**	where knowledge is openly
spread around the	**world**	as more will through the clean
to people around the	**world**	—and particularly those who
big cities around the	**world**	by the end of this year.
apparently lucrative	**world**	of the dot.coms . . . we do not
to the progress of the	**world**	in which they live. And if
sensitive areas of the	**world**	be permitted? Companies
a green revolution the	**world**	couldn't have fed the 2 billion
and cities of the	**world**	would have been overwhelmed
and developing the	**world's**	natural resources. We are by
quality of air in the	**world's**	cities. Let me start with
to me when I travel	**worldwide**	that it is the cumulative
—80,000 people	**worldwide**	in our case. These people

Brundtland has two uses out of nine of 'around the' (Table 7.5). This too gives rise to a fixed phrase, expressing an unspecific entity, 'all over the world'. Prince Charles uses this fixed phrase once, as we see in Table 7.6. Brundtland also has a third related collocate, namely 'all over the'.

The other left collocates employed by the Prince of Wales are exclusively of the form determiner plus modifier(s): 'the natural world' (8 occurrences out of 16, 50%), 'our entire world', 'the living world', 'one or the world', 'our world', 'the empirical world', 'living and spiritual world' and 'visible and invisible worlds'.

Table 7.7 shows Lovejoy's use of 'world'.

Lovejoy uses 'natural' once as a left collocate. Otherwise the lemma 'share' (sharing) is the only item with multiple use (twice). A glance at his concordance gives us physical references of the term and one with 'agencies' as a near collocate to 'World Bank'. This will be compared with the other uses by Patten and Shiva below.

But first look at Shiva's left collocates in Table 7.8.

Eight instances of the lemma 'feed' occur as mainly left but also as right collocates. There are also terms from the same broader lexical field. These

Table 7.5 'World' Concordance in Brundtland's Lecture

must be to create a	**world**	where we all can live well fed
Let us look around the	**world**	as it is now. About three
In actual fact the	**world**	average is now closer to 0.2
cities around the	**world,**	the quality of life among the
change. In the modern	**world,**	bacteria and viruses travel
meant being local	**world-wide.**	True. Companies that
as to believe that our	**world**	has, all of a sudden, become a
us all is to look at the	**world**	through the eyes—and spirit—
people all over the	**world**	dread being ill. It can so easily
At the same time, the	**world's**	capacity to produce food has
rice to becoming the	**world's**	second largest exporter.
to stabilising the	**world's**	population. We do not yet,
by most of the	**world's**	people threatens their
worth of 45% of the	**world's**	population, we start to see a
the health of the	**world's**	poorest billion and a half

Table 7.6 'World' Concordance in Prince of Wales' Lecture

people around the	**world**	I've been fascinated to hear
with the natural	**world,**	and with each other. If
us treating our entire	**world**	as some "great laboratory of
in the natural	**world**	which set limits to our
to reduce the natural	**world**	including ourselves to the
design of the natural	**world,**	scientists like Bertrand
we do, for the natural	**world**	is, as the economist Herman
will win—the living	**world**	as one or the world made up of
world as one or the	**world**	made up of random parts, the
for the natural	**world,**	irrespective of its usefulness
parts of the natural	**world**	are connected through an
don't know about our	**world**	and the life forms that inhabit
place in the empirical	**world**	yet traditional wisdoms would
just about the natural	**world,**	but about people too. This
living and spiritual	**world**	—as in the case of organic
visible and invisible	**worlds**	that inform the entire

Table 7.7 'World' Concordance in Lovejoy's Lecture

birth we grow up in a	**world**	of difference. Very early we
learn we share this	**world**	not just with our family but
the river water in the	**world**	reside around 3000 species of
people realize. The	**world**	is literally melting: tropical
time". The natural	**world**	in which we live is nothing
great joy in sharing a	**world**	with the shimmering variety
agencies like the	**World**	Bank, the InterAmerican
the largest of the	**world's**	forests, the largest
wilderness and the	**world's**	single greatest repository of

Table 7.8 'World' Concordance in Shiva's Lecture

Who feeds the	**world?**	My answer is very different
our fields and in our	**world.**	The Mayan peasants in the
. . . tification. What the	**world**	needs to feed a growing
peasants feed the	**world**	through biodiversity we are
of agriculture the	**world**	will starve. In spite of all
I ask, who feeds the	**world?**	This deliberate blindness to
consumer prices and	**world**	prices is the presence of large
food processors in the	**world.**	However, their work in
for feeding the	**world,**	but stealing livelihoods from
into the picture. The	**world**	can be fed only by feeding all
beings that make the	**world.**	In giving food to other beings
Seattle and the	**World**	Trade Organisation protests
providers in the Third	**World,**	and contrary to the dominant
farmers in the Third	**World**	—farmers like those in my
production by Third	**World**	farmers allows destruction
"Feeding the	**World"**	becomes disassociated from
the incomes of Third	**World**	farmers through a combination
too much." And a	**World**	Bank report has admitted that
being forced on Third	**World**	people through dumping of
Rights Agreement of	**World**	Trade Organisation forcing
innovations of Third	**World**	communities. Patents and
the poor of the Third	**World**	and making it the exclusive

include the right collocates 'starve' and 'giving food'. The collocation the 'Third World' occurs seven times and 'The World Trade Organisation' twice and 'a World Bank report'. It would be interesting to demonstrate in more detail how the semantic prosodies (see Sinclair 1987 and Partington 1998: 66ff) of the latter items compare with those in Patten (Table 7.9).

If we look at Patten's eleven right collocates of 'world', six are the names of agencies, organizations or official entities: 'World Trade Organisation'

Table 7.9 'World' Concordance in Patten's Lecture

will look after the	**world**	with all due care and
States leads the	**world.**	Yet its contribution to the
the rich developed	**world**	can lecture poor developing
the degradation of our	**world,**	its natural environment and
democracy to save our	**world,**	with its shadows of death and
global bodies like the	**World**	Trade Organisation, the
Monetary Fund and the	**World**	Bank. Into the gaps, the
was written 'The	**World**	Wide Movement Against
this year of the	**World**	Bank and the International
it. To their credit the	**World**	Bank have moved some way
and after Seattle the	**World**	Trade Organisation clearly
of Band-Aid to the	**world's**	wounded. In the course of my

(two), 'World Bank' (three) and 'World Wide Movement Against' (one). The establishment politician's conception of the world as an ordered political entity is possibly being underlined, if we consider the semantic prosodies in the wider co-texts of these occurrences. This is immediately contrastable with Shiva's two occurrences of 'World Trade Organisation' (protests) (forcing) and 'World Bank report' (has admitted). Her discourse does not take things at face value and does not view the world in a top-down fashion. By contrast, two right collocates of the Prince of Wales' use of 'world' include environmentally friendly items 'which set limits to our' and 'as one or the world made up of'.

6   DIFFERENCES IN REALIZATION OF THE INTERACTIONAL OR INTERPERSONAL FUNCTION?

All the examples I have discussed focus on the ideational function or the experiential dimension (Halliday 1985), pinpointing the themes and topics treated by the lecturers. But naturally enough an important perspective on a topic and an element of every position taken up by a speaker can be adduced from the way the interactional or interpersonal function is structured. So I will briefly refer to signallers of the interpersonal function. Personal pronouns and modal verbs provide a fairly swift entry-point if we are using a

Table 7.10 Frequencies of Personal Pronouns in All Lectures

Name	I (%)	My	We (%)	Our	You (%)
Patten	26 (0.5)	9	32 (0.67)	7	17 (**0.36**)
Lovejoy	28 (0.85)	5	23 (0.70)	14	4
Browne	27 (0.82)	7	35 (1.05)	17	3
Brundtland	24 (0.68)	1	27 (0.76)	15	3
Shiva	9 (0.24)	3	21 (0.57)	13	0
Prince Charles	14 (0.59)	0	45 (**1.9**)	30	0

concordancing programme. The pronouns 'I' and 'we' can give us some idea of the way a speaker argues or their mode of reasoning. Table 7.10 displays the result of counting the personal pronouns 'I', 'we' and 'you' and the possessives 'my' and 'our'.

Even without an analysis of the concordances for these items, we can draw a number of preliminary conclusions. Patten appears to be the only speaker who 'addresses' his audience directly ('you'). Prince Charles potentially makes quite excessive use of what could turn out to be the 'royal we' (including his audience, perhaps). Note, too the parallel use of 'our'. The relative shares of the word counts (in percentage terms) for 'I' and 'we' are given in brackets. In the case of Vandana Shiva the minimal use of 'I' appears to parallel an 'impersonal' and 'factual' tone which several other features reflect and which correspond to the serious and very radical, political contribution she makes to the series.

7 'SUSTAINABLE DEVELOPMENT' IN ALL THE LECTURES COMPARED

In this section I intend to compare an item and its related collocates which we might expect all the lecturers to use in some form or other. I am referring to a major buzzword of environmentalists which appears to have become so debased in the course of its 'integration' into many other domains of discourse—'sustainable development'. In one respect, then, the Reith Lectures serve as kind of benchmark for how widely diverging interest groups have colonized and exploited the concept (see also chapter 5). In absolute figures we find the instances for each speaker in Table 7.11. Patten and the Prince of Wales stand out from the rest with the considerable use they make of the collocation 'sustainable development'.

Looking at Browne's use of 'sustainable' (Table 7.12), we can see that he has 'societies' as a right collocate. He also uses 'sustainable' twice predicatively.

Table 7.11 Occurrences of 'Sustainable Development' of All Speakers

Speaker	Total (Sustainable Development)
Browne	3
Brundtland	3
Lovejoy	5
Patten	11
Shiva	1
Prince of Wales	13

Each of the uses, as we can see in the concordances themselves, has positive and confident collocates like 'deliver'. It is all very business-like. And indeed the word 'business' is always close by in the co-texts, as can be seen below (19, 20, 21). Only business can deliver 'sustainable development' is the clear and uncompromising message Browne is delivering!

(19) Business is not in opposition to, but has a fundamental role in delivering sustainable development—to meet the needs of today's world without depriving future generations of their means to do so.

(20) The relationship I've talked about should give society the confidence to trust business to deliver sustainable development—on the basis of enlightened self-interest. But of course this means that companies must play their full role.

Table 7.12 'Sustainable' in Browne's Lecture

20	Is development	**sustainable?**	Or is one strand of
62	we now live is not	**sustainable.**	America still remains
131	role in delivering	**sustainable**	development—to meet
143	is that business needs	**sustainable**	societies in order to
495	business to deliver	**sustainable**	development—on the
383	new technology.	**Sustainable**	development requires
533	of development can be	**sustained—**	it clearly can't and

(21) So it will be clear to you that I believe technological change will help us avoid the harsh trade off which some deem inevitable, between the desire to increase living standards and the desire to preserve a clean environment. But only if we don't kill off our ability to develop new technology. Sustainable development requires successful companies.

In the case of Brundtland, 'economic growth' is a right collocate of 'sustainable' (not shown here). And not surprisingly Brundtland makes the close connection between her preoccupation with health and 'sustainable development' or links it with other speakers' definitions (23). The broader co-texts make this visible (22, 23, 24).

(22) I want health to be at the heart of our struggle for sustainable development.

(23) We also find it hard to work for people ruled by corrupt despots, by weak leaders caught up in power-struggles, or by plain war-lords. As Chris Patten has already argued in this lecture series, sustainable development cannot work without good governance.

(24) Are we ready to scale up our investments in poor people's health?—investments vital for sustainable development?

Looking at how the Prince of Wales' fifteen instances of 'sustainable' are used, all except two have 'development' as right collocate. What is striking is how he attempts to demonstrate a degree of commonality in the term's usage. His generous reference to other speakers is seen in the co-text (25).

(25) Like millions of other people around the world I've been fascinated to hear five eminent speakers share with us their thoughts, hopes and fears about sustainable development based on their own experience. All five of those contributions have been immensely thoughtful and challenging.

The co-texts (26) and (27) both show the Prince is referring to the negotiation of meaning that surrounds this compound phrase.

(26) There have been clear differences of opinion and of emphasis between the speakers but there have also been some important common themes, both implicit and explicit. One of those themes has been the suggestion that sustainable development is a matter of enlightened self-interest. Two of the speakers used this phrase and I don't believe that the other three would dissent from it, and nor would I.

(27) Self-interest is a powerful motivating force for all of us, and if we can somehow convince ourselves that sustainable development is in

all our interests then we will have taken a valuable first step towards achieving it.

In occurrence (28) it becomes clear that Prince Charles sets out to provide his own interpretation of the notion, introducing moral and spiritual aspects.

> (28) I am convinced we will need to dig rather deeper to find the inspiration, sense of urgency and moral purpose required to confront the hard choices which face us on the long road to sustainable development. So, although it seems to have become deeply unfashionable to talk about the spiritual dimension of our existence, that is what I propose to do.

He extends the notion to include 'a sense of the sacred'. This is to be seen in extract (29).

> (29) It is only recently that this guiding principle has become smothered by almost impenetrable layers of scientific rationalism. I believe that if we are to achieve genuinely sustainable development we will first have to rediscover, or re-acknowledge a sense of the sacred in our dealings with the natural world, and with each other.

Occurrence (30) is a further enhancement of his 'reading' of the concept. Here it is striking how he appears to relativize the 'scientific-sounding' left collocate 'parameters'.

> (30) Fundamentally, an understanding of the sacred helps us to acknowledge that there are bounds of balance, order and harmony in the natural world which set limits to our ambitions, and define the parameters of sustainable development. In some cases nature's limits are well understood at the rational, scientific level.

Prince Charles' critique of lack of action is quite marked as (30) reveals. Here 'sustainable' is paired with 'outcome'. The implicit double standards towards 'scientific issues' are brought out by his contrasting the acceptance of genetic engineering and the neglect of climatology's findings. This is indicated in (31) by the 'insufficient' vs. 'sufficient' parallelism.

> (31) And we are beginning to comprehend the full, awful consequences of pumping too much carbon dioxide into the earth's atmosphere. Yet the actions being taken to halt the damage known to be caused by exceeding nature's limits in these and other ways are insufficient to ensure a sustainable outcome. In other areas, such as the artificial and uncontained transfer of genes between species of plants and animals, the lack of hard, scientific evidence of harmful consequences is regarded in many quarters as sufficient reason to allow such developments to proceed.

Such personal defining takes place also in co-text (32). That it resorts to the authority and the quotation of another person is a quite legitimate rhetorical procedure, of course.

(32) So which argument do you think will win—the living world as one or the world made up of random parts, the product of mere chance, thereby providing the justification for any kind of development? This, to my mind, lies at the heart of what we call sustainable development. We need, therefore, to rediscover a reference for the natural world, irrespective of its usefulness to ourselves—to become more aware in Philip Sherrard's words of 'the relationship of interdependence, interpenetration and reciprocity between God, Man and Creation.'

Then by using 'achieve' (33) the Prince of Wales places 'sustainable development' in the pragmatic context of goal-setting.

(33) In suggesting that we will need to listen rather more to the common sense emanating from our hearts if we are to achieve sustainable development, I'm not suggesting that information gained through scientific investigation is anything other than essential. Far from it. But I believe that we need to restore the balance between the heartfelt reason of instinctive wisdom and the rational insights of scientific analysis.

By virtue of being the final, summarizing speaker, Prince Charles refers again to the other discussions of the notion, as several instances (including 34) show.

(34) As Gro Harlem Brundtland has reminded us, sustainable development is not just about the natural world, but about people too. This applies whether we are looking at the vast numbers who lack sufficient food or access to clean water, but also those living in poverty and without work.

As he says, historical contextualization will be necessary (35).

(35) So if we are serious about sustainable development then we must also remember that the lessons of history are particularly relevant when we start to look further ahead.

Arguments are presented for a specific orientation towards education to enable it to come about (36).

(36) They won't, I believe, unless there are increased efforts to develop an approach to education which balances the rational with the intuitive. Without this truly sustainable development is doomed. It will merely

become a hollow-sounding mantra that is repeated ad nauseam in order to make us all feel better.

In (37) his respect for and humility before nature is contrasted with a reductionist tendency he sees elsewhere.

> (37) The future will need people who understand that sustainable development is not merely about a series of technical fixes, about redesigning humanity or re-engineering nature in an extension of globalised, industrialisation—but about a re-connection with nature and a profound understanding of the concepts of care that underpin long term stewardship.

His final sentence (38) is itself a summary of the semantic re-negotiation he has been engaging in throughout the lecture:

> (38) Taking a cautious approach or achieving balance in life is never as much fun as the alternatives, but that is what sustainable development is all about.

As can be expected for a professional biologist view of 'sustainable development', Lovejoy argues for and sees diversity playing a central role (39).

> (39) Biological diversity lies at the heart of sustainable development.

Moreover, Lovejoy, like the Prince of Wales, makes his interpretation of 'sustainable development' explicit (40).

> (40) There certainly can be locations (cities for example) where there is very intense use and low biological diversity. It does mean enough wild places and enough connections between them so all the species can make it in the long term.

> These two measurable goals provide an operational definition for sustainable development within that piece of geography.

His biological focus is repeated with regard to the future (41), as he defines nature as all embracing, rather than separated from humanity.

> (41) The moment is at hand to take the right steps to underpin a sustainable future biologically. Certainly, the challenge is highly complex, and it must work locally everywhere so that it all adds up to sustainable development. Yet it could be summed up by saying we need to live within nature rather than think of it as something which is taken care of, almost in token fashion, with fenced off areas while humanity operates without restraint in the rest of the landscape.

In (42) Lovejoy inserts the notion of 'ecosystem' as a model for 'sustainable development'.

> (42) Classical conservation is not in fact enough. Honoring the Patrick Principle through ecosystem management means we have to live in ways that won't degrade the biology of areas of strict preservation, but also won't degrade that of the landscapes in which we live. That is why sustainable development is so important. It is also why it is so complex to grasp.

At the same time Lovejoy does, and, presumably given his consultant status to various organizations, cannot neglect to, inject a political dimension (43) into his perspective on 'sustainable development'.

> (43) I believe it could happen and I know that multilateral agencies like the World Bank, the InterAmerican Development Bank, UNDP and UNEP plus civil society would jump at the chance to support such an effort. Sustainable development takes good governance as well as good science.

We see Patten employing 'sustainable' fourteen times, eleven with 'development'. An analysis of the wider co-texts of this pairing in Patten's lecture can be quite instructive. He first (44) situates its usage historically.

> (44) The 'sustainable development' to which this series of lectures is devoted is a phrase first coined by the United Nations Conference on the Human Environment—The Stockholm Conference—in 1972.

But clearly Patten re-negotiates 'sustainable development' to fit in with his arguments about what counts as 'good governance'. It is very much a status quo view of the world (45). Recall the discussion of 'good governance'.

> (45) I think that we understand today that sustainable development is about much more than environment policy defined in terms of departments, ministers and white papers. It requires a mosaic of institutions, policies and values.

He makes much of what can only be seen as a somewhat surreal anecdotal example of the role played by landrovers in developing countries. This juxtaposition (46) supports what he means by 'sustainable development'.

> (46) Now what, you may ask, does a motor vehicle have to do with sustainable development and good governance? Simple. The Land Rover is the heroic war-horse of development policy. As a donor of aid we had given fleets of those splendid vehicles to poor countries.

At the same time, for Patten (47) 'sustainable development' is not a simple and straightforward concept.

(47) And note that sustainable development is challenged even by the practices of liberal, pluralist democracies.

And his clear moves incorporating the semantic negotiation of 'sustainable development' continue throughout the lecture, as (48) shows.

(48) Concepts of good governance or democracy were arguably implicit in the earliest definitions of sustainable development. In recent years, the references have been explicit.

Moreover, the argument he advances (49) is enhanced by his rather patrician view of democracy:

(49) Democracies are not corruption-free zones, either in business or public administration. Yet the scale of corruption and its corrosive impact on sustainable development is limited by democratic practice and a free judiciary. In an open, plural society even where there is still no cultural recognition of the primacy of public responsibility over private gain, corrupt practices . . .

This does not prevent his emphasizing (50) the close link he sees between 'sustainable development' and democracy.

(50) Democracy is more likely to produce better government on the side of sustainable development. But to borrow the song title, "It ain't necessarily so".

When he does not approve of something, Patten (51) employs a passive to avoid naming his opponents.

(51) And this is specially relevant to the area we are discussing, since democratic governments have not always been conspicuously good at meeting their environmental responsibilities. So to secure sustainable development, it is suggested that traditional notions of good governance must take far greater account of civil society.

The people he opposes are again left unnamed in the clause 'what is thought essential' (52) with its impersonal and unspecific passive:

(52) The cutting edge of all this civil society activism has been environmental, the campaign in various ways to save what is thought essential

for sustainable development. But I find myself asking the awkward question—is it actually very sustainable given that it isn't obviously democratic?

Avoiding, again, naming his opponents, Patten employs the nominalization of 'demonisation' (53), but he makes his point by suggesting that people who oppose globalisation cannot be in favour of 'sustainable development'.

(53) But is the demonisation of global trade and technological progress good for sustainable development and how democratic is it?

Turning now to Vandana Shiva, we see that she has five occurrences of 'sustainable', one of which precedes 'development'. As we saw in chapter 7, she uses 'sustainability' more (ten times), like Lovejoy, and 'sustainably' once. Shiva is extending the meaning potential of the concept.

In the one occurrence of 'sustainable development' in Shiva's lecture (54) she refers anaphorically to other speakers' discussion of the notions. She emphasizes that she will 're-evaluate' what is going on.

(54) Throughout this lecture series people have referred to different aspects of sustainable development taking globalisation for granted. For me it is now time radically to re-evaluate what we are doing. For what we are doing in the name of globalisation to the poor is brutal and unforgivable.

For her re-evaluation Shiva does not explicitly even use the phrase 'sustainable development', preferring extensive use of the word 'sustainability.'

8 OMISSIONS CAN TELL US SOMETHING ABOUT HOW DISCOURSE IS SHAPED

What remains unmentioned can tell us something about the shaping of discourse too. A search for two seemingly significant items 'climate change' and 'global warming' might tell us something about the orientation of the lecturers. Who mentions these items? Table 7.13 summarizes the result of a computer search.

The discussions turn out to be very non-committal however, as these wider co-texts make clear! Note, interestingly, that Browne (55) has the only instance of 'global warming'. (See chapter 11 for a discussion of the semantic engineering engaged in by multinational corporations to replace 'global warming' by the less threatening phrase 'climate change'.) Note how Browne immediately de-emphasizes the issue by means of an agentless nominal, 'environmental concern'.

Table 7.13 Occurrences of 'Climate Change' and
'Global Warming'

Lecturer	Climate Change	Global Warming
Browne	3	1
Brundtland	1	0
Lovejoy	2	0
Patten	1	0
Shiva	0	0
Prince of Wales	0	0

(55) One way of seeing this is to focus on two of the problems at the very heart of environmental concern—climate change or global warming—and the quality of air in the world's cities.

Browne perhaps generously, and certainly strategically, uses intertextual reference to an earlier speaker's contribution (56). Yet prior to that his use of merely the word 'mounting' to denote the 'human effect' serves to play down its significance.

(56) The latest authoritative scientific reports on climate change make clear—in the most careful, rigorous language—that indications of a human effect on the climate are mounting. Tom Lovejoy, in this lecture series, has already referred to this.

Brundtland's use of 'climate change' (57) predictably links it to its propensity for affecting abilities to combat illnesses.

(57) More people are suffering from this killing and debilitating disease now than ever before, and deforestation, climate change and breakdowns in health services have caused the disease to spread to new areas and areas that have been malaria-free for decades, like in Europe.

Lovejoy uses 'climate change' twice (58 and 59) distinguishing it from low-level or local environmental problems requiring immediate solution because they are 'intrinsic'. By contrast the broad issue of 'climate change' is aligned with the class of 'extrinsic factors'.

(58) because it means taking on all environmental problems intrinsic to the area as well as those like acid rain and climate change which are extrinsic.

(59) One of the most important extrinsic factors for ecosystem management is that of climate change.

Patten's comment hingeing on 'climate change' (60) appears remarkably low-key, with him only just falling short of expressing criticism of the USA.

(60) Yet its [USA] contribution to the global struggle against climate change is hamstrung by the seeming political imperative of keeping energy prices low.

Shiva's focus on poverty clearly relegates issues such as a focus on climate change or global warming elsewhere, for the purposes of her lecture. In retrospect it seems somewhat strange that at the time of the Millennium Reith Lectures climate change did not apparently play such a central role when people were asked to discuss the state of the world.

9   ON THE STRUCTURE OF POWER
THAT SHAPES MEDIA CHOICES

The analysis of the majority of the lectures in the Reith 2000 series serves, if anything, to underline how complexly science and politics interlock. They involve the discourse of politics and how appeals can be made to science to try and 'understand', construct and, I would argue, 'shape' specific perspectives on the environmentally and ecologically degrading state of the world. We need not be surprised that all the speakers take on an anthropocentric standpoint.[1] These are leading figures. We find business, politics and world governance (in the form of the WHO) represented, in the person of their spokespeople. It suffices to repeat the litany of their names here: Patten, Lovejoy, one-time special adviser to President Clinton, Browne, CEO of BP, Brundtland, head of the WHO, and His Royal Highness, The Prince of Wales, to demonstrate my point. Only Vandana Shiva stands out as the token 'outsider', selected to prove the BBC's balance, as always!

As John Berger says (2003), speaking about politics in the late 20th century: for the powerful it is about 'management' in this consumerist age. Little, if anything has changed, in the 21st century. Crisis management is the name of the game. But top-down 'solutions' are not genuine solutions. They are short-term massaging of the populace, with the kinds of assuaging and semi-bureaucratese, such as at least five of these speakers engage in from their various constituencies.

Giving space to speakers like the BP chairman John Browne is a part of the massive campaign to control the agenda and to crowd out critical voices. Commercial corporations do this almost by definition; but also public broadcasters like the BBC, we now see. Browne once more has space to sing the praise of and promote the claimed benign intents of companies.

People need to be helped to become aware of the techniques of persuasion that are being employed here. This can hardly stop the extension of corporate hegemony over what we get to hear, see, read, know and think. Herman and Chomsky's (1988) *Manufacturing Consent* is not out of date. But as critical scholars and critical linguists we must persist in encouraging listeners and readers to employ their common sense to peer through this mush or smog of ideology.

10 EDWARD HERMAN'S "POWER LAWS"

Edward Herman (1992: 14) has discussed the relation between power and who gets to wield the influence to shape public discourse through the media. In a democracy not everyone has access to the media. It is the case that the most powerful have ease of access and can tell lies. It is important, moreover, to note that "the more powerful they are, the more easily they can lie and the less likely it is that their lies will be corrected". The close correlation between status and the likelihood of counting as "credible" is equally obvious. And it is precisely this "credibility" which grants the most powerful in Western democracies "freedom to lie"—a freedom not enjoyed by 'normal' citizens. Herman derives from this power structure two laws: a 'power law of access' and an 'inverse law of truthfulness.' In chapter 10 we return to this situation and discuss it in more detail. Suffice it, at this stage, to note what responses we can encounter from the media in 'free' societies like the US and the UK. As the war in Iraq has demonstrated most tellingly, the evidence for untruths and deceit was too obvious to be overlooked. Nonetheless the media's representatives meekly and slavishly were prepared to fall in with the powerful, in the form of the US and UK governments, and to 'support' their actions. Edwards and Cromwell (2006) have trenchantly dissected the servant role the British media played in bolstering the lies to the British public purveyed by the UK government, despite the prominent liberal self-image of 'freedom of expression'.

It is to be hoped that in the case of environmental issues, rather than war and peace or power politics, media reporting and discussion is more reliable. Since most people have been noticing, perhaps physically, the increase of rainfall, storms and flooding, even now in Europe, maybe this position will begin slowly to change. But as critical observers we have to be aware that, if this is the case, this will not automatically mean that these issues will still be openly debated and indeed necessarily understood by the recipients of this environmental discourse.

My hypothesis is that there are forces (contesting and competing in this area) which shape and engineer how they wish the processes of environmental degradation to be viewed, conceptualized and presented in public discourse domains.

11 CONCLUSION

I am not necessarily saying that the speakers, the Reith lecturers, were all dissimulating. Indeed it is beyond the scope of this study to seek to verify or to test the validity of the statements of fact that some of them activate. What is important is the framework within which such presentations are mediatized. The BBC is nominally a not-for-profit organization. Nonetheless the trends that could be observed during the past thirty years demonstrate that the BBC operates in essentially the same fashion as many purely commercially run mass media businesses. Moreover there are now commercial divisions and associated businesses and companies that have been 'hived off' to the private sector. Most 'content' programming on TV channels and radio channels is now produced by commercial businesses as commissions for 'producers' of the BBC! Similar trends are to be seen in the public broadcasting sectors of many other European countries.

8 Resisting Imposed Metaphors of Value

1 INTRODUCTION

Vandana Shiva is a committed scientist and environmental activist from India. She uses her analytical ability to uncover the semantic engineering that goes on when global corporations colonize and destroy traditional agriculture in the Third World. This is evident in her 2000 BBC Reith lecture (Shiva 2000a). It is a sustained critique of how global corporations, with the active support of many politicians, are forcing genetic engineering and commercial agriculture on rural communities.

Shiva denounces the eradication of a sustainable way of life in the name of modernization and science. Shiva's work (2000b and 2002a) uncovers the metaphors and the models underlying the so-called modernization of agriculture. This is designed to benefit nobody but the Western corporations which are pursuing it. This process parallels one already far developed in Europe (Trampe 2001).

Shiva's approach can be read on two levels. First we have the factual, objective analysis of how rural traditions in India are being dismantled and the call to resist physically and politically. Then, on the meta-analytical level, Shiva critically delineates how the myths associated with neo-liberal projects and 'solutions' are being formulated. From a critical discourse analytical standpoint it is significant to note that Shiva is a discerning observer of how language is employed in this process. As Shiva (2000a) says:

> The global free trade economy has become a threat to sustainability and the very survival of the poor and other species is at stake not just as a side effect or as an exception but in a systemic way through a restructuring of our worldview at the most fundamental level. Sustainability, sharing and survival is being economically outlawed in the name of market competitiveness and market efficiency.

2   STATEMENT OF THE INTENTION OF SHIVA'S REITH LECTURE: AN ARGUMENT

The phrase "restructuring of our worldview at the most fundamental level" recalls the 'structural' metaphorical level and the well-known truism uttered by Lakoff and Johnson (1980: 157): "[W]hether in national politics or in everyday interaction, people in power get to impose their metaphors". This is what Shiva's (2000a) Reith lecture goes on to demonstrate. That a worldview is in part a metaphorical conceptual system seems to be beyond doubt. The interaction between cognitive systems and language to construct such features of human existence is likewise beyond dispute nowadays.

Generalizing her specific theme of poverty and globalisation, Shiva states the intention of her lecture:

> It is experiences such as these which tell me that we are so wrong to be smug about the new global economy. I will argue in this lecture that it is time to stop and think about the impact of globalisation on the lives of ordinary people. This is vital to achieve sustainability.

The first two pivotal sentences capture the gist and mode of operating she sets out to pursue in her lecture. In stark summary: she sets out to 'argue/ stop/and think about something'. Later she reiterates the gist of her lecture and underlines her approach:

> I want to argue here tonight that we need to urgently bring the planet and people back into the picture.

Again we may note the verbs of saying and inert cognition used: 'argue/ bring people back into the picture'. They are a key to her intention and also the clue to her achievement.

3   ON THE NATURE OF SHIVA'S ACHIEVEMENT

This chapter investigates how language is used in argument and how Shiva actively focuses on this very feature. The 'content' of her Reith lecture (2000a) does not necessarily, or even mainly, treat facts about the world. It seems instead to be about 'ideas'. She uses terms like 'myth', 'worldview', 'view', 'claim' and others. Her Reith lecture is peppered with verbs of reporting, saying and related modes. Her interest is equally directed at the linguistic structure of the ideas which she is criticizing. The actions which she is opposing, she suggests, are linked to worldviews. Hence to combat them we need to re-formulate or unpack some of the semantic processing that is involved. The next step is to present counter-concepts, alternative metaphors and a different view of the world.

Shiva manifests a critical capacity to see through language employed in the service of industrial and commercial agriculture. She uncovers the ideologies and values which specific terminological or lexical choices encode. Shiva's lecture is a sustained, committed and very eloquent analysis of what the impact of globalisation means for the poor peasants and especially the women of India. She begins her lecture with a very dramatic opening paragraph:

> Recently, I was visiting Bhatinda in Punjab because of an epidemic of farmers' suicides. Punjab used to be the most prosperous agricultural region in India. Today every farmer is in debt and despair. Vast stretches of land have become water-logged desert. And as an old farmer pointed out, even the trees have stopped bearing fruit because heavy use of pesticides have killed the pollinators—the bees and butterflies.

The restructuring of the worldview on the part of multi-national companies like Monsanto and Cargill affects these people. It results in the ecological degradation and destruction of their natural resources and hence the material bases of their lives. Shiva's is an exposition which is unusual for such Reith Lectures: it is committed, it represents the interests of women, the poor, the down-trodden. She is not oblique and evasive in pinpointing where the causal agent for certain developments are concerned. She names names, for example Cargill and Monsanto. We find five instances of Monsanto and two of Cargill. The concordances for Monsanto and Cargill allow us to rapidly access the critical points she makes about the actions of these global multis. She makes her partiality and partisanship clear. The other Reith lecturers all represent the rich and powerful and claim to be speaking for the whole world. Unlike them, Shiva is direct and polemical. She says uncomfortable things, calls a spade a spade and unearths the hypocritical stance of the vertically integrated global pesticide, seed and biotechnology corporation, Monsanto, as in this passage:

> The recent announcement that Monsanto is giving away the rice genome for free is misleading, because Monsanto has never made a commitment that it will never patent rice varieties or any other crop varieties.

Shiva critiques the 'announcement' (a reporting verbal noun) of Monsanto's. She questions the very language used by Monsanto and its intention, calling it 'misleading'. She also interrogates the related verb of saying 'commit', calling into question the sincerity of the commitment!

4   CONCEPTUAL ANALYSIS IN VANDANA SHIVA'S WRITING

What do we call it when in addition to arguing a case writers start to scrutinize the language used especially by their (supposed) opponents? Is it metadiscourse analysis? Looking at the terms used? Critiquing the terminology, the wording chosen? In Shiva's work we encounter semantic analysis as well as objective political and scientific reasoning. In Shiva (2000a) this can be seen by highlighting how often she talks about 'defining' or by focusing on a number of lexical items which can serve to uncover the 'linguistic' and 'conceptual' praxis she can be shown to be engaged in. Taking issue with definitions, sense, meaning and the 'values' assigned to terms, words and concepts is to contest, argue against and to present alternatives. Fairclough (1992: 122) discusses a related and complementary activity:

> Metadiscourse is a peculiar form of manifest intertextuality where the text producer distinguishes different levels within her own text, and distances herself from some level of the text, treating the distanced level as if it were another, external, text.

One way this is achieved is to paraphrase or reformulate an expression or to mark sections as being metaphorical. Fairclough comments (ibid.: 122): "Metadiscourse implies that the speaker is situated above or outside her own discourse, and is in a position to control and manipulate it." This basically is what a major portion of Shiva's Reith lecture is about.

For our purposes a convenient way of tapping into this metadiscourse analysis took the 'as' concordance (Table 8.1) as a starting point. This uncovered a number of verbs of saying, reporting or inert cognition like 'define', 'characterise', 'promote', 'project', 'treat', 'count', 'perceive' and 'redefine' as the concordance for 'as' shows.

What the narrow concordance does not reveal can be shown by consulting the text more closely. In the broader co-text of the first instance (1) we find 'referred to' just to the left of 'by'.

> (1) pulses and millets and paddy have been lured by seed companies to buy hybrid cotton seeds referred to by the seed merchants as 'white gold'

For the second instance (2) 'defining' can be found five words to the left of 'local'.

> (2) A global monoculture is being forced on people by defining everything that is fresh, local and handmade as a health hazard.

Table 8.1 'As' Concordance in Shiva's Reith Lecture

by the seed merchants	**as**	"white gold", which were supposed
local and handmade	**as**	a health hazard. Human hands are
defined in such a way	**as**	to make the food production on
are characterised	**as**	unproductive because they produce
constantly promoted	**as**	the only alternative available for
to be projected	**as**	creation. Take the case of the
are treated	**as**	'non-productive' and
itself is counted	**as**	growth. And women themselves
do it and is projected	**as**	dependent on global agribusiness
are defined	**as**	"wealth creators", something has
are being defined	**as**	the worst contaminants, and work
are being perceived	**as**	parasites, to be exterminated for
theft is defined	**as**	creation, and saving and sharing
seed is defined	**as**	theft of intellectual property.
has been redefined	**as**	a crime. This makes us all poor.
defines pollination	**as**	"theft by bees" and claims

If we now look more closely at the concordance for 'defined' (Table 8.2), it is clear how Shiva takes issue with the way certain concepts and propositions are interpreted by corporations. Here Shiva engages in the meta-communicative, 'metadiscourse' or meta-linguistic level of analysis (see Fairclough 1992: 122). The preponderance of this dimension in Shiva's (2000a) lecture is most striking. I have located numerous instances of this meta-level. Running through Shiva's work is a sharp insight into the fact that 'what people say' or the propositions they advance are closely inter-related, if not always dependent on 'how' they say things, or how they package their concepts, 'what words they choose' to encapsulate their thoughts and ideas, right down to the very definitions of the words they are using.

A closer examination of the broader co-text of these items brings out the systematic fashion in which Shiva analyzes the conflicts of interest between the rural agriculture of India and global corporations propagating 'modernization'.

Table 8.2 'Defined' Concordance in Shiva's Reith Lecture

food. Yields have been	**defined**	in such a way as to make the
and speculators are	**defined**	as "wealth creators",
hands are being	**defined**	as the worst contaminants,
of basmati, theft is	**defined**	as creation, and saving and
and sharing seed is	**defined**	as theft of intellectual
A worldview that	**defines**	pollination as "theft by bees"
forced on people by	**defining**	everything that is fresh,

Passage (3) skilfully takes issue with the term 'yield'. Shiva argues for the re-definition of this term in an ecologically sustainable fashion as the highlighted elements show.

(3) Planting only one crop in the entire field as a monoculture will of course increase its individual yield. Planting multiple crops in a mixture will have low yields of individual crops, but will have high total output of food. Yields have been defined in such a way as to make the food production on small farms by small farmers disappear.

Passage (4) stakes a claim for the validity of human labour as paramount in the agricultural process against the chemical and machine-driven process being thrust upon the Third World producers.

(4) Human hands are being defined as the worst contaminants, and work for human hands is being outlawed, to be replaced by machines and chemicals bought from global corporations.

Passage (5) deals with 'wealth creation' addressing directly the conceptual and categorial level. This turns out be a central issue in Shiva's writing and will be examined more closely below.

(5) More food is being traded while the poor are consuming less. When growth increases poverty, when real production becomes a negative economy, and speculators are defined as 'wealth creators', something has gone wrong with the concepts and categories of wealth and wealth creation.

Passage (6) discusses definition issues and addresses in two instances the structural metaphorical level of wealth creation. Shiva acknowledges that production of sense is taking place here. Firstly with wealth being metamorphosed or metaphorized as patents—a clear case of 'theft' for Shiva! Secondly, by contrast, the sharing of seed is criminalized as theft of intellectual property with sense transformation being involved again!

(6) When patents are granted for seeds and plants, as in the case of basmati, theft is defined as creation, and saving and sharing seed is defined as theft of intellectual property.

Shiva discusses in (7) the topsy-turvy world of global corporations that defines pollination as "theft by bees". The re-sensing of the world accompanies the industrialization of agriculture and provides the justification for subsequent actions. I return to the 'theft' metaphor below.

(7) A worldview that defines pollination as 'theft by bees' and claims biodiversity 'steals' sunshine is a worldview which itself aims at stealing nature's harvest by replacing open pollinated varieties with hybrids and sterile seeds, and destroying biodiverse flora with herbicides such as Roundup.

A further example of Shiva's meta-analytical method can be seen in (8). For Shiva it is evident that force and persuasion (via definitions) are close comrades in the globalising of agribusiness. This reminds one of Humpty-Dumpty semantics (see chapter 5); it all depends on who is master.

(8) A global monoculture is being forced on people by defining everything that is fresh, local and handmade as a health hazard.

This kind of examination of 'define' could be extended to other items. Lack of space does not allow us to observe Shiva's close meta-discursive analysis of 'name', 'refer', 'call', 'basis' and 'pseudo'. Taking issue with definitions, senses and the 'values' assigned to terms is to contest people's categories of thought and to present alternatives. As we see, a major portion of Shiva's Reith lecture is about conceptual analysis.

5   METAPHORICAL BLINDNESS: A MODE OF SENSE PRODUCTION

Sometimes Shiva comments on the semantic veracity or the truth value of a proposition differently, saying 'X is not Y but Z', as in (9).

(9) The poor are pushed into deeper poverty by making them pay for what was theirs. Even the rich are poorer because their profits are based

on the theft and on the use of coercion and violence. This is not wealth creation but plunder.

A further technique used by her is explicit metaphor choice. In one section of her lecture she suggests that 'metaphorical blindness' is a way people ignore what is extant. It is like a manifestation of 'cognitive dissonance', of not accepting what exists and viewing it in another fashion. It is a 'failure' to see or to look. In discourse it takes the form of redefining phenomena or concepts. Shiva several times imputes this tendency to unspecified but implied actors, to generic 'humans'. But the allusion to the corporations she is opposing is clear, when she speaks of 'This deliberate blindness to diversity'.

In the concordance for 'blind' and 'blindness' (Table 8.3) the last two examples interestingly refer to literal blindness, thus re-engaging with the material problems of poor Indian people.

But if we examine the broader co-texts of the first four examples we will see the behaviour I have been referring to in action. In (10) not acknowledging the role of species other than humans is a problem for Shiva:

(10) As humans travel further down the road to non-sustainability, they become intolerant of other species and blind to their vital role in our survival.

In (11) Shiva contrasts 'biodiversity' and 'monoculture' and metaphorically transfers the latter to mental constructs.

(11) From the biodiversity perspective, biodiversity based productivity is higher than monoculture productivity. I call this blindness to the high productivity of diversity a 'Monoculture of the Mind', which creates monocultures in our fields and in our world.

Table 8.3 'Blindness' Concordance in Shiva's Reith Lecture

of other species and	**blind**	to their vital role in our
. . . ductivity. I call this	**blindness**	to the high productivity of
This deliberate	**blindness**	to diversity, the blindness
to diversity, the	**blindness**	to nature's production,
A rice as a cure for	**blindness.**	It is assumed that without
A rice and prevent	**blindness**	in children and anaemia in

In (12) Shiva lists four crucial elements which in her opinion are deliberately ignored or 'not seen'.

(12) This deliberate blindness to diversity, the blindness to nature's production, production by women, production by Third World farmers allows destruction and appropriation to be projected as creation.

6   WHAT IS VALUE? NEGOTIATION OF SENSES AND METAPHOR

Much political debate revolves around who causes what and with what result. The ensuing assessment of the relative shares in the process of value creation is the issue that Shiva addresses. The crux is one of agency. In this area the debate about the factors of production and their relative shares in economic activity and, hence, in the creation of value comes to mind. Joan Robinson (1962: 1ff) has documented tellingly and ironically how widely variant notions as to what constitutes everyday 'value' among economists can be found. Metaphorical structuring is endemic to its definition. The debate about worth and value forms an important part of Shiva's Reith lecture. She arrives at the VALUE IS SHARING or SHARING IS VALUE metaphor by means of a chain of arguments. These include a discussion of 'wealth creation', bringing in the law and legal processes (WTO 'orders'), patents and property 'rights'. A side-argument related to the legal domain addresses the sub-domain of 'theft'.

The neo-liberal concept and metaphor, MARKET IS VALUE, is the very antithesis of SHARING. The concordance for 'market' (Table 8.4) shows that bringing out this distinction is of central importance in Shiva's chain of argument. The collocations associated with Shiva's antipathy to markets in their globalised form can be seen in the highlighted items.

Table 8.4 'Market' Concordance in Shiva's Reith Lecture

to the dominant	market	driven 'development' and
It destroyed the	market	for our diverse oilseeds—
in the name of	market	competitiveness and market
competitiveness and	market	efficiency. I want to argue
We have to move from	market	totalitarianism to an earth
. . . rnational commodity	markets."	While farmers earn less,
the poor to create	markets	for the powerful. People are

In the question session Shiva is asked about her 'negative' views of markets. This triggers an explicit positioning and differentiation (13) between the 'physical market' and the 'organizing principle for life' from Shiva.

(13) Let me first respond by saying—I love markets. I love my local market where local 'subgees' are sold, and one can chat with the women. The tragedy really is that the market is being turned into the only organising principle for life, and Wall St is being turned into the only source of value, and it's the disappearance of other markets, other values that I am condemning.

By stressing 'competitiveness' and 'totalitarianism' in connection with the market idea she is condemning, Shiva sets off her VALUE IS SHARING metaphor in sharp contrast.

7 A WORLD TURNED 'UPSIDE DOWN' IN THE NAME OF MODERNIZATION

Running through the lecture is the central metaphor SHARING IS VALUE. A superficial glance at the 'sharing' concordance (Table 8.5) and its collocations show that in Shiva's eyes VALUE IS SHARING for the Indian subcontinent.

This is, as stated, the very antithesis of contemporary globalising tendencies which are being forced upon Indian farmers and especially their womenfolk. The highlighted left and right collocates underline the complex 'value' metaphor Shiva is promoting. It is noteworthy how out of eight occurrences of 'sharing' seven contribute to the positively loaded semantic

Table 8.5 'Sharing' Concordance in Shiva's Reith Lecture

have saved seed or	shared	it with neighbours. The
and saving and	sharing	seed is defined as theft of
create growth through	sharing.	The poor are pushed into
level. Sustainability,	sharing	and survival is being
abundance is based on	sharing	and on a deep awareness of
on abundance and	sharing,	diversity and
of compassion and	sharing.	We have to move from
other crop varieties.	Sharing	and exchange, the basis of

prosody surrounding Shiva's use of the word. A closer look at some extended co-texts will make this more explicit.

Shiva comments in (14) on the questionability of the Western metaphor of 'exclusive property' (via patents) for common knowledge and how this leads to the act of 'sharing' becoming 'theft' for Westerners.

(14) Instead they are becoming the instruments of pirating the common traditional knowledge from the poor of the Third World and making it the exclusive 'property' of western scientists and corporations. When patents are granted for seeds and plants, as in the case of basmati, theft is defined as creation, and saving and sharing seed is defined as theft of intellectual property.

It is most significant that in several (three) instances (15), (16) and (17) 'sharing' has near collocates of 'abundance', 'worldview', 'view' and 'nature', thus underlining a number of related concepts and radial categories which Shiva counterbalances against the capitalist expropriation view.

(15) Nature has given us abundance; women's indigenous knowledge of biodiversity, agriculture and nutrition has built on that abundance to create more from less, to create growth through sharing.

(16) This worldview of abundance is based on sharing and on a deep awareness of humans as members of the earth family.

(17) The sustainability challenge for the new millennium is whether global economic man can move out of the worldview based on fear and scarcity, monocultures and monopolies, appropriation and dispossession and shift to a view based on abundance and sharing, diversity and decentralisation, and respect and dignity for all beings.

In (18) Shiva appeals to 'the rules of justice', among other related facets, as endangered by globalisation.

(18) The rules of globalisation are undermining the rules of justice and sustainability, of compassion and sharing. We have to move from market totalitarianism to an earth democracy.

In (19) Shiva reiterates that 'sharing' is being redefined as a crime.

(19) Sharing and exchange, the basis of our humanity and of our ecological survival has been redefined as a crime.

Straightforward, traditional agricultural practices such as saving seed have been criminalized under the WTO regime. The genetic engineering corporations are using 'intellectual property rights' to destroy small farmers. Shiva states in (20):

> (20) Patents and intellectual property rights are supposed to prevent piracy. Instead they are becoming the instruments of pirating the common traditional knowledge from the poor of the Third World and making it the exclusive 'property' of western scientists and corporations.

The usurping of value by capital is the praxis of corporations. As Shiva notes in (21), this constitutes the annihilation of all that stands in its way.

> (21) Since Seattle, a frequently used phrase has been the need for a rule based system. Globalisation is the rule of commerce and it has elevated Wall Street to be the only source of value. As a result things that should have high worth—nature, culture, the future are being devalued and destroyed.

The Western metaphor CAPITAL IS VALUE is predicated on the implication that 'value' is caused by 'capital' or that 'capital produces value'. We are dealing here with Humpty-Dumpty semantics once more (see chapter 5).

As we saw, Shiva argues for the metaphor SAVING SEED IS WEALTH CREATION. A look at the concordance for 'theft' (four occurrences) demonstrates how Shiva views the activities of corporate agriculture. In a passage (22) which has two occurrences of 'theft' she addresses the issue of patents. She shows how the failure to use patented seed is declared to be illegal! One is reminded of Proudhon's famous slogan PROPERTY IS THEFT, in this connexion, as one continues to disentangle how Shiva contests the CAPITAL IS VALUE metaphor. As we have seen, at several points, she invokes metaphors of 'piracy' and 'theft' to characterize the activities of multis. This is to underline how they employ the law to legitimate their commercial power.

> (22) When patents are granted for seeds and plants, as in the case of basmati, theft is defined as creation, and saving and sharing seed is defined as theft of intellectual property. Corporations which have broad patents on crops such as cotton, soya bean, mustard are suing farmers for seed saving and hiring detective agencies to find out if farmers have saved [. . .] .

The metaphor of 'crime' and 'stealing' is used by Cargill to describe 'sharing', as Shiva shows (23) by quoting the Cargill Chief Executive.

> (23) In 1992, when Indian farmers destroyed Cargill's seed plant in Bellary, Karnataka, to protest against seed failure, the Cargill Chief Executive stated, 'We bring Indian farmers smart technologies which prevent bees from usurping the pollen'.

Table 8.6 'Stealing' Concordance in Shiva's Reith Lecture

feeding the world, but	**stealing**	livelihoods from the poor to
prevent "weeds from	**stealing**	the sunshine". But what
which itself aims at	**stealing**	nature's harvest by

We can see (Table 8.6) how this metaphor is modified to STEALING IS WEALTH CREATION. According to Shiva this is the case for the corporate interests like Monsanto and Cargill expanding in India.

She ironically quotes the absurd claim (24) made in a Monsanto leaflet.

(24) When I was participating in the United Nations Biosafety Negotia-tions, Monsanto circulated literature to defend its herbicide resistant Roundup-ready crops on grounds that they prevent 'weeds from steal-ing the sunshine'.

This provides the cue to consider the term 'theft' and the related semantic field, with items like 'steal', 'usurp', 'piracy' and 'pirating'. We see also how the discourse of 'law and order' and 'crime' has colonized the dealings with industrial agriculture. In Shiva's words: "Sharing and exchange, the basis of our humanity and of our ecological survival has been redefined as a crime. This makes us all poor."

When giant corporations view small peasants and bees as thieves, the world is being 'turned upside down' in the name of modernization, busi-ness and science. The Uruguayan writer Eduardo Galeano has analyzed this "looking-glass world" (1998: 5), writing about "Los modelos del éxito [Models of success]": "El mundo al revés premia al revés: desprecia la hon-estidad, castigo el trabajo, recompensa la falta de escrúpulos y alimenta el canibalismo. Sus maestras calumnian a la naturaleza; la injusticia, dicen, es ley natural." ["The upside-down world rewards in reverse: it scorns honesty, punishes work, prizes lack of scruples, and feeds cannibalism. Its professors slander nature: injustice, they say, is a law of nature."]

8   RE-INVIGORATING UNDER-RATED CHARACTERISTICS OF THE WORLD

As a counter-weight to these developments Shiva stresses alternative meta-phorical concepts and configurations. In her own discourse Shiva re-invig-orates belittled (sic!), depreciated or devalued notions like smallness. 'Small farmers' is a positively loaded, affirmative term as used by Shiva. Shiva re-writes and re-iterates a counter-current to structural metaphorical thought, namely: SMALL IS GOOD (and by implication LARGE IS BAD).

Table 8.7 'Small' Concordance in Shiva's Reith Lecture

It is women and	**small**	farmers working with
biodiversity based	**small**	farms are more productive
the food production on	**small**	farms by small farmers
on small farms by	**small**	farmers disappear. This hides
into account. In Java,	**small**	farmers cultivate 607 species
FAO has shown that	**small**	biodiverse farms can produce
While women and	**small**	peasants feed the world
local economies and	**small**	autonomous producers is by
impossible for	**small**	farmers to survive. The
level, or by the	**small**	cottage industry because it is
. . . ntionally kept at the	**small**	level. Now , under the pressure
local economies and	**small**	scale processing. In August
In August 1998,	**small**	scale local processing of
corporations view	**small**	peasants and bees as thieves,
to stamp out the	**smallest**	insect, the smallest plant,
smallest insect, the	**smallest**	plant, the smallest peasant
smallest plant, the	**smallest**	peasant comes from a deep

To illustrate this let us consider the concordance (Table 8.7) for 'small' and 'smallest' (from Shiva 2000a).

If we list the immediate right collocates of 'small' (14 instances) and 'smallest' (3), we find what Shiva sees as valuable: 'farmers' (4), 'farms' (2), 'biodiverse farms' (1), 'peasants' (2), 'peasant' (1), 'scale processing' (1), 'scale local processing' (1), 'insect' (1), 'plant' (1), 'autonomous producers' (1), 'cottage industry' (1) and 'level' (1).

This reminds one somewhat of E. F. Schumacher (1973), the title of whose book was also the very predication of an alternative metaphor: "Small is beautiful". In the question session after her Reith Lecture Shiva underlines (25) the different state of affairs and how much this alternative needs to be upheld since modern global corporations have expanded.

(25) For the first time we have a system where no-one needs the peasants, unless we realise as societies we need them, that we've reached a

Table 8.8 'Local' Concordance in Shiva's Reith Lecture

prudent food crops for	local	needs. It is experiences such
destruction of nature,	local	economies and small
. . . obalisation destroys	local	economies and destruction
uses to shut down	local	economies and small scale
1998, small scale	local	processing of edible oil was
the diversity of	local	food cultures and local food
food cultures and	local	food economies. A global
that is fresh,	local	and handmade as a health

period where people are actually talking in India, in other countries that you can get rid of small producers.

Her emphasis on 'local' unearths the same value system at work. A consideration of the right collocates in the concordance (Table 8.8) shows positive semantic prosodies, while the left collocates even in the small span visible here indicate the threats to which they are being subjected.

The right collocates are: 'needs', 'economies and small', 'economies', 'economies and small scale', 'processing of edible oil', 'food cultures and local food', 'food economies' and 'handmade as a health'. There are three negative left collocates, representing a threat to 'local' in the form of: 'destruction of nature', 'globalisation destroys', 'uses to shut down'. But these are countered by two positive collocates: 'the diversity of', 'that is fresh'. In two sentences both 'small' and 'local' come together underlining the positive semantic prosody.

'Large', by contrast, seems to be negative, judging by its right collocates (Table 8.9).

Table 8.9 'Large' Concordance in Shiva's Reith Lecture

times more food than	large,	industrial monocultures. And
is the presence of	large	trading companies in

9   WHAT ARE THE ALTERNATIVE METAPHORS FOR VALUE?

Together with her contempt for and critique of largeness, Shiva notes explicitly a further 'phrase'. She shows in (26) how this refers to value, its sole origin being Wall Street. Here too the meta-comment on the specific kind of rule system contests the very validity of 'commerce'.

(26) Since Seattle, a frequently used phrase has been the need for a rule based system. Globalisation is the rule of commerce and it has elevated Wall Street to be the only source of value.

How do we ascertain what the further alternative metaphors are? We can start with word frequency lists. In chapter 6 it was found that the seven most frequent items were 'food' (40), 'farmer/s' (26), 'being/s' (23), 'world' (22), 'production' (20), 'women' (19) and 'globalisation' (16). These can give us a first approximation to the centres of interest of Shiva's lecture. Certainly 'food' (40), 'farmer/s' (26) and 'women' (19) are recurrent topics and actors Shiva focuses on, as we have already seen.

A second approach is to search for how the author presents items she criticizes directly or indirectly. A heuristic employed here entails searching with a listing and concordancer programme for further multiply employed lexical items from selected spheres. Given the interest in 'value' I selected 'devaluation' and 'devalue' as a starting point. As highlighted collocates in the concordance (Table 8.10) show, Shiva demonstrates what things are being systematically ignored or 'devalued'.

I then examined the broader co-texts of the first two occurrences of 'devaluation'. Shiva makes it clear (27) that 'women' and 'women's work' are underrated. Also, 'work' in general in sustainable economies is downplayed.

Table 8.10 'Devalu***' Concordance in Shiva's Reith Lecture

inactive. The	devaluation	of women's work, and of
support systems. The	devaluation	and invisibility of
a combination of	devaluation	of currencies, increase
themselves are	devalued.	Because many women in the
ensures sustenance is	devalued	in general, there is less
the future are being	devalued	and destroyed. The rules of

(27) Women who produce for their families and communities are treated as 'non-productive' and 'economically' inactive. The devaluation of women's work, and of work done in sustainable economies, is the natural outcome of a system constructed by capitalist patriarchy.

In another section (28) Shiva elaborates on this point, linking it more closely to patriarchal structures. These effectively devalue food production to make it invisible.

(28) The devaluation and invisibility of sustainable, regenerative production is most glaring in the area of food. While patriarchal division of labour has assigned women the role of feeding their families and communities, patriarchal economics and patriarchal views of science and technology magically make women's work in providing food disappear. 'Feeding the World' becomes disassociated from the women who actually do it.

We can perhaps make the link here to feminist economics. Feminist economists such as Marilyn Waring (1988) and Julie A. Nelson (1996) have commented on primary production. The consumption of their own produce by non-primary producers, normally women, is considered to be of little or no importance by mainstream economists.

10   RE-DEFINITIONS OF VALUE

The two extracts (27) and (28) have enabled us to isolate at least two major strands of the life-work sphere which Shiva rates highly by contrast to what she downrates (like patriarchal division of labour). These are (1) sustainable, regenerative production and (2) women's work. In this context she employs the 'orthodox' phrase 'wealth creation' but then proceeds to redefine the whole complex to the point where it can be seen as an aspect of 'value'. Starting with the equation WEALTH CREATION IS X, we can list some of the 'values' X may receive in Shiva's discourse. X is 1) sharing, 2) diversity, 3) sustainability, 4) working co-operatively with nature's processes, 5) food processing, 6) local economies and small scale processing, 7) women as the primary food producers and food processors in the world.

The next evident item to locate was 'wealth' itself. Table 8.11 allows us to identify Shiva's counteracting definitions and her contestation of existing patriarchal and capitalist metaphors.

Shiva demonstrates what the metaphor of wealth creation really means. The concordances with the left collocations 'defined as', 'categories of' and 'This is not' clearly testify to her disputing the one-sided semantic engineering she sees in the field of agriculture.

Table 8.11 'Wealth' Concordance in Shiva's Reith Lecture

are defined as "	**wealth**	creators", something has gone
and categories of	**wealth**	and wealth creation. Pushing
of wealth and	**wealth**	creation. Pushing the real
route to instant	**wealth**	creation. Women—as I have
on the poor. The	**wealth**	of the poor is being violently
violence. This is not	**wealth**	creation but plunder.

It is worth mentioning in connection with 'wealth' what Shiva writes in *Stolen Harvest* (2000b: 57): "In India, cows have been treated as sacred—as Lakshmi, the goddess of wealth" among other things. This aspect of Indian culture is developed in more detail in Shiva (2000b).

The collocation of 'wealth' with 'creation' leads us to consider the verb 'create'. And 'creation' also brings to mind 'causation'. Do we have a simple case of a synonym pair or a case of a radial category being expanded metaphorically? We have mentioned the widely used expression 'wealth creation' in the mouths of politicians and economists. This is also a notion Shiva (2000a) looks at critically. The relatively high frequency of these terms (circa twenty-three) is also evidence of her preoccupation with the concept, we might note. Observing the concordance (Table 8.12) for the lemma 'create' and the related items, including 'creation', we find immediately an ambiguous and negative semantic prosody surrounding them, reflected in some of both the right and the left collocations (highlighted below).

Here is one of two broader co-text samples (29) in which Shiva engages with and contests the very categorization systems and naming conventions involved.

(29) When growth increases poverty, when real production becomes a negative economy, and speculators are defined as 'wealth creators', something has gone wrong with the concepts and categories of wealth and wealth creation.

Example (30) is triggered by following up synonyms for wealth like 'white gold'. The latter is clearly in itself a superficial metaphor for a commodity being promoted by the seed companies, serving merely a persuasive function in the selling process.

(30) Farmers who traditionally grew pulses and millets and paddy have been lured by seed companies to buy hybrid cotton seeds referred to by the seed merchants as 'white gold', which were supposed to make them millionaires. Instead they became paupers.

Table 8.12 'Creat**' Concordance in Shiva's Reith Lecture

from the poor to	create	markets for the powerful.
waste parts that	create	a threat to our culture and
myth of creation to	create	new property rights to life
Humans do not	create	life when they manipulate it.
on that abundance to	create	more from less, to create
more from less, to	create	growth through sharing. The
that Ian Wilmut "	created	" Dolly denies the creativity
the ecological poverty	created	by the new biotechnologies.
of the Mind", which	creates	monocultures in our fields
are recipes for	creating	hunger, not for feeding the
services is declining,	creating	deeper poverty for the
global corporations,	creating	a situation where the poor
to be projected as	creation.	Take the case of the much
few. But the myth of	creation	presents biotechnologists
of wealth and wealth	creation.	Pushing the real production
to instant wealth	creation.	Women—as I have said—
Such false claims to	creation	are now the global norm,
patriarchal myth of	creation	to create new property
theft is defined as	creation,	and saving and sharing seed
This is not wealth	creation	but plunder. Sustainability
Dolly denies the	creativity	of nature, the
. . . technologists as the	creators	of Vitamin A, negating
defined as "wealth	creators",	something has gone wrong

11 DISTURBED HARMONY AFFECTS SOCIETY AS WELL AS NATURE

A further element in Shiva's SHARING IS VALUE metaphor is touched upon by her in an article (2002b) entitled "On Pests, Weeds And Terrorists: Weaving Harmony Through Diversity".

In Shiva (2002b) we find mention of reductionist trends in science, as the concordance (Table 8.13) illustrates.

Shiva continues (31) to contest the 'modernization' of science.

(31) This non-relational absolutised approach aggravates the problem instead of solving it because it deepens the disharmony which creates pests instead of recovering harmony, the only lasting solution for preventing insects from becoming 'pests'.

'Harmony' is the name for this state to which we need to return. This echoes much ecological thinking on the biosphere, of course. It is a term used often in Shiva (2002b) (Table 8.14).

The collocation of 'harmony' with 'diversity' is intended to underline this point. To set up 'diversity' as a metaphor for 'harmony' as an alternative to the narrow, reductionist idea of harmony as 'conformism' demonstrates the political nature of Shiva's writing. In times when 'fundamentalist' and militant religious precepts are being imported into daily politics, especially foreign policy discussions, this may sound idealistic. But Shiva knows (32) what she is up against.

(32) Non-sustainability, injustice, war are different expressions of disharmony which has its roots in a world view that blocks out relationships and essentialises characteristics and properties that are relational properties.

Against this Shiva (2002b) sets relations and relationships, criticizing this 'non-relational absolutised' approach. She attacks reductionism in science. 'Relationships' is a term she uses three times. The article deals in several

Table 8.13 'Reductionist' Concordance in Shiva (2002b)

of disharmony but as	reductionist,	essentialised,
offered in the same	reductionist	approach, with the new
"weeds". Instead, the	reductionist,	essentialised approach
. . . tialising violence of	reductionist	thought. It is time to
enemies of pests.	Reductionist	science which fails to

Table 8.14 'Harmony' Concordance in Shiva (2002b)

Shiva Lack of	harmony	characterizes our times—
ecosystems. Weaving	harmony	in agriculture implies
instead of recovering	harmony,	the only lasting solution
instead of recovering	harmony	will deepen the pest
context of creating	harmony,	a war is declared against
Diversity creates	harmony,	and harmony creates
creates harmony, and	harmony	creates beauty, balance,
Terrorists: Weaving	Harmony	Through Diversity December

ways with the pervasive nature of the phenomenon of how everything hangs together.

As Shiva says: "The most effective pest control mechanism is built into the ecology of crops, partly by ensuring balanced pest-predator relationships." She refers to "invisible relationships of the plant to its environment". It is interesting how this expression echoes the perception of insightful scientists and artists of the 20th century, such as Piet Mondrian, who saw their task as uncovering and making observable these very relations and relationships. According to Herbert Read (1968: 200), for example, "Mondrian defines Neo-plasticism [his aesthetic theory: RJA] as a means by which the versatility of nature can be reduced to the plastic expression of definite relations. Art becomes an intuitive means, as exact as mathematics, for representing the fundamental characteristics of the cosmos."

What happens in the case of failing to acknowledge such relationships is what we see now happening in the world of agriculture, but also more generally in society, in Shiva's estimation. Reductionism in science and the accompanying technological praxis is one of the problems that prevent us dealing satisfactorily with such obstacles. The 'reductionist' concordance (Table 8.13) shows that Shiva sees this as a central problem too. She has harsh words for Western science: "Reductionist science which fails to perceive the natural balance, also fails to anticipate and predict what will happen when that balance is disturbed."

12 CONCLUSION: SHIVA'S WORK IS DISTURBING AND IRRITATING

Shiva's work is disturbing and irritating in several respects. First at the 'level' of meta-commentary, as we have seen. But her major influence will undoubtedly be at the face value level, where she addresses the objective situation. And here her work is equally, if not more, disturbing. It disturbs the Northern (First World) reader or listener precisely because it reminds him or her that the repression and exploitation at work in the Third or Majority World, such as India, is largely the result of individuals, international organizations and corporations that originate in the North.

People still tend to under-estimate the extent and the powers of the forces of repression at work in the world. It is perhaps more comforting to accept the illusions propagated by the Western media and lie-machines, that suggest the roots of poverty in the world lie solely in the countries where it exists. The global trading system will, by definition, solve all the world's problems. Environmental and ecological degradation will cease once Western technologies, scientific method and cultivation procedures developed by 'philanthropic' and socially responsible corporations can be put in place. So goes the Washington Consensus argument.

The failure to appreciate the desperation that exists in some countries and parts of the world and which seems to express itself in a millenarian nihilism or in religious fundamentalist movements can be seen to mask insight into the true causes of that desperation. The lack of will to engage with human history in the recent past is symptomatic of this failure of understanding.

The rush to generalize, to abstract and to impose new metaphorical concepts developed elsewhere on societies which have long possessed their own appropriate ways of living is what Shiva attacks in her work. The material conditions of being, of very existence are at stake in the Third World. In terms of the capitalist system, promises or expressions of trust are meaningless. Capital knows no promises. Capital answers only to the logic of accumulation. This entails taking away surplus value wherever it can be generated and repatriating it as profit to the investor. Nowhere is this more brutally obvious than in the relationship with the factor of land or the physical environment. As we argued in chapter 5, 'sustainable development' has become a kind of magic wand to spirit away opposition to normal capitalist practices of exploitation and accumulation.

What 'counts' as valuable is what can be counted on the profit and loss statement, as long as it is my profit and someone else's loss. The loss of the Third World farmers is converted into the profit of the multinational corporations! This is the state of affairs that Shiva is censuring or arraigning in her lecture.

Finally, what is the significance of the fact that Shiva is the only BBC Reith lecturer in 2000 who originates from a Third World country? Different metaphors and 'worldviews' take on a new meaning when this point has been digested.

9 Engineering Agriculture
Who Pays the Price?

1 INTRODUCTION

The collapse of the talks at the WTO meeting in Cancún in September 2003 underlined how urgent the issue of agriculture and food production is for Third World countries. Third World activists like Vandana Shiva commented on the impact of the trade policies. They are said to be driven and practically dictated by multinational corporations (Shiva 2003d) and to be profoundly unfair and unjust. People like her and the International Farmers' and Indigenous Forum—an alliance of small farmers, peasants and landless people, with a global membership of 100 million—are trying to change priorities away from benefiting the rich farmers and rich countries. In their opinion the WTO should play no role in food and agricultural issues at all. Local production and local trade should be encouraged and supported. Instead the expansion policies of largely US- or European Union (EU)-based agribusinesses and farmers are subsidized.

This chapter scrutinizes publicity material employed by global genetic engineering corporations to justify selling their agricultural products in the Third World. A critical discourse analytical approach is adopted. It is complemented by the use of concordancing techniques which help to uncover specific linguistic features accompanying more extensive discourse processes typical of corporate public relations and advertising materials.

2 THE POLITICAL ECONOMY OF GENE-BASED CORPORATIONS

This section sketches the background to global biotech or genetic engineering corporations. Agriculture has become capitalist business in most of the world; hence the use of the English word 'agribusiness' to describe the commodification of food production. Cash crops, planting and harvesting for a distant 'market' has become the 'developmental' path that the Washington Consensus of the World Bank, IMF and also the WTO has imposed via structural adjustment programmes and now through trade agreements on most Third World countries. There is little doubt that this process is powered by

Western multinational corporations. We know from history that this is not a specifically recent development. The 501 years of European imperialism previous to 1993 have been documented in detail by Chomsky (1993).

In the popular imagination India is a country which represents complete opposition to the Western world. But this is a superficial view. For nearly 400 years India has been in the sphere of influence of Western imperialism. With its own special mix of casteism and feudal society it is no less inegalitarian than anywhere else is. And the British understood how to utilize the domination structures in place and how to win over the Moguls for their own commercial purposes. Till this day the route to profit making for Western capital has built on this inequality. Using the powers of the élite to subordinate the poor and the less rich to their requirements is what Western corporations have been doing ever since the East India Company established itself in 1601. The Company saw the rise of its fortunes from 1608 and its transformation from a trading venture to a ruling enterprise. In 1858 the East India Company was officially dissolved, but its heritage lived on in the form of the British Empire. One might ask what has changed since the 19th century. As the field of agriculture shows, perhaps very little!

If we take a brief look at how the agribusiness market is organized, it is noticeable how certain names recur, among them the one time seed giant and now major pesticide producer Monsanto and the grain giant Cargill. They form a vertically integrated alliance today, combining to sell the seeds, biotechnology and the agrochemicals said to be needed to grow them (New Internationalist 2003: 20). Cargill is perhaps the largest private company in the USA (Kidron and Segal 1987: 18–19). In its corporate adverts it claims to "have been in the food and nutrition business for more than a century." It is the largest grain trader in the USA. "Some of our best customers have never heard of us," it says in a Cargill brochure. Yet in the 1970s it controlled US grain exports to the tune of: 42% barley, 32% oats, 29% wheat, 22% sorghum, 18% soya beans and 16% maize.

But only 40% of Cargill's business is in grain. Its conglomerate expansion has propelled it into cotton and metal trading, flour processing, chemicals, steel manufacturing, poultry processing, salt mining, sunflower and other oilseed processing, meat, cocoa, sugar, molasses, barge construction, waste disposal, fire protection systems, scientific research installations. In 1996 its transnational empire comprised over 140 subsidiaries in 66 countries. It has 14 ocean vessels, 3,000 rail cars, 400 river barges and 40 port elevators in the USA. Recently it has closely cooperated in strategic alliances with Monsanto.

3   MULTINATIONAL AGRIBUSINESS IN THE FIELD OF SEED PRODUCTION

Focussing now explicitly on the genetic or biotech side of seed production the following six multinational agribusinesses can be distinguished: Bayer

CropScience, Syngenta, Monsanto, Pioneer Hi-Bred (DuPont), Dow Agro-Sciences and BASF. Recently in the EU there have been innumerable new applications to import, market or trial previously unapproved GM crops. These six companies made nineteen new applications. Behind this strategy was the desire to stop the four-year de facto EU moratorium on the approval of new GM crop varieties. The applications came from subsidiary or partner seed companies or from the genetic engineering companies directly (CorporateWatch 2003).

Many of the applications concerned the import into the EU of new types of GM soya and maize for use in food and animal feed. This is a prelude for what has been happening all around the Third World in the past decade. Already GM crops imported from the US, Argentina and Canada have flooded those markets. And they have led to considerable problems that we shall return to in the final sections.

For the purposes of this chapter I have chosen to look at and compare the material of two of these companies. A few preliminary remarks on these global players are perhaps in order.

4　MONSANTO AND PIONEER HI-BRED: LINGUISTIC ENGINEERING AT WORK

I have selected Monsanto and Pioneer Hi-Bred (a DuPont subsidiary) to analyze briefly how their websites manifest linguistic engineering at work. The first, Monsanto, has gone through various transformations in the past three decades. The company, once a chemical company producing polychlorinated biphenyls (PCBs), dioxins and the defoliant/chemical weapon Agent Orange (notorious for its military use in Vietnam), later moved into genetically modified (GM) crops. Monsanto was involved in agrochemicals, seeds, chemicals, sweeteners, GM bovine growth hormone (BGH), polymers and pharmaceuticals. The company now bearing the name is now a relatively small stand-alone agricultural company, a fraction of its size in the mid 1990s. The majority of its income comes from sales of Roundup herbicide and GM crops. Monsanto is the biggest seller of GM crops in the world, with big sales in the USA, Canada and Argentina and smaller sales in India and South Africa.

Pioneer Hi-Bred is the second firm I look at. At the time of writing (August 2003) Pioneer Hi-Bred was the largest seed company in the world. It was founded in the USA in 1926. Pioneer was bought by DuPont in 1998. Pioneer markets GM crops including many containing licensed GM crop traits from Monsanto and Bayer/Aventis. Pioneer has conducted a small number of GM crop trials in the UK.

Taking up a critical discourse analytical stance I now want to look at some of the publicity material employed by the global genetic engineering corporations. I analyze the recent websites of Monsanto and Pioneer

Hi-Bred. How they present, showcase and position themselves is my interest. The following remarks are based on quantitative analyses generated by a concordancer program. I aim to bring out how discourse processes and rhetorical tactics typical of corporate public relations are linked to linguistic and specifically, in this chapter, lexical features of the texts.

The Monsanto material has sections entitled 'Products & Solutions', 'Integrated Businesses' and 'The Monsanto Pledge 2003' (Monsanto 2003). The Pioneer material consists of a report, entitled 'Company Philosophy—The Long Look' (Pioneer 2003).

5   LINGUISTIC ANALYSIS OF MONSANTO WEBSITE

A website is a means for firms to present themselves in a benevolent and self-endorsing light. We have to be aware of this proviso when looking at them. Here I consider the section of Monsanto's website which a few years ago would explicitly have been termed the 'mission statement'. Interestingly the word 'mission' occurs only once in a section called 'The Monsanto Fund mission is global'. Certainly, were one to read this document purely superficially, one could gain the impression that Monsanto was one of the world's greatest philanthropic foundations, rather than one of the world's most rapacious multinationals. Here are the quantitative statistics of the text. A computer word count of the web-pages gave a total of 2,149 words with 933 different words, i.e. word-forms. This gives a type-token-ratio (TTR) of for the Monsanto text of 0.434.

For this brief analysis I concentrate on keywords employed to focus and emphasize Monsanto's image. The positively connoted items are highlighted in the text. A central element in this process is 'The Monsanto Pledge'. The website states:

> The Monsanto Pledge was announced two years ago. It was based on interviews with hundreds of stakeholders who met with people from many departments across Monsanto, gave us their time, explained their concerns and offered their ideas. Their feedback helped us to better understand public expectations and suggested to us what corporate social responsibility might look like for a company solely focused on leading-edge agriculture.

> The Pledge represents our stake-in-the-ground. It shows what we stand for as a company. It confirms our commitment as capable stewards of the technologies we develop, addressing tough issues honestly and openly, and delivering on values-based as well as science-based commitments.

As the text goes on to comment: "We have also made Our Pledge a substantial part of our Corporate Web site, expanding in many ways on the latest

Table 9.1 'Commit**' Concordance of Monsanto

273	Respect We	Commit	in the Pledge to deliver
57	It confirms our	commitment	as capable stewards of
82	made in each of the	commitment	areas. We have also
226	Fossil Fuels.	Commitment	to Stewardship: Efforts
59	well as science-based	commitments.	Over the last two
71	sites. Some of our	commitments	preceded the Pledge.
88	part of our corporate	commitments	in the future. Last
98	deliver on our Pledge	commitments	and whether they are
110	Sincerely,	Commitments	to Our Stakeholders
142	on food labels.	Commitments	to Our Stakeholders
214	I Legal Notice	Commitments	to Our Stakeholders
270	I Legal Notice	Commitments	to Our Stakeholders
326	I Legal Notice	Commitments	to Our Stakeholders
90	one year after we	committed	to the Pledge and then
217	the Pledge, Monsanto	committed	to provide high-quality

report." So it is not surprising that there are fourteen occurrences of the word 'pledge'.

However, more interesting for our purposes is the near synonym 'commitment'. As the concordance in Table 9.1 shows, there are three occurrences of the verb 'commit' and twelve cases of the noun. At least three are in titles—perhaps a by-product of the hypertext genre. Right collocates include 'stewards' and 'stewardship'. Note also the use of the phrase 'capable stewards'. 'Our' or 'we' occur as near collocates twelve times. I discuss the role of personal pronouns below.

6   THE PRONOUNS 'OUR' AND 'WE' AND THE INTERACTIONAL AND INTERPERSONAL ASPECT

Sometimes we can get an idea of the interpersonal feel of a text by considering how personal pronouns are employed. They play a major role in managing relational aspects of communication (Fairclough 1989: 111). What kind of relationship do the authors of the Monsanto text set out to create with

Table 9.2 Frequencies of Personal Pronouns in Pioneer and Monsanto Websites

	We	*Our*	*Us*	*You/Your*	*Total*
Pioneer	67 (2.08%)	59 (1.84%)	10 (0.31%)	0	3206
Monsanto	23 (1.07%)	32 (1.45%)	6 (0.27%)	5 (0.23%)	2149

their readers? Is it a 'distanced', objective, formal or 'authority'-based one? Or is it a close, informal, personal or equal-terms one? I return to this aspect below.

First, I consider the statistics for both Monsanto and Pioneer together. One question we can pose is whether the reader is 'addressed' directly by using 'you'. Pioneer has zero instances of 'you' or 'your', whereas Monsanto has five. 'We' occurs sixty-seven times in Pioneer's website, and twenty-three in Monsanto's (2.08% as against 1.07% of total words used); 'us' has ten instances in Pioneer (0.32%) and six in Monsanto (0.27%). Table 9.2 summarizes these data.

The figures might lead us to conclude that Pioneer focuses on itself more than does Monsanto, which at least addresses a potential reader by means of the single 'you' and the five instances of 'your'. Table 9.3 gives the concordance for these items. The single 'you' is here a generic 'one' rather than an intimate 'you'. But the five instances of 'your' explicitly seek to stimulate interaction with right collocates like 'feedback', 'product' and 'comments'. The process of 'talking to' their potential customers is seen in the other three cases.

Turning now to the first person pronouns, it is clear that all twenty-three cases of 'we' are exclusive, and the use of 'our' also. The following is typical for Monsanto usage: "The Pledge represents our stake-in-the-ground. It shows what we stand for as a company." The phrase "as a company" underlines this. In the case of the possessive 'our' there are thirty-two occurrences. They are all exclusive, as are the five instances of 'us'.

Table 9.3 'You' and 'Your' Concordance of Monsanto Text

353	or marketer will tell **you,** the key to being successful is
109	forward to hearing **your** feedback on this report, on our
110	click here to send **your** Comments. Sincerely,
354	is assessing **your** customers' needs and adding
355	enough value to **your** Product to make it more
356	to them than are **your** Competitors' products. Cost

Table 9.4 'Our' Concordance of Monsanto Text (Selected)

56	The Pledge represents	our	stake-in-the-ground. It shows
57	company. It confirms	our	commitment as capable stewards
63	to challenge	our	thinking and suggest new
71	web sites. Some of	our	commitments preceded the
73	continue as pillars in	our	Pledge. Through ongoing programs
75	held respect for	our	employees, communities and
87	an explicit part of	our	corporate commitments in the
93	still surround	our	products and that we should
98	things to deliver on	our	Pledge commitments and whether
218	products that benefit	our	customers and the environment.
274	that are beneficial to	our	customers and the environment
276	We show respect to	our	employees, communities,

A closer look at the 'our' concordance in Table 9.4 allows us to see two other features worth mentioning. I select only twelve items for illustrative purposes. The first concerns agents or people in the text. These can give some idea of which 'persons', such as 'customers', are addressed on the website and are significant for Monsanto.

The second feature concerns those areas or aspects of the world, of business, which are rated highly by the company and in particular the purr-words chosen to express this evaluation. When one has read several company websites, one acquires a 'feel' for these recurring items, which a concordancer programme can then deliver the objective evidence of.

7   PURR-WORDS USED IN THE TEXT

Purr-words (as non-linguists call them) are positively sounding or euphemistic words. They are fairly transparent and recognizable indicators of self-representation. When one analyzes how purr-words are employed in corporations' discourse one can uncover a number of features they have in common. The use of such words and phrases, and, particularly, their tendency to cluster, or their cumulative effect when used often with each other, reflects a self-assured, unquestioning and practically incontestable perspective. They convey a confident and categorical note to the discourse.

These are essentially the characteristics of discourse that aims to transmit an authoritative message to its readership or audience. It is not surprising that corporate business and powerful agencies of governments employ these tactics. They aim to give the impression of decisiveness.

Typical examples, both left collocates of 'our', are 'benefit' (12 instances) and 'beneficial' (one). I have highlighted some of the collocates in Table 9.5 that refer to the types of benefits entailed. These include 'biotech' or 'biotech crops' (five times). Several beneficiary groups are explicitly mentioned, 'smallholder farmers', 'Our Stakeholders', 'our customers' and 'farmers'.

Some other collocates of 'our' are 'respect', 'deliver', 'steward', as already mentioned, 'sharing' and 'shared', but also 'improve' and 'solutions'. Several concordances of such purr-words can be displayed together. In this way it becomes clear how they co-occur to a great extent and with other terms and phrases which are positively loaded for Monsanto. The highlighting in Tables 9.6–9.9 serves to show this close interconnection explicitly—a feature one otherwise might just 'feel' as a reader.

The lemma 'share', with its variants 'shared' and 'sharing' (eight instances), is a purr-word that forms part of the Monsanto Pledge. Six of the eight instances occur in the Pledge section, as the 'cluster' of line numbers in the concordance show. What the company really means by this appears to be a very concrete element, as this extract from the broader co-text demonstrates:

Table 9.5 'Beneficial/Benefit(s)' Concordance of Monsanto

274	products that are	**beneficial**	to our customers and the
218	products that	**benefit**	our customers and the
219	are recognizing a	**benefit**	from biotech crops is
79	. . . ortunities to deliver	**benefits**	to smallholder farmers,
242	and economic	**benefits**	from the use of biotech
261	the potential	**benefits**	that biotechnology holds for
215	to Our Stakeholders	**Benefits**	In the Pledge, Monsanto
221	the world. More On	**Benefits** . . .	Download Benefits (pdf)
221	Benefits . . . Download	**Benefits**	(pdf) 913k Renewable
233	Conservation Tillage	**Benefits**	Farmers, the Environment
241	Studies: Biotech	**Benefits**	Demonstrated.Recent
251	Biotech Crop	**Benefits.**	The Council for
259	Scientific Studies:	**Benefits**	of Biotechnology for

Table 9.6 'Respect' Concordance of Monsanto

79	a deeply held	**respect**	for our employees,
293	stewardship. We show	**respect**	to our employees,
135	Fosters Mutual	**Respect.** A second successful year of
288	to Our Stakeholders	**Respect**	We commit in the Pledge to
295	environment. More On	**Respect.** Download Respect (pdf)
295	Respect . . . Download	**Respect**	(pdf) 929k Monsanto Has

Table 9.7 'Deliver' Concordance of Monsanto

83	more opportunities to	**deliver**	benefits to smallholder
104	the right things to	**deliver**	on our Pledge commitments
290	in the Pledge to	**deliver**	high-quality products that
61	and openly, and	**delivering**	on values-based as well as

Table 9.8 'Improve' Concordance of Monsanto

12	solutions that	**improve**	productivity and simplify
307	Safety Program:	**Improved**	Driving Safety For
326	for Environmental	**Improvement.** Eco-Efficiency Data

Table 9.9 'Solutions' Concordance of Monsanto

2	products and unique	**solutions**	to farmers. The full value
8	to offer integrated	**solutions**	that combine our seeds,
12	can offer integrated	**solutions**	that improve productivity
1	Products &	**Solutions**	Integrated Businesses

Table 9.10 'Shar***' Concordance of Monsanto

76	past 10 years, we've	shared	our technologies with
151	of 2002, Monsanto	shared	important soybean genetic
195	used repeatedly and	shared	or replicated with few
145	As part of the	sharing	element of the Monsanto
143	to Our Stakeholders	Sharing	As part of the sharing
148	nations. More On	Sharing	... Download Sharing (pdf)
148	On Sharing ... Download	Sharing	(pdf) 675kk Donating
150	Genetic Information:	Sharing	Technologies for a Healthier

> Donating Genetic Information: Sharing Technologies for a Healthier Soybean. In the spring of 2002, Monsanto shared important soybean genetic information developed by its researchers in cooperation with the U.S. Department of Agriculture (USDA).

The collocates highlighted in Table 9.10 underline this orientation in part. Here, as elsewhere, there are several instances which are artefacts of the hypertext format.

'Steward(ship)' is also used interestingly or intriguingly. In addition to a 'predictable' left collocate, 'environmental' for 'stewardship', we find 'technologies' as a right collocate for 'stewards' (Table 9.11). The broader co-text of the phrase 'effective stewardship' gives no hint as to its concrete semantics. It seems to be being used as a 'positive'-sounding, PR icon, only:

> We commit in the Pledge to deliver high-quality products that are beneficial to our customers and the environment with sound and innovative science and thoughtful and effective stewardship.

A keyword in Monsanto's lexicon is 'integrated'. It has the two right collocates of 'businesses' and 'solutions' (Table 9.12).

Table 9.11 'Stewards(hip)' Concordance of Monsanto

57	... mitment as capable	stewards	of the technologies we
72	environmental	stewardship	and diversity are long
275	and effective	stewardship.	We show respect to our
226	Commitment to	Stewardship:	Efforts Focus on

Table 9.12 'Integrated' Concordance of Monsanto

4	. . . sinesses Monsanto's	**integrated**	businesses offer
7	value of Monsanto's	**integrated**	businesses comes from
8	our ability to offer	**integrated**	solutions that combine
9	chemicals. Monsanto's	**integrated**	businesses provide
12	we can offer	**integrated**	solutions that improve
2	Products & Solutions	**Integrated**	Businesses Monsanto's

As the broader co-text of lines 7, 8 and 9 in Table 9.12 makes clear, there is one sentence (the third) which 'explains' what this means:

> Monsanto's integrated businesses offer high-value products and unique solutions to farmers. The full value of Monsanto's integrated businesses comes from our ability to offer integrated solutions that combine our seeds, traits and chemicals. Monsanto's integrated businesses provide farmers with high-value Roundup® agricultural herbicides and other herbicides, top brand seeds, and biotechnology traits. By combining these capabilities, we can offer integrated solutions that improve productivity and simplify farming.

Lots of claims are made in this text for Monsanto's abilities to 'help' farmers. Notice in the highlighted items how 'help' is itself used in Table 9.13.

Take, by way of illustration, one example of the broader co-text of 'help': "Monsanto traits help farmers reduce their tillage and their pesticide use."

A still current buzzword, apparently, in company websites, is 'new'. It is well known how quickly this can 'age'. The politicians of the British Labour Party now seldom use the phrase 'New Labour'. It has long ago passed its

Table 9.13 'Help' Concordance of Monsanto

22	Monsanto traits	**help**	farmers reduce their tillage and
147	and know-how to	**help**	growers in developing as well as
171	of Illinois, will	**help**	researchers understand key
161	Imperative to	**Help**	Poorer Countries: In our world
51	ideas. Their feedback	**helped**	us to better understand public
200	Company, has been	**helping**	people since the mid 1960s.

Table 9.14 'New' Concordance of Monsanto

17	—to develop	**new**	varieties for our brands and
35	Mr. Zoerb tested	**new**	Roundup WeatherMAXTM in 2002.
67	thinking and suggest	**new**	approaches. Several technology
121	They provide	**new**	perspectives and give us
128	and discussed	**new**	products, company policies, and
136	looking forward to a	**new**	year and the challenges it holds.
281	it possible to produce	**new**	therapies from plants . . .
347	Achieve Results This	**new**	element, borrowed from a set of
307	as "Star" Sites.	**New**	Vehicle Safety Program:
319	Eco-Efficiency to a	**New**	Level: Redesigned Monsanto
186	Technology:	**New**	Leaf Potatoes Fight Pests in

'best by date'. Comparing Monsanto's website with Pioneer's we see that 'new' was used fifteen times by Pioneer (text of 3,206 words (= 0.467%)). It is used ten times by Monsanto in a shorter text (2,149 words (= 0.465%)), thus giving almost exactly the same percentage, as luck would have it! So what is 'new' for Monsanto? The highlighted right collocates in Table 9.14 manifest a maximally varied range of items.

A related positively tinged 'everyday' or orientational metaphor (Lakoff and Johnson 1980) is 'high'. It collocates on the left four times with 'quality' and twice with 'value' in this text (Table 9.15).

The fairly public controversies in recent years over genetic modification of crops seem to have led on the part of corporations to a desire to play down its use. 'Biotech/biotechnology' is clearly 'preferred', with 12 occurrences, over the term 'genetic' (only 3 uses) (Table 9.16). These modify only 'material' and 'information'. As the analysis in Table 9.31 shows, Pioneer uses 'genetic' more frequently, although they comment on this very usage, attributing it to others.

Perhaps 'biotech' is thought to sound more 'scientific' in the pro-GM constituency or else it represents an avoidance strategy. The concordance in Table 9.17 shows that three occurrences are part of an organizational name and two more are possibly artefacts of the hypertext format, being in titles of quoted literature listed at the end, as the high line numbers (generated by the computer) show. Otherwise, the four right collocates of 'biotech' are 'issues', 'products', 'ingredients' and 'crops'. More confident signals are given out with 'benefit(s)' occurring both to the right and left. From Table

Table 9.15 'High' Concordance of Monsanto

4	businesses offer	high-	value products and unique
10	provide farmers with	high-	value Roundup(r) agricultural
15	serves farmers with	high-	quality brand-name seeds, such
16	We also use a broad,	high-	quality collection of genetic
217	committed to provide	high-	quality products that benefit
273	the Pledge to deliver	high-	quality products that are
223	Renewable Fuels:	High-	Fermentable Corn Replacing
35	. . . atherMAX provides a	higher	level of weed control than its
163	in the 42 so-called	highly	indebted poor countries

Table 9.16 'Genetic' Concordance of Monsanto

17	Collection of	genetic	material—called germplasm
163	Important soybean	genetic	information developed by its
161	(pdf) 675kk Donating	Genetic	information: Sharing

Table 9.17 'Biotech' Concordance of Monsanto

128	company policies, and	biotech	issues. In November, 2002,
131	about the challenges	biotech	products bring to their
150	or not to note	biotech	ingredients on food labels.
234	a benefit from	biotech	crops is increased usage. For
235	year, acreage of	biotech	crops has increased around
259	from the use of	biotech	crops. Scientific Studies:
271	In 2001, eight	biotech	crops approved and used in
65	have in the past. The	Biotech	Advisory Council, formed
120	Monsanto formed the	Biotech	Advisory Council, a group of
127	Dialogue (pdf) 419k	Biotech	Advisory Council: The council
257	Scientific Studies:	Biotech	Benefits Demonstrated.Rece . . .
266	Review Confirms	Biotech	Crop Benefits. The Council

Table 9.18 'Biotechnology' Concordance of Monsanto

11	top brand seeds, and	**biotechnology**	traits. By combining
277	benefits that	**biotechnology**	holds for the European
280	Advances in	**biotechnology**	have made it possible
20	companies' brands.	**Biotechnology**	traits, such as
275	Studies: Benefits of	**Biotechnology**	for European

9.18 it is clear (see the highlighted items) that 'biotechnology' has more positively connoted left collocates.

8 SUMMARY OF MONSANTO ANALYSIS

What I have analyzed above is very much the 'soft sell' tactic that Monsanto adopts. It presents itself as a benevolent and philanthropic outfit. But the Janus-like characteristics are only too evident, when you look away from the PR and see how Monsanto 'really' treats its potential customers. In the alternative CropChoice network for North American farmers Paul Beingessner (2003), a Canadian farmer and writer, refers to the other side of their activities, which naturally do not find any mention in Monsanto's own material. "Monsanto and President George Bush have one thing in common. Both have a liking for the 'walk softly and carry a big stick' form of public relations." Beingessner states (2003):

> Monsanto is very determined to defend its position that farmers must buy new seed of its patented genetically modified crops each year. Monsanto has built a whole department to enforce its seed patents and licensing agreements. It has 75 employees and an annual budget of $10 million.

In India and the Third World the activities of Monsanto and its fellow transnational corporations are perhaps currently less successful in terms of market penetration, but no less 'effective' in profit terms.

9 LINGUISTIC ANALYSIS OF PIONEER HI-BRED WEBSITE

I now analyze the website of Pioneer Hi-Bred. Here are the basic statistics. The sum of different words (word-forms) (981) divided by the total number of running words (3206) gives a TTR for the Pioneer text of (0.306). I concentrate on one section of the website, a report, entitled "Company

Table 9.19 'Involve' Concordance of Pioneer Hi-Bred

419	on programs that	**involve**	its customers, growers,
240	research locations	**involved**	in developing and testing
325	Pioneer has been	**involved**	in the study and

Philosophy—The Long Look The Pioneer way of doing business" (Pioneer Hi-Bred 2003), in the following. This is basically the company's mission statement. It has separate pages with the following headings: 'The Pioneer way of doing business', 'Preface', 'We Strive to Live Up to It', 'Who We Are', 'Statements of Business Policy', 'Quality Products', 'Honesty and Fairness', 'Sales Representation', 'Customer Service', 'Our Commitments'.

The rubrics listed give an idea of the informational purpose it sets out to fulfil. As with Monsanto and like most company websites, this one is self-eulogizing, if not self-adulation, incarnate. Pioneer praises its own long-term philosophy. The use of purr-words in the text is an index of such self-representation. One of the first is 'involve'. Its right collocates (Table 9.19) include, naturally, their 'customers' and 'growers'.

Further purr-words, which the concordances show go together, are 'honest' and 'fair' and their related adverbs. One would expect the use of such self-ascribed epithets not to be used by business organizations among sophisticated potential customers. But nonetheless there are, rather surprisingly, at least five occurrences each of these items, as Tables 9.20 and 9.21 show. The verbs that appear as highlighted left collocates show that Pioneer refers to behaviour in commercial areas, namely 'be', 'deal', 'sell' and 'treat'. The actors involved are 'employees' or, as the broader co-texts show, related commercial partners. The observer can only wonder at the reason for the hedging 'try': "We try to deal honestly and fairly with our employees, sales representatives, business associates, customers and stockholders."

A further popular purr-word of Pioneer's turns out to be 'enhance' (see Table 9.22). This item appears to be much loved, with its nominal derivative, as it is to be found twelve times. By contrast, Monsanto does not use

Table 9.20 'Honest**' Concordance of Pioneer Hi-Bred

104	a company should be	**honest**	and fair out of a sense of
79	2. We try to deal	**honestly**	and fairly with our
99	is: "We try to deal	**honestly**	and fairly with our
204	best product, sold	**honestly**	but aggressively, to
97	important of all.	**Honesty**	and Fairness The second

Table 9.21 'Fair**' Concordance of Pioneer Hi-Bred

103	of being honest and	**fair.**	An individual or a company
104	should be honest and	**fair**	out of a sense of human dignity,
79	to deal honestly and	**fairly**	with our employees, sales
100	to deal honestly and	**fairly**	with our employees, sales
204	whom we treat	**fairly,**	and to whom we give superior

the term once. It has close right and left collocates such as 'sustain', 'value' (twice), 'continue', 'offer better performance', 'potential', 'a wider range of traits', etc.

The broader co-text of one entry shows how far the positive semantic prosody reaches: "Longer-term, genetically enhanced crops will likely be a source for high value products such as pharmaceuticals, polymers, renewable fuels and a host of others."

One of the most frequent content items in the text is 'increase' and its variants. This too may well be considered a purr-word in business circles. The concordance (Table 9.23) contains both the noun and the verb forms. There are five occurrences of the noun; twice with the left collocate 'significant'.

Table 9.22 'Enhance**' Concordance of Pioneer Hi-Bred

314	To sustain or	**enhance**	profitability include
348	Biotechnology, will	**enhance**	the nutritional value of
386	Will continue to	**enhance**	the genetic performance of
349	Genetically	**enhanced**	crops will likely be a
368	Have been genetically	**enhanced**	to offer better performance
384	They provide	**enhanced**	nutritive value for
400	Crops genetically	**enhanced**	through new technology are
294	. . . nologies for genetic	**enhancement**	represent another step
309	Modification and	**enhancement**	are now being used to
248	Supply of product that	**enhances**	the company's ability to be
311	Productivity and	**enhancing**	the abilities of farmers to
328	The potential of	**enhancing**	a wider range of traits and

Table 9.23 'Increase**' Concordance of Pioneer Hi-Bred

288	the first significant	increase	in corn production during
291	another significant	increase	in yield potential and
286	the mainstay of these	increases.	The transition from
337	use of insecticides,	increases	in productivity from
338	be dramatic. These	increases	will more than offset the
371	reliably and safely	increase	the productivity of each
380	the potential to	increase	their productivity and
271	improved crops and	increased	the productivity of
284	the history of	increased	agricultural productivity.
307	keeping the trend of	increased	production on track. New
314	profitability include	increased	productivity and
339	more than offset the	increased	cost that may be
354	these crops will offer	increased	productivity that will
355	more food. That	increased	productivity will not only
25	and stockholders by	increasing	the profitability of our
282	viable options for	increasing	productivity, do not offer
282	the potential for	increasing	productivity offered by
303	and the rapidly	increasing	populations we
311	potential for	increasing	productivity and
399	the environment and	increasing	the productivity of

Of the fifteen cases of the verb, eleven have 'productivity' as a right collocate (or as an object). This is an indication of how 'growthism' (see Halliday 1990: 23ff.) and emphasis on quantity still rules in US farming circles. 'Sustainability' in ecological terms remains unmentioned in Pioneer's website although 'sustain' does have four mentions. But see Table 9.26 for how they are employed.

The right collocates of 'significant', 'increase' and 'productivity gains' reveal a company still tied to growthism in the metaphorical sense of growth. So it is perhaps worth looking at the 'growth' and 'significant' concordances (Tables 9.24 and 9.25) to see what this orientation refers to.

Table 9.24 'Growth' Concordance of Pioneer Hi-Bred

31	committed to patient **growth** from our research activities.
61	support the personal **growth** of our employees around the
68	problem-solving and **growth** comes not only from the
142	help to sustain our **growth** in the 21st century. Sales

Table 9.25 'Significant' Concordance of Pioneer Hi-Bred

49	our products make	**significant**	differences in the
288	corn caused the first	**significant**	increase in corn
290	initiated another	**significant**	increase in yield
332	to safely provide	**significant**	value to farmers,
297	technology products.	**Significant**	productivity gains can be

Table 9.26 'Sustain***' Concordance of Pioneer Hi-Bred

142	century will help to	**sustain**	our growth in the 21st
332	the opportunities to	**sustain**	or enhance profitability
33	well be essential to	**sustaining**	humanity. We are
212	well be critical to	**sustaining**	humanity in the future.

The left and close right collocates of 'growth' turn out to be ambiguous: 'patient' (a feature of the 'long look' approach, perhaps?), 'personal' and 'our' plus 'our employees'. In the case of 'significant' three out of the five instances modify quantitative concepts, as Table 9.25 makes clear.

As noted in chapter 5, almost everyone seems to employ the term 'sustain' in business today. Four instances (Table 9.26) occur in this text.

The broader co-texts of 'sustain' are interesting, precisely because the collocates, sometimes 'profitability' at others 'humanity', again prove to be ambiguous in their reference:

1 "The kind of reputation we build in the 20th century will help to sustain our growth in the 21st century."

Table 9.27 'Superior' Concordance of Pioneer Hi-Bred

31	to developing	**superior**	products with efficiencies
42	resources are	**superior**	germplasm and dedicated
199	to the development of	**superior**	products through research;
205	and to whom we give	**superior**	service. We hope that all

2 "Some of the opportunities to sustain or enhance profitability include increased productivity and production of grain with specialty or value-added traits."

3 "We are committed to developing superior products with efficiencies which may well be essential to sustaining humanity."

4 "and we are committed to working on problems and products which may very well be critical to sustaining humanity in the future."

However they leave the concept of 'problems' (in 4) unexplained.

A further businessy purr-word is 'develop'. Note the positive prosodies or collocational chains in which it appears. Consider this example with its cumulative or incremental cluster of affirmative sounding items 'superior products', 'efficiencies', 'essential' and 'humanity': "We are committed to developing superior products with efficiencies which may well be essential to sustaining humanity." We find several occurrences in Tables 9.27 and 9.28 (on 'superior' and 'commitment').

The word 'superior' is a useful way of demonstrating a degree of linguistic or ideological engineering at work in the text. We can safely call this Pioneer's ideological construction of reality. With Kress and Hodge (1979: 15), I am of the opinion that: "[i]deology involves a systematically organized presentation of reality." Pioneer's PR department overtly and patently presents its own view of reality by carefully choosing how to arrange words. The non-comparative use of 'superior' gives it the status of a superlative. Everything else that does not come up to Pioneer's standard is subtly and implicitly being 'rubbished'.

10 'COMMITMENT' IN THE PIONEER HI-BRED WEBSITE

For Monsanto, the term 'commitment' played a role in the text. So it might be interesting or even insightful to compare how Pioneer uses the same lexical group. It appears in the discussion of Pioneer's 'philosophy'. Consider this extract:

Table 9.28 'Commit**' Concordance of Pioneer Hi-Bred

396	a seven-decade old	commitment	to preserving the
399	extension of that	commitment	as we move into the
201	future. These three	commitments,	these "Long Look
192	by our research. Our	Commitments	We are a business . . . a
30	the "long look." We are	committed	to patient growth from
31	activities. We are	committed	to developing superior
33	humanity. We are	committed	to developing these
61	possible. We are	committed	to continuing the
184	to organizations	committed	to expanding usage of
197	expectations, we are	committed	to the development of
199	within; and we are	committed	to working on problems
404	International, Inc. is	committed	to helping improve the

These three commitments, these 'Long Look' approaches to business, are coupled with the four operating policies: best product, sold honestly but aggressively, to customers whom we treat fairly, and to whom we give superior service.

Let us look at the 'commit**' concordance (Table 9.28). Invoking some of the broader co-text elements brings out the almost religious rhythm. Like religious creeds or the pledge of allegiance ("I pledge allegiance to the Flag of the United States of America, and to the Republic for which it stands, one Nation under God, indivisible, with liberty and justice for all.") this has pious, liturgical overtones. A parallel structure with a repetitive syntactic pattern—'we are committed to'—is reiterated twice after the first time:

We are committed to patient growth from our research activities. We are committed to developing superior products with efficiencies which may well be essential to sustaining humanity. We are committed to developing these products through the work of people developed from within the organization wherever possible.

The 'we' pronoun usage also serves to underline this personal trust element. (See also section 11 below.)

The verbs and nominals which figure as right collocates of the phrase 'committed to' are nearly all actions with positive connotations in the business world—'patient growth', 'developing superior', 'developing', 'continuing', 'expanding usage', 'development', 'working on problems' and 'helping improve'. The effectiveness of Pioneer is clearly being underscored here.

In comparison to Monsanto and its 'Pledge', Pioneer has its 'long-look business philosophy'. The concordance in Table 9.29 shows that the collocation of the eighteen occurrences (= 0.56%) of 'long' is mostly 'look' (fourteen cases); there are three cases of 'term' and one of 'time'. The corporation clearly wishes to impress upon the reader its temporally 'sustainable' policies.

Table 9.29 'Long' Concordance of Pioneer Hi-Bred

16	to be essential to our	**long-**	term success. Our long-look
16	Success. Our	**long-**	look business philosophy has
31	We Are We take the "	**long**	look." We are committed to
50	great faith and the "	**long**	look" can hope to succeed. At
68	employee. Our	**long-**	term approach to
176	the community. Our	**long-**	time success in selling Pioneer
438	Pioneer takes a	**long**	look at problem solving, it is
2	Philosophy—The	**Long**	Look The
8	Preface "The	**Long**	Look" was originally written in
73	have understood the "	**Long**	Look" and held to it
77	for humanity. The "	**Long**	Look" has led us to set forth
99	other points in the "	**Long**	Look" formula, but for us a good
104	second point in "The	**Long**	Look" formula is: "We try to deal
182	The last point in our "	**Long**	Look" formula for business
213	commitments, these "	**Long**	Look" approaches to business,
224	always be sound. "The	**Long**	Look" was originally written by
218	"Do I have the	**'Long**	Look?' Will this thing that I am
370	livestock and people.	**Longer-**	term, genetically enhanced

11   PRONOUNS 'WE' AND 'OUR'
IN THE PIONEER WEBSITE

As became clear above in the case of the Monsanto text, the personal pronouns 'we' and 'our' can be used inclusively, to relate to the reader or listener more closely, or exclusively, to refer to the speaker or writer. The latter mode predominated in Monsanto's usage. In the Pioneer website nearly all sixty-seven instances of 'we' refer exclusively to Pioneer, with, interestingly, perhaps only the following single instance expressing inclusiveness: "As the world looks toward the future, and the rapidly increasing populations we must feed . . ."

'Our' or 'ours' occurs fifty-nine times. As this passage, with three occurrences, shows, Pioneer is interested in self-presentation, in creating a specific view of reality.

> When we write a catalog or an ad for magazine, newspaper, radio or television, or when we are selling face-to-face, we want to picture our products as they are, without misrepresentation.

Two of the section headings—'We Strive to Live Up to It' and 'Who We Are'—contain the pronoun 'we'. The large number of occurrences of 'we' (sixty-seven in all, 2.08% of the total text) should alert us to the role it plays. Looking at the extract in Table 9.30, it is striking how large a proportion of the right collocates of 'our' refer to the philosophy, reputation or 'long-term approach' adopted by the company, namely 8/59 in all. Alongside these items are two related instances of 'success'. This self-eulogizing or self-praise makes up a large proportion of the right collocates of 'our' too, with items like 'attitudes', 'research activities', 'products' and 'most valuable resources'. Nine of fifty-nine have 'employees' (and 'sales force') as a right collocate, whereas only eight of fifty-nine surprisingly have 'customers'.

Third person reference in the shape of 'our customers' etc. is the preferred form of address to their readers and potential customers and stakeholders for Pioneer. There is no instance of 'you' or 'your' (see Table 9.2 above). Yet the 'our' concordance enables us to isolate the actors or people who figure as Pioneer's addressees.

12   THE USE OF 'GENETIC' BY PIONEER HI-BRED

Let us take a look at the keyword 'genetic'. It is a central term in this area. There are twelve occurrences of it. There are also five occurrences of 'genetically' (see Table 9.31).

Genetic has 'improvement(s)' as its immediate right collocate four times, 'technologies' three times, 'modification' twice, 'attributes of plants', 'performance' and 'enhancement' once each. As immediate or near left collocates

Table 9.30 'Our' Concordance of Pioneer Hi-Bred (Extract)

8	in 1952. It reflected	**our**	business philosophy, one that had
26	achieving success for	**our**	employees, sales force, seed
54	We are pleased by	**our**	success and are excited by our
74	for our customers,	**our**	employees, our sales force, seed
88	possible profit from	**our**	products. Quality Products
117	the word about us and	**our**	reputation. If good, we have a
146	to advertise and sell	**our**	products vigorously but without
183	suggestions to	**our**	customers to assist them in
199	and trained to assist	**our**	customers in realizing the
316	in the process. It is	**our**	responsibility to provide
45	units worldwide.	**Our**	most valuable resources are
203	by our research.	**Our**	Commitments We are a business

it has 'new' five times and the verb 'enhance' two words to the left also. It is worth mentioning that 'new' occurs fairly frequently in the text—fifteen times in all. Note also that 'genetically' is followed by 'enhanced' three times (as shown in Table 9.31) and by 'modified' twice.

The right collocates of 'genetic' are interesting, especially the purr-words 'enhanced' and 'improvement'. One can see their euphemistic function. This demonstrates some cunning linguistic and ideological engineering at work, in addition, to physical genetic engineering! As this extract demonstrates, 'genetically modified' is placed in quotes. Why? It is a term attributed to others as the left collocate 'called' makes evident, functioning as a meta-discoursal comment.

> Pioneer agrees with and wants to ensure that all those interested in new genetic technologies understand the value of plants that are now being called 'genetically modified.' Pioneer supports the right of everyone to examine and debate the relative merits of any new technology. Pioneer has been involved in the study and development of new products utilizing the tools of biotechnology for more than 15 years. During that time it has become apparent that biotechnology offers the potential of enhancing a wider range of traits and methods in crops than was previously available.

Table 9.31 'Genetic/Genetically' Concordance of Pioneer Hi-Bred

270	of farmers through	**Genetic**	modification of plants. By
270	plants. By modifying	**Genetic**	attributes of plants, Pioneer
277	fertilizers, and	**Genetic**	improvement. Tillage, pest
281	. . . ductivity offered by	**Genetic**	improvements. This has been
284	productivity. New	**Genetic**	technologies have been the
292	new technologies for	**Genetic**	enhancement represent
303	it is apparent that the	**genetic**	improvement portion of this
307	New technologies for	**genetic**	modification and
320	interested in new	**genetic**	technologies understand the
337	with these new	**genetic**	technologies. Some traits
345	Other products with	**genetic**	improvements, made possible
384	to enhance the	**genetic**	performance of crops
321	are now being called "	**genetically** modified." Pioneer
347	people. Longer-term,	**genetically** enhanced crops will
358	class of so-called	**genetically** modified organisms. As
366	crops that have been	**genetically** enhanced to offer better
398	everywhere. Crops	**genetically** enhanced through new

Is 'biotechnology' used as a euphemism in this extract? Looking at the concordance in Table 9.32 we find a series of both positive left collocates 'tools of, various methods, possible, aid' and right 'potential, safely, enhance, safe'. As the final sections show, the work of the seed transnationals is not without its critics, in both the First and the Third Worlds.

13 THE VIEW FROM THE THIRD WORLD: SHIVA AND OTHER CRITICS

After considering the glossy and flickering image of corporate agriculture which such websites project, it is necessary to ask what the results of the industrialized agriculture they represent are really like. Companies like Monsanto, Pioneer and Cargill are well known in agricultural circles in India. And not everyone is happy with what they find.

Table 9.32 'Biotechnology' Concordance of Pioneer Hi-Bred

326	utilizing the tools of	**biotechnology**	for more than 15
327	become apparent that	**biotechnology**	offers the potential of
331	various methods of	**biotechnology**	will continue to safely
348	made possible through	**biotechnology,**	will enhance the
364	with the aid of	**biotechnology**	will offer only safe,
387	. . . hnologies, including	**biotechnology.**	We will, as we have
267	people worldwide.	**Biotechnology**	-Open Letter on
267	—Open Letter on	**Biotechnology**	Pioneer Hi-Bred

In the past two or three decades many claims have been made about how world hunger can be avoided. Elsewhere it might be worthwhile to investigate the role that Western food aid programmes have played in sometimes 'destroying' agricultural markets in Africa and Asia or by 'not' helping countries in need, like Bangladesh in 1974. (See a report of the British journalist John Pilger's films in Hayward 2001: 153 and Curtis 2003b: 209ff. on so-called 'development aid' offered by Britain.) The often praised 'transfer of technology' slogan promises more than it can and does deliver. It tends to favour rich farmers at the expense of relatively poor farmers who cannot afford the investment in the high inputs (Millstone and Lang 2003: 8).

Strangely, and perhaps in a rather inflationary fashion, many Western-led agricultural developments have been termed 'revolutions'. The observer of these developments can be forgiven for wondering what the hidden agenda really is when politicians and public relations activities appear to 'talk up' and 'hype' these, literally, 'colourful' revolutions. The close cooperation with governments in some countries is evident, as the self-congratulatory quotation from Rajnath Singh, Union Agriculture Minister, about India shows (2003):

> The technology-led developments in agriculture have made India self-sufficient in foodgrains and a leading producer of several commodities in the world. The green revolution in crops, yellow revolution in oilseeds, white revolution in milk production, blue revolution in fish production and a golden revolution in horticulture bear an ample testimony to the contributions of agricultural research and development efforts undertaken in the country.

Behind the phrase "the contributions of agricultural research and development efforts" lie the unmentioned efforts of Western-based corporations which are attempting to persuade the world's peasant farmers and fishers to give up their traditional ways of life and work. Large multinational corporations, whose expansion in the world has accelerated in the past three decades, market genetically engineered crops and the accompanying chemical and technological products needed to 'industrialize' agriculture. 'GM', genetically modified, plants are the latest fashion.

At the same time the public and consumers in some countries like France, Germany and the UK are unconvinced of the need for genetically engineered or modified crops (George 2003). Third world farmers likewise remain sceptical and resistant to the often misleading claims made by the 'gene-based corporations' (Shiva 2003b and passim; see also New Internationalist 2003).

The near rainbow-like revolutions which Third World agriculture has already experienced were supposed to aid poor countries to feed their own populations. The outcome has been a quite different one however. Cash crops for global markets have usually formed the heart of each of these revolutions. Acquaculture and shrimps in particular are an example for the real, destructive results of the 'blue revolution' (Limberger 2003). So what is the true price that the Third World is paying for effectively feeding the world?

The rules of the WTO demand that support for farmers in the Third World is cut and their agricultural markets are opened to rich countries, or more specifically to the surplus production and the multinational corporations of these countries.

Particularly the work of the Indian physicist and activist scholar, Vandana Shiva, has provided ample evidence of the destructive effect this is having on small farmers, as we saw in chapter 8. Shiva (2003b) writes:

> The dysfunctionality of agriculture under globalisation is leading to farmers paying with their very lives. However, this dysfunctionality is beneficial to agri-business which is harvesting the artificially accumulated stocks and artificially manipulated collapse of domestic markets to make super profits.

She goes on to comment on the tragic and extreme lengths to which this process is leading: "In March 2001, Punjab became the first state to admit the fact that farmers, unable to clear their debts, have started committing suicide" (Shiva 2003b). She presents a dramatic example of the irresponsible way some orthodox academics respond to this situation (Shiva 2001b):

> When thousands of our farmers are committing suicide, when millions of our women and children are facing hunger and starvation, a leading economist said that, "The poor can buy Barbie dolls". This statement was made when I was on a T.V. panel with him to discuss and debate the impact of the removal of import restrictions (Quantitative Restrictions or QRs).

14 VANDANA SHIVA: HER CRITICISMS OF CORPORATE ACTIVITIES

Vandana Shiva's work can serve as a counterweight to the corporate exposi-
tions analyzed above. The juxtaposition of these opposing views of agricultural development in the Third World illustrates how closely, and at times
bitterly, opposing ways of life, culture and work confront each other around
the world.

Her work stands out like a beacon or a lighthouse. Chapter 8 has already
analyzed in detail both the politics and language of Shiva. Here it will suffice to give a brief selection of the theses she puts forward. The titles of her
regular articles in *ZNet Commentary* give a flavour of these ideas, as can
be seen by consulting the bibliography. In (2001a) Shiva writes graphically
about globalisation, which she sees as containing violence as an intrinsic
component:

> Globalization is a violent system, imposed and maintained through use
> of violence. As trade is elevated above human needs, the insatiable appe-
> tite of global markets for resources is met by unleashing new wars over
> resources. The war over diamonds in Sierra Leone, over oil in Nigeria
> has killed thousands of women and children. The transfer of people's
> resources to global corporations also makes states more militaristic as
> they arm themselves on behalf of commercial interests, and start wars
> against their own people.

Shiva (2003a) talks of how we need to act in the face of globalisation and
writes:

> The response to globalization is the protection and defense of our di-
> verse economies at local and national levels. The response to fundamen-
> talism is celebrating our cultural diversities. The response to war is the
> recognition that the 'other' is not a threat but the very precondition of
> our being.

But she recognizes that we must stand firm against globalisation. She demonstrates what the movements of poor farmers represent and what they are
trying to achieve (2003c):

> Our movement in India seeks to defend our seed freedom (Bija Swaraj)
> and food freedom (Anna Swaraj) by defending our rights, and refusing
> to cooperate with immoral and unjust laws (Bija Satyagraha). We save
> and share our seeds, we boycott corporate seeds, we are creating pat-
> ent free, chemical free, genetic engineering free zones of agriculture to
> ensure our agriculture is free of corporate monopolies and chemical and
> genetic pollution.

Here is a situation in which two opposing cultural views of agricultural development in the Third World clash. Some of the horrendous consequences of this repressive system can be seen in reports from India. The American journalist John Biewen reports (2000) on how "India has emerged as a leading hotspot in the worldwide battle over GM crops." He interviewed Indian farmers who had to sell one of their kidneys to pay for the loan they had made to a moneylender for worthless seeds from a crooked salesman. He details, like Shiva, the increasing numbers of suicides among poor farmers in India.

Talking about organizations like the World Trade organization (WTO) Shiva does not hesitate to name names or to beat about the bush, as noted in chapter 8. Shiva writes (2003a):

> The Agreement on Agriculture should be called a Cargill Agreement. It was former Cargill Vice-President, Dan Amstutz, who drafted the original text of the Uruguay Round Agreement on Agriculture. Opening Southern markets and converting peasant agriculture to corporate agriculture is the primary aim of Cargill and hence the Agreement on Agriculture.

The targets Shiva attacks are always shifting. Coca Cola is just the most recent to be criticized for their polluting the water in some parts of India, as well as contributing to tooth decay and the bad diet of many Indians (Shiva 2003e).

Naturally Shiva and her supporters have plenty of critics. Disinformation, flak or hostile publicity are techniques Beder (1997) has analyzed in relation to the combating of environmentalist organizations by big business and industry. The same techniques are used against the 'bio-activists', as they are sometimes called. One can find many websites like <http://reason.com/0101/fe.rb.dr.shtml> and <http://eagle.westnet.gr/~cgian/bleifuss2.htm>. These provide a positive and affirmative presentation of the biotech industry.

Typical sentences to be found are: "If the activists are successful in their war against green biotech, it's the world's poor who will suffer most." This reference to the future is extremely cynical since it ignores the fact that the poor are actually suffering right now. They do not need to wait until the unforeseeable future. In short, it is evident how key notions of 'value', nature and sustainable development are being contested in ecological and environmental discourse today.

The English writer, John Berger (2003) describes the basic processes and mechanisms that underlie current globalisation trends:

> Those who hold the power and they are not all heads of state, see themselves as saviours of the world, offer the population the opportunity of becoming their clients. The global consumer is sacred, but what these people do not say is that he or she only is important because they generate profit.

The neo-liberal economists claim that for every buyer, there must be a seller. They neglect to add that under most capitalist circumstances these roles are hardly every symmetrical. And they repeat the neo-classical truisms about 'a buyer's market' or 'a seller's market', claiming that they are the exceptions to the otherwise perfectly functioning market! However, surplus value continues to be extracted asymmetrically by one side in every such commercial 'exchange'. 'Fair' exchange is, by definition, excluded, since, as the true meaning suggests, it would lead to cooperation and egalitarian outcomes. The essential priority of capitalist exchange with or without a human face remains the creation of unilateral profit.

In advanced or late-monopoly capitalism large corporations are able to 'create' nearly permanent sellers' markets. This, as this chapter has shown, is particularly the case in the agricultural seed business. The future outcome of this struggle for the existence of autonomous agricultural production is uncertain. The forces opposing the WTO and their sponsors, the transnational corporations, are slowly grouping and building coalitions across the continents. However, First World consumers still need more education about why their food is so plentiful and comparatively 'cheap'. They need to be helped to begin to think about where the true costs lie and to whose disadvantage it is for consumers and producers in the West to continue to exploit the Third World.

10 Language and Orwell's Problem

1 INTRODUCTION

Eric Hobsbawm's 1994 Amnesty International lecture in Oxford was entitled 'Barbarism: A User's Guide'. In the lecture, Hobsbawm, an eminent British social and economic historian, takes a look at the 'short twentieth century, 1914–1991' (see Hobsbawm 1997). According to Simon Targett, who was in the audience, Hobsbawm characterized the achievements of the 20th century as 'astonishing'. Nonetheless, Hobsbawm (1997: 253) argues that "we have all adapted to living in a society that is, by the standards of our grandparents or parents, even—if we are as old as I am—our youth, uncivilised." Targett goes on to summarize Hobsbawm's general assessment, that "we all have become relatively insensitive to human atrocity, our voice of moral outrage has been silenced, things that would once have caused an outcry now pass by without so much as a raised eyebrow. And, in Hobsbawm's book, this is barbarism" (Targett 1994: 19).

Many years later observers of international relations in the current world against the backdrop of the 'war on terror' still under way might wish to reflect on phrases like 'insensitive to human atrocity', 'moral outrage', 'things that would once have caused an outcry' or 'barbarism'. Echoes of such phrases today can be heard to justify illegal bombings or occupations of countries, like Yugoslavia, Afghanistan or Iraq. This is to focus merely on the political dimension. The role which corporate globalisation is playing simultaneously in contributing to the general degradation of the biosphere, and the ways in which this is justified as normal or natural or 'inevitable', as previous chapters have outlined is undoubtedly closely linked.

We might wonder why, in Hobsbawm's words so many "things [. . .] now pass by without so much as a raised eyebrow". What part is played, especially in the Western world, by the misrepresentation of what is going on in the world? What role are the modern media and their owners and patrons (frequently political and economic élites in major countries) playing in perhaps preventing people from seeing the wood for the trees? And we might wonder how this takes place despite the 'flood of reporting' and news churned out daily in the Media Age.

Noam Chomsky has referred to this apparent paradox, namely, how it transpires that we know so little about the (social and political) world, while being surrounded by so much 'information' as 'Orwell's problem' (1986: xxvii)[1]. One of the major contentions of this chapter will hold that part of explanation for this outcome is relatively simple, namely, that given the configuration of the corporate and governmental set-up in the so-called Western democracies, Edward Herman's 'power laws' operate.

2   IF YOU WANT TO LIE, IT HELPS TO HAVE POWER

Herman and Chomsky demonstrated in their book *Manufacturing Consent* (1988) how closely the press and other media contribute to the 'distortion' of real events. We can concur with them that various techniques of 'news management' unite both government self-presentation and corporate self-images (see Greer and Bruno 1996, on 'greenwash'). Truth and reason play no role in these matters. Powerful interests have no need to be consistent. Consider, for example, the ways in which Western governments (most notably the US and UK) have provided support for unelected 'dictators' often selling them large amounts of weapons, until they are abandoned for reasons of 'realpolitik'. See the case of Noriega in Panama, who was built up and sustained by the CIA until 1989 (Blum 2003: 305–14), and that of Saddam Hussein, who was granted massive military aid in his war against Iran in the 1980s.

Herman has characterized the situation that permits this, as follows (1992: 14): "The structure of power that shapes media choices and determines who gains access also affects truthfulness in the mass media. Those who have assured access can lie; the more powerful they are, the more easily they can lie and the less likely it is that their lies will be corrected. The higher the rank, the more 'credible' the statement; the more credible the speaker, the greater the freedom to lie."

In the days before commercial mass media existed, at least fictionally, Hans Christian Andersen's 'The Emperor's New Clothes' story was imaginable. The difference today is that the modern 'power law of access' excludes small children in the crowd from shouting 'But he doesn't have any clothes on!' Herman formulates two laws to capture this state of affairs: a 'power law of access' and an 'inverse law of truthfulness.'

> The first law says that the greater your economic and political clout, the easier your access to the mass media; the less your power, the more difficult the access. At a certain point on the declining power scale, access falls to zero. The fall to zero is accelerated if the message is discordant and would offend the powerful. The second law says that the greater your economic and political power—hence, access—the greater your freedom to lie; the smaller your power, the less your freedom to

Table 10.1 Edward Herman's Power Laws

Herman's First Law Says	*'Power Law of Access'*
1) the greater your economic and political clout,	2) the easier your access to the mass media;
3) the less your power,	4) the more difficult the access.
The Second Law Says	*'Inverse Law of Truthfulness'*
1) the greater your economic and political power—hence, access—	2) the greater your freedom to lie;
3) the smaller your power,	4) the less your freedom to prevaricate.

prevaricate. The second law follows in part from the first, as those who would be most eager to refute the lies of powerful are weak and have limited access, further reduced by their discordant messages. Their messages can be ignored without cost to the mass media (whose biases would incline them toward avoidance anyway). (1992: 14)

The laws can be laid out in tabular fashion to underline their close correlation (see Table 10.1).

When we factor in discordant messages, a corollary of the second law can be seen in Table 10.2.

Why do reporters and commentators fall in with this set up? After all, Herman notes: "The media's gullibility and groveling before the powerful occurs despite recognition by media personnel, in principle, that governments lie." The high degree of mutual support shows in Chilton's words (1988: 54) how "dependencies between media, political and commercial institutions can act as effective filters and censors." How such general processes of disinformation and so on can reign supreme on a societal plane will require some explanation.

As the quotation from Hobsbawm at the beginning made clear, the stance taken up in this chapter is not primarily oriented at language in isolation. The position we adopt here, as in the previous chapters, accepts that language and its use is intimately and intrinsically connected with social processes.

Table 10.2 The Corollary of the First Law for the Weak

The Second Law Follows in Part from the First, as		
1) those who would be most eager to refute the lies of powerful	2) are weak and have limited access,	3) further reduced by their discordant messages.

But more importantly, language use is a result of social processes. The recognition of the primacy of the social clearly has methodological consequences for those of us who are interested in or concerned with the workings of the socio-economic and political 'real' world.

3   WHAT SORT OF SOCIETY DO WE LIVE IN?

How does the real world function? Clearly, a socio-economic or historical grounding for the investigation of disinformation and related processes is needed, or at least might be helpful. It can be useful to bring in Herbert Marcuse at this point. Marcuse's (1964) analysis of modern technological society, *One Dimensional Man*, was published over forty years ago. Yet, on re-reading it today, it remains remarkably apposite and relevant to our current world. In the first place, he painted a portrait of a technologically overdetermined society, a totalitarian post-industrial world, with its "comfortable, smooth, reasonable, democratic unfreedom". As Stephen Amidon (2000: 56) notes: "A cold Marcusian look at our world indicates we are trapped in one-dimensionality deeper than ever."

Several aspects of what has become 3rd millennium society were early pinpointed by Marcuse. We might mention the childishness and semi-infantilism which is being induced by consumerism as one feature. Also 'off-job control' has increased as a result of casualization of the work force. But we see too that 'prefab leisure activities' are still very much a reality. This Taylorization of consumption was a feature Marcuse comments on in his book. Less and less time seems to exist in the 'wired up', digitalized and mobile phone age of the young today! With this technological infrastructure of control, we have reached the hyperindustrial époque. Consciousness is overdetermined by 'tertiary retentions' of experienced events. By means of information technology (IT) (numerical or digitalized) in the form of camera-enhanced mobiles, webcams and audio and video recordings, traces of the 'flux of consciousness' can be recorded. The increasing surveillance via closed circuit TV and computer and satellite technology in the 'public sphere' accompanies the personal overloading of both the senses and the central nervous system. Together we thus have elements of external control which provide a far more ubiquitous, material basis for Orwellian 'thought control'.

Alongside the evolving regimes of surveillance and spying currently being put in place we might also adduce the internalization of commercial 'branding' as a further example of "this tightening one-dimensionality" that Marcuse prophetically predicted long before 9/11. Whether we view this as comprehensive moronization is clearly a matter of judgement. The seed for this can be seen in Marcuse's analysis of the universe of discourse of a one-dimensional society. Marcuse provides a sketch of the ideological and cultural atmosphere which a one-dimensional society has succeeded in constructing (1964: 77): "The Happy Consciousness—the belief that the real is rational and that the system delivers the goods—reflects the new conformism which is a facet of technological rationality translated into social behaviour."

4　ON THE RELATIVE WEIGHTING OF MATERIAL AND LINGUISTIC FACTORS

Marcuse focuses on "The Language of Total Administration" (1964: 77ff.), pinpointing the jargon that reflects what he terms (ibid.: 82) "the authoritarian character of this language." He details some of the features it manifests, such as "concreteness" (ibid.: 84): "This language, which constantly imposes *images*, militates against the development and expression of *concepts*. In its immediacy and directness, it impedes conceptual thinking; thus, it impedes thinking" (emphasis in original). In this connection it is insightful to compare what the American photographer, concept artist and academic Allan Sekula says about the limited representational range of the camera. In one of his exhibition projects from the 1970s he claims: "One cannot photograph ideology" (2003: 161).

To quote a few sentences of Marcuse is to notice how reminiscent they are of the passages in Orwell's *1984* (1949) discussed below. "The war of annihilation has not yet occurred; the Nazi extermination camps have been abolished. The Happy Consciousness repels the connection. Torture has been re-introduced as a normal affair, but in a colonial war which takes place at the margin of the civilized world. And there it is practiced with good conscience for war is war. And this war, too, is at the margin—it ravages only the 'underdeveloped' countries. Otherwise, peace reigns" (Marcuse 1964: 77).

As we shall see in later sections the authoritarian resonances of this appear to have multiplied in contemporary times. At the time writing we see that 'plus ça change, plus c'est la même chose'. For example one of the practices Marcuse was targeting was operationalism. And certainly, there are many aspects of current academic, business and media discourse which show its persistence today. The superficial discourses need to be 'read' carefully. One might ask how such 'social behaviour' can come into being. Perhaps at this point we can briefly refer to 'ideologies' and how they play a part in maintaining society. Discourse-oriented linguists like Chilton (1988: 79) have addressed this issue. He argues that "[t]o start with, a language like English is not an entirely neutral system. Whole chunks of vocabulary and grammatical habits are produced by groups with special interests (politicians, bureaucrats, advertisers, and so on). The consumers of language then consume it, by and large unconsciously and uncritically." As Van Dijk notes (1995: 33), we need to tease out how discourse structures are linked to these ideological structures.

In view of our earlier reference to how governments present themselves we can agree with Van Dijk (1995: 32) that "[o]verall, we find that preferred, consistent or otherwise self-serving information will be emphasized, highlighted, focused upon, and made explicit and prominent, whereas the converse is true for dispreferred information." The fact that one-sided or biased mental models can be created in this way is a truism well understood by the hidden persuaders. It leads to recipients working in concert with or agreement with the goals or interests of speakers. And Van Dijk (1995: 32) underlines what might transpire: "There will be a higher chance that recipients will activate preferred old models or construct new models in agreement with the goals or interests of the speaker, if no alternative information is present." There are a number of ways of preventing alternative information from being attended to in so-called 'democratic' societies. To these we now turn.

5   INSTITUTIONAL OBFUSCATION: HERMAN ON DOUBLESPEAK

The power laws relating to prevaricating in high places and the ability to publish opinions based on untruths were discussed by Herman in a book entitled *Beyond Hypocrisy. Decoding the News in an Age of Propaganda. Including the Doublespeak Dictionary*. He says (1992: 1) it is: "about doublespeak, the misuse of words by implicit redefinition, selective application of 'snarl' and 'purr' words, and other forms of verbal manipulation."

These techniques flourish in advertising, public relations and media news provision. So clearly commercial agents are no strangers to what we might call propaganda. As Herman (1992: 1) states, "the growth of doublespeak also results from intensifying market pressures, along with the challenge of selling indistinguishable, if not downright noxious, goods as exceptionally worthwhile." Orwell is adduced as an early commentator on how in political propaganda language serves to obfuscate an indefensible reality (1992: 3). Clearly self-deception and internalization play a role. Several US presidents before George W. Bush are cited as examples. But Herman rightly emphasizes the role of the media in a capitalist society (1992: 5): "Media collaboration with the government in fostering a world of doublespeak is essential to its use and institutionalization, and this collaboration has been regularly forthcoming." During Reagan's presidencies Herman noted "a huge increase in what was officially called 'public diplomacy,' a new doublespeak term for what used to be known as government propaganda" (1992: 18). Similarly, the British linguist, Paul Chilton, sees a propaganda function of media as dealing with "awkward facts and events which conflict with what the dominant view of the social reality is or ought to be" (1988: 81).

Together with Herman, Chomsky's social and political work is worthy of mention. We might bring in Chomsky's testimony over the years as an index of 'stability' and continuity in real world politics. His writings demonstrate that the imperialist tendencies in Western 'democracies' have continued to exist since 1945 and never went away. As a political thinker and activist, in an interview on 11 April 1968 (published 1988) during the Vietnam War, Chomsky feels the need to draw attention (1988a: 98) to "the present state of the world and America's role in the world." Nearly four decades later his commitment to telling the truth about American power and its abuse by certain groupings continues. Now Iraq replaces Vietnam as the point of shame and reference. As we know, Chomsky is systematically 'silenced' or snubbed by the mainstream media in his own country. He is frequently on the TV and radio and in the press in the UK, Canada and other countries. This appears very strange and perhaps tells us more about people's, even intellectuals' and certainly the US media's ability to conceal or ignore what has been going on in the world for the past sixty years. And yet, despite the seemingly 'peaceful' developments in Europe and the 'unfortunate' uncivilized conflagrations in the Balkans in the 1990s, works by Chomsky, Johnson, Pilger, Curtis etc. show that the world has been experiencing on many continents (at a distance from us in Europe) a pretty barbaric set of events. Pilger (2004: xxv) brings this home pointedly and sardonically in introducing a selection of investigative journalists who have gone against the grain: "What is almost never reported in the United States is the pattern of American colonial interventions. Only 'anti-Americans', it seems, refer to the hundreds of illegal 'covert operations', many of them bloody, that have denied political and economic self-determination to much of the world." As Pilger notes, a "voluntary system of state-sponsored lies" has long suppressed knowledge of these barbarities.

Edward Herman himself demonstrated the brutal contempt for truthfulness on the part of the powerful. Writing about the Kosovo War, Herman states (1999b: 1):

> War, propaganda, and the proliferation of doublespeak have always gone hand-in-hand. As was the case during the Persian Gulf war, the NATO war against Yugoslavia witnessed a collapse of mainstream media integrity and a new surge of doublespeak in the service of the war party. It was grimly humorous that NATO and its compliant media partners justified the bombing of Serbian radio and TV on the grounds of propaganda service to Milosevic's war machine. In reality, the parallel service of the U.S. and British media differed from that of the Serbs mainly in their ludicrous self-designation as objective and propaganda-free.

This is an instance at the macro-level of the point Van Dijk (1995: 33) makes about the micro-level of discourse: "As is the case for virtually all strategic choices at the semantic level, such 'forms' will signal and emphasize *our* good actions, and *their* negative actions" (emphasis in original).

6 COMMUNICATIVE AND DISCOURSE STRATEGIES EMPLOYED: PROPAGANDA, AND THE PROLIFERATION OF DOUBLESPEAK

In view of the foregoing, it seems evident that enlightened citizens should cast a critical eye over the methods employed by certain political and corporate bodies to sustain their hegemonic hold over the current 'globalised' world and international political and economic order. In previous chapters we examined some of the communicative and discourse strategies employed by the powerful to present a view of or a perspective on this world that is favourable to their interests. Indeed, to a large extent, this very discourse aims to constitute the interpretation or ideology presented by such bodies to the 'public', 'voters' or external world generally.

We have analyzed examples of the language or discourse used by selected multinational (or transnational) corporations (MNCs or TNCs) in earlier chapters. These studies have demonstrated that the role played by MNCs or TNCs is central to the ongoing social engineering and economic and industrial project which is the complete domination of all countries in the world by corporate capitalist institutions. As we know, corporations such as Bechtel, General Electric, ExxonChevron, BP-Amoco, etc., rely to a great extent on the backing by, if not the instrumentalization of, national governmental institutions (see Chomsky 2000: 192–8). Simultaneously, the major economically 'regulatory' international agencies—the Bretton Woods institutions, such as the International Monetary Fund (IMF), the World Bank and later the World Trade Organization (WTO)—were set up under the aegis of both corporations and governments. Indeed, the WTO is partially a creation of the very bodies which are set to benefit most from its activities. In Johnson's telling characterization (2004: 269): "The WTO was created because the United States discovered that it could be created." (For discussion of how such organizations might be brought under more democratic control see the papers in Cavanagh, Wysham and Arruda (1994) and also George (2004) and Petras and Veltmeyer (2001).)

7 EUPHEMISMS, JUST A FORMALIST INTERLUDE?

In seeming to highlight communicative and discourse strategies, one could run the risk of reducing analysis of real world actions and events to merely formal patterns. A further danger is to be seen to be just seeking universal elements of human behaviour, perhaps in the service of supposedly disinterested science and scholarship. Ayto (1993: 1) in his dictionary of euphemisms might be an example of this tendency, where he states: "Euphemism is the set of communicative strategies we have evolved to refer to a topic under a taboo, without actually contravening its terms." This is to occupy an apolitical and neutral position. Later he rather euphemistically characterizes them as "the various ingenious lexical formulae that speakers of English have come up with to tiptoe around conversational danger areas." Despite this diffuse characterization his book does contain two sections which could be of interest to us: '11 Government and Politics' and '12 Warfare'. The mention of these subjects shows that there may be specific views of the world or ideologies at work in certain quarters.

A more robust approach to this issue is to ask (after Wenden 1995: 221) what aspects of the language system are utilized to communicate propositions or proposals and to convey the ideology that underlies them? Schäffner and Wenden, in the introduction to their volume on "Language and Peace", emphasize the not always explicitly stated truism that, in addition to providing access to our experience of the world, "[l]anguage can also disguise the world. It can channel access to it in a specific way or structure it according to particular and not always honourable aims and purposes" (1995: xiii). In contrast to Ayto, Wenden (1995: 223) is far less formal and abstract. Her definition gets straight to the point. "A euphemism is an alternative choice of word used to disguise something unpleasant or undesirable."

What speakers or writers wish to disguise are issues of a substantial nature. This is something both analysts and critically disposed citizens also need to sceptically scrutinize and question. There are parallels to be seen in observing the role of artistic activity in societies through history.

8   FORM VERSUS SUBSTANCE: A DIALECTICAL RELATIONSHIP?

'Impressing' is the first step towards 'suppressing' people, seen in terms of maintaining order by an authoritarian social or political élite or order. The role art plays in socialization is clearly significant, although it will vary and change from age to age and from society or culture to society or culture.

One might consider art and its historical function as a hegemonic statement in the service of domination. Monuments and spectacles come to mind. Consider the Mayan temples, the Aztec pyramids or the Incan palaces as examples. In Mesopotamia and in Egypt there are similar monuments. In medieval Europe we can adduce cathedrals, castles, palaces. The 17th century brought with it the Baroque churches in Austria and Bavaria. The idea that the 'whole' is greater than the sum of its constituents bringing in the phenomenon of the 'Gesamtkunstwerk' plays its part. The opera is a similar form, cf. Bayreuth and Wagner. Consider the Nürnberg Rally and films during the Third Reich (Leni Riefenstahl) and the similar employment in monarchical Britain of British pomp and circumstance. And now in the Media Age we have the orchestrated party conventions on TV or mass rock concerts. The semiotic modalities intermingle. Signs proliferate and predominate. What the *significance* of the signs is becomes secondary. Indeed signs turn out to be strangely 'immaterial'. As Fairclough (1995b: 150) asks with reference to the promotional function discourse may take up: "Does meaning [. . .] have primacy or is it subordinated to effect." Is language referring to an event, a book, an idea, or constructing it? It is interesting to see how swiftly these patterns have invaded or colonized all walks of life, as we once called them.

The role of photography and design also are examples of how art can be used in the service of power and/or persuasion. Alongside this we have also the creation of images, presentation of pictures and films in news broadcasts in the electronic media. Does the nature of the accompanying language serve to enhance and support the images or vice versa? Fairclough (1995b: 150) has commented on this contemporary trend: "the giving of information is taking place in a context where there is a premium on winning people to see things in a particular way." He observes that increasingly 'telling' is simultaneously 'selling'. It is as if the two activities are gelling! Clearly, the position of 'news', of 'information' in a Media Age is also undergoing a shift when seen against this background.

How something is said affects or influences what is said. Additionally, in keeping with Herman's power laws, 'who' says something clearly also affects 'what' is said and more importantly its probability or possibility of being said. This relational angle is linked or makes up part of the formal nature of signs. But to underline this link between the 'who', the 'how' and the 'what' is to show that the distinction between form and substance is not hard or fast.

In persuasive rhetorical terms this prevalent analytical or heuristic dichotomy is often invoked to allow people to shift the premises of their arguments or contributions in debates or conversations. Modern linguistics, informed by discourse analysis, takes as axiomatic or truistic that all language production or interaction with others involves 'evaluation'. The lexical or syntactic choices made by a writer or speaker are made (mostly?) unconsciously to encourage or influence in some way evaluatively tinted effects.

A seemingly extreme instance can serve to illustrate this. 'Name-calling' is an everyday activity which tends to directly demonstrate the close fit or even direct mapping between substance and form. On the other hand, euphemistic choices are a way of shifting focus from the substance to the forms and thus, for example, to displace the thrust of a dispute or distract the recipient's attention. It is a technique developed in persuasive rhetoric. Pragmatics shows how we gauge an audience, listeners and readers and how we stretch their credibility. Apologists for power interests employ oblique, vague and intractable language for the purpose of distracting, 'persuading' and leading up to their conclusions.

It is the way you do something that is focussed and rated highly in the Media Age. It is a throwback to pre-democratic, less rationally oriented societies and cultures, where the 'show', the manner in which something is presented or produced, is elaborated by rulers, priests, emperors to support the enforcement of obedience or deference. The shock and awe producing techniques have developed and adjusted to the predominantly electronic media. The imposition of capitalist consumerist 'values' serves to embody infantilistic, servile, and essentially subaltern behaviour patterns on the general populations of Western capitalist societies. The growth of what C. W. Mills (1959) refers to as the 'cultural apparatus' and others have closely analyzed, including Herbert Marcuse (1964) and Raymond Williams (1962), that is to say, the means of 'mass distraction' in the entertainments and sports sectors, is well-attested. The invasion of private space no longer takes place via the churches, but by means of the 'Taylorization' of leisure and the self-service mentality, which often entails the externalization of multiple costs from the seller to the buyer, in the last analysis.

All these elements function as it were in concert to 'pacify' and control the population. To take active citizenship out of everyday politics and replace it by the receptive and passive consumer, whose role echoes that of the command and control hierarchies of feudal and pre-feudal, tribal societies. The net results are to stabilize and reproduce almost neo-baroque and neo-conservative times. New Times really means nothing other than new forms for old substance. Nothing of substance is 'new'; it is simply form that is 'new'. Old wine in new bottles is the order of the day. The forces of mass distraction thus divert attention to 'brands', to labels, to images. As the Germans say, 'Etikettenschwindel' (manipulating the label) becomes the name of the game, and also the aim and substance of the game.

9 EUPHEMISMS AND PROPAGANDA: THE INTERCONNECTION

This section looks at the origins of propaganda and its institutional grounding today. We can begin by considering an obscene, propagandistic euphemism the US military have established, namely 'collateral damage'. In view of the Pentagon and the media using such phrases, David Barsamian asks Chomsky in an interview to talk about "the role of language in shaping and forming people's understanding of events." Linguistically trained discourse analysts unfamiliar with Chomsky's political writings might be surprised by the answer he gives—although on closer reflection, there need be no contradiction with discourse analysis at all. Chomsky answers (2005: 18–19):

> It has nothing much to do with language. Language is the way we interact and communicate so, naturally, people use the means of communication to try to shape attitudes and opinions and to induce conformity and subordination. This has been true forever, but propaganda became an organized and very self-conscious industry only in the last century.

He then makes a significant comment on where and when the propaganda 'industry' originated. "It is worth noting that this industry was created in the more democratic societies. The first coordinated propaganda ministry, the Ministry of Information, was set up in Britain during the First World War. Its 'task,' as they put it, was 'to direct the thought of most of the world'" (2005: 19). In the USA, as Chomsky then notes, "[t]he Wilson administration reacted by setting up the first state propaganda agency here, the Committee on Public Information. This is already Orwellian, of course." He talks about the work of Lasswell and how the term 'propaganda' was used in the 1930s. "People used the term *propaganda* openly then, before the association of the word with the Nazis; now people use various euphemisms" (2005: 23).

The discussion of Lasswell is reminiscent of Carey, who demonstrates the role of academia and academics in controlling and limiting democracy (1995: 81):

> From 1930 to 1960 Professor Harold Lasswell held a position of academic leadership in the field of propaganda and communication comparable with Bernays's leading role as a practitioner in the business world [. . .]. In 1933, in an article for the *Encyclopedia of the Social Sciences*, Lasswell *cynically observes that since the 'masses are still captive to ignorance and superstition', the arrival of democracy, in America and elsewhere, has 'compelled the development of a whole new technique of control, largely through propaganda'*. For propaganda, Lasswell continues, is 'the one means of mass mobilization which is cheaper than violence, bribery or other possible control techniques'. Moreover he held (in conformity with the corporate view) that *propaganda was essential in a democracy because 'men are often poor judges of their own interests' and must therefore be swayed by propaganda* to make choices they would otherwise not make. (my emphasis, RJA)

Carey goes on to comment that by 1947 social scientists and university departments were largely working on behalf of corporations.

10   ORWELLIAN: THE WORD

It is undoubtedly the case that George Orwell's novel *1984* has left a lasting impression on people in the English-speaking world who are sensitive to doublethink and its linguistic manifestation. This is also often called 'doublespeak', which is not a word Orwell used himself. One superficial indicator of his influence can be gauged simply by considering how widespread the notion and the use of the word 'Orwellian' have become in English.

The number of writers on politics and current affairs who employ the word might be cited, such as two whom I have already frequently referred to. Notice above that Chomsky called Wilson's Committee on Public Information "Orwellian". The US public relations industry was already developing the tools of propaganda in the 1920s "long before Orwell was writing", notes Chomsky (1988a: 671). Even Edward Herman uses it when commenting on one of the corporate-government euphemisms referring to a law which enables corporations to be free of legal sanctions for environmental infringements. He writes (1999a): "A federal version is being offered in the Senate under the Orwellian title 'The Environmental Protection Partnership Act'". And here is Robert Fisk, an intrepid British reporter on the illegal Iraq occupation, using the term in 2001: "We are engaging—an Orwellian cracker this, from the Pentagon on Friday night—in 'protective retaliation'." This itself comes in an article entitled "Locked in an Orwellian eternal war".

Given its currency it is not surprising to find the word glossed in Advanced Learners' Dictionaries for foreign learners of English. Oxford (2005: 1973) has the following entry: "adj. used to describe a political system in which a government tries to have complete control over people's behaviour and thoughts ORIGIN From the name of the English writer George Orwell, whose novel *1984* describes a government that has total control over the people."

To get an idea of its contemporary usage, I did a search of the Collins Wordbanks Online 45 million word corpus.[2] 'Orwellian' appeared 264 times. Several entries turn out to be double entries, but still the frequency of 5.8 per million (as contrasted with 'Orwellism' occurring only once!) shows that it is firmly established in the English-speaking world.

Looking at some of its collocations can tell us something about its associations (see Table 10.3 for a thirty-three-line extract). One of the most frequent right collocates is 'nightmare(s)' (with eighteeen occurrences). A selective extract from the concordance with some collocations highlighted can demonstrate the negative evaluative loading caused by right collocates such as nightmare(s), etc. The left collocates 'bleaker', 'chillingly', 'sinister', 'frightening', 'hideously' and 'grim' illustrate the horror vision associated with certain social and political developments. Predictably, 'newspeak', 'doublethink' and even 'doublespeak' (even though not coined by Orwell) occur in the concordance. The notion of rewriting history and also the names of public figures whom observers see as employing similar measures to those described by Orwell are also found in the concordances (see Table 10.3).

11 EXCURSUS: THE CONCERN WITH INEQUALITY AND FREEDOM OF SPEECH AND THE CONNECTIONS WITH LINGUISTICS

It is evident that to a great extent the way we relate to and participate as social beings in historical circumstances proceeds via language. But in the first instance our lives are lived in specific social formations in which extra-linguistic constraints may be held to be primary. Sociologists will speak of social structure, class and status groups. Economists will focus on property

Table 10.3 'Orwellian' Concordance from Collins Wordbanks Online (Extract)

out of Terry Gilliam's far bleaker	Orwellian satire, Brazil. However, like
January 17), is a classic piece of	Orwellian doublethink. <p> He wants us to
security. <p> Arguably the stuff of	Orwellian nightmares, biometrics is based
witnessing an intriguing case of	Orwellian double think, the famous ability
Blairite lexicon, priority is an	Orwellian word: all spending is prior but
Trying to rewrite history in this	Orwellian way will not help avoid the
Middle East. There was a chillingly	Orwellian quality to his proposal that
stick recently, for being sinister	Orwellian tools which not only monitor your
Big Brother lived up to the full	Orwellian horror of its name would be an
to the wider game as well as an	Orwellian corruption of language. <p> It
mature democracy. <p> A frightening	Orwellian world confronts us. We are
seen the beginnings of a kind of	Orwellian doublethink. Social inclusion
spokesman, said: 'This is an	Orwellian nightmare which the viewer would
Sir: There is something hideously	Orwellian about a situation in which
altered to fit the military junta's	Orwellian rewriting of Egyptian history.
of identity cards would not be some	Orwellian surveillance nightmare-it will
sized tapes. Ironically, such	Orwellian surveillance will be of little
We are being sucked into an	Orwellian nightmare," says one US-based
Give us bombs for peace." It is an	Orwellian juxtaposition. Yet the answer to '
David Andrews, as hypocrisy on an	Orwellian scale. There is no appeal
that would free people from a grim	Orwellian future. This year, Hotjobs, a
Nowhere to hide Are we living in an	Orwellian nightmare? Only the brave should
President Bush sounds distinctly	Orwellian when he urges Americans: 'Go
reread as a war against memory, an	Orwellian falsification of reality . . ."
for everyone else's statism. The	Orwellian 'New World Information Order"
the potential exists for an	Orwellian nightmare if the databases are
to a propaganda barrage of	Orwellian proportions. <p> On television
creating," he wrote. <p> 'One is an	Orwellian dimension of Authoritarianism
pure wind' rises to whirl away this	Orwellian shopping-list of Rightspeak. <p>
police the Eyes; this theological	Orwellian newspeak filters down into the
s part? Classic Newspeak in the	Orwellian mold? <p> In a brilliant public
with quite open U.S. consent, the	Orwellian name of "Peace for Galilee
Centre, which opened in 1986, is an	Orwellian sign: "Education Is Growth."

relations, connections between producers, as either capital holders or wage earners, and how the socially generated product is distributed and consumed. Linguists of the 'London School' (inspired by Firthian sociological linguistics)[3] will foreground how the context of situation of human interaction needs viewing against a much extended context of culture; both constituting the non-verbal environment of discourse and texts.[4] It is part of the professional deformation of academic disciplines which can lead scholars to consider as primary those objects they focus their attention on. When it is a matter of responding to the ways in which world events are mediated a plurality of methods is available.

We could take the issue of freedom of speech as a test case. What do linguists have to say about it? Very little, we might concur with Harris (1990). Indeed the preoccupations with universal grammar and the link with the underlying neurobiological bases that make language possible might appear to have removed freedom of speech from the agenda of a narrowly conceived linguistics. Harris accuses linguists of shirking their responsibility.[5] By focusing on abstract models and disregarding the particularized and contextualized nature of language use, considerations of speakers' rights and freedom of speech simply fail to show up on the radar of a 'linguist'. At no point in his essay does Harris mention Chomsky. The model he invokes is one of 'speech communication' associated with Saussure, Katz, Chafe, Denes and Pinson (see Harris 1990). That Chomsky frequently dons a philosopher's hat and reflects on language and freedom might appear to absolve him from criticism; see the 1970 paper 'Language and Freedom' reprinted in Chomsky (1973: 167–86). In this early talk Chomsky sets out his rationalist and libertarian credentials, quoting Descartes, Wilhelm von Humboldt and Jean-Jacques Rousseau among others.[6] As Harris argues, also invoking Rousseau alongside John Stuart Mill, the question of who is allowed to speak, how and about what is a valid set of issues for linguists to tackle (1990: 159). These issues relate to power and the nature of society.

So it is interesting to consider what the man whose work on generative grammar to a great extent reinforced this formal and inward turn in linguistics, Noam Chomsky, might have to say. Given that he has published more books on politics than linguistics, for many readers the connexion between the two fields of his very active life remains fascinating and even enigmatic. Social and political analysis requires little special knowledge, Chomsky claims. Asked about the connection between his linguistics and his politics, Chomsky (1979: 3) concedes that to a certain extent "they perhaps derive from certain common assumptions and attitudes with regard to basic aspects of human nature." And then he delivers an assessment of relevance to studying social and political issues. He says: "Critical analysis in the ideological arena seems to me to be a fairly straightforward matter as compared to an approach that requires a degree of conceptual abstraction. For the analysis of ideology, which occupies me very much, a bit of open-mindedness, normal intelligence, and healthy skepticism will generally suffice." Several scholars have attempted to make more explicit where the origin for this bifurcation in Chomsky's thinking is located. McGilvray (1999: 25) has highlighted the clear distinction Chomsky makes between common sense and scientific understanding. McGilvray maintains that once one grasps the scope of this divide, it "should make it easy to see why Chomsky thinks his political and his linguistic work are in different intellectual universes. Politics turns out to be within the intellectual range of all people" (1999: 25). Chomsky has been scathing about the role 'intellectuals' play in US life (see his earliest political essays in 1969). And he has often attacked status quo oriented scholarship because "quite commonly, social and political analysis is produced to defend special interests rather than to account for the actual events" (1979: 4). The conclusion to be drawn is that as a critical intellectual Chomsky cares very much indeed for issues such as inequality and freedom of speech around the world, as his innumerable appearances in, and participation in campaigns on, disparate countries such as Nicaragua, Turkey and East Timor are testimony to.

The position I would take is that the stance of activists (such as Chomsky, Curtis and others who are cited in this chapter) is complementary to the descriptive and analytical critical discourse work coming from academia. The synthesis between investigative journalists and publicists and broadcasters, on the one hand, and the critical, reflective and dialectical scholars on the other is most worthwhile and enlightening. It can provide a necessary and well-rounded out picture of the social, economic and political world (with all its real, material antagonisms and disharmonies)—a far cry from some of the ideological nonsense that academia, the media and political and commercial élites would prefer us to accept at face value.

And after all, there are academics, like Halliday, whose work sets out to demonstrate the explicit link between linguistic mechanisms and political processes in the broadest sense. Moreover it can be interesting to compare the views of Halliday and Chomsky on certain topics. For some readers the closeness of their insights might appear remarkable. Let us first take the "unmentionable five-letter word" (Chomsky 1994a)—'class'—as the first example. The emphasis made in the following extracts is mine.

Halliday on social classes	Chomsky on the "unmentionable five-letter word"—class
Halliday writes (1990: 16–7): "When Hasan shows that mothers of boys use a different code from mothers of girls, she is praised for having added a new dimension to our understanding of language and	Chomsky (1994b: 106): "*In the United States you're not allowed to talk about class differences*. In fact, only two groups are allowed to be class conscious in the United States. One of them is the business community, which is rabidly class conscious. When you read their literature, it's all full of the danger

sex. When she shows by the same linguistic techniques that working class mothers use a different code from middle class mothers, *she is criticized on the grounds that there are no such things as social classes*, and (somewhat self-contradictorily) that anyway mothers and children do not belong to them."

of the masses and their rising power and how we have to defeat them. It's kind of vulgar Marxist, only inverted. The other is the high planning sector of the government. So they're full of it too. [. . .] But it's extremely important to make other people, the rest of the population, believe that there is no such thing as class. We're all just equal. We're all Americans. We live in harmony. We all work together. Everything is great."

Secondly consider Halliday and Chomsky on racism and sexism vs. class differences. Note the identical assessment of how they relate to the capitalist political economy.

Halliday (1990: 16–7):

David Barsamian says, "You say that class transcends race, essentially."

"It is acceptable to show up sexism—as it is to show up racism—because to eliminate sexual and racial bias would pose no threat to the existing social order: *capitalist society could thrive perfectly well without sex discrimination and without race discrimination*. But it is not acceptable to show up classism, especially by objective linguistic analysis as Hasan as done; because capitalist society could not exist without discrimination between classes. Such work could, ultimately, threaten the existing order of society."

Chomsky answers (1994b: 109–110): "For example, *the United States **could** become a color-free society*. It's possible. I don't think it's going to happen, but it's perfectly possible that it would happen, and *it wouldn't change the political economy, hardly at all. Just as you could remove the 'glass ceiling' for women and that wouldn't change the political economy at all*. That's one of the reasons why you quite commonly find the business sector reasonably willing, often happy to support efforts to overcome racism and sexism. *It basically doesn't matter that much*. You lose a little white male privilege, but that's not all that important. On the other hand, basic changes in the core institutions would be bitterly resisted, if they ever became thinkable."

What these quotations show when displayed together is a singularly close political agreement on the structure of capitalist society. At the same time they arguably support what the linguist Raphael Salkie has written on the connections between politics and linguistics in Chomsky's work (1990: 203):

The ways in which language is used in society, and the ways that social class distinctions and other oppressive structures are encoded and reproduced by language, are not matters that Chomsky's linguistics concentrates on. So even if linguistics can be connected with politics, there are good reasons not to look for close parallels between *Chomsky's* linguistics and his politics.

For Chomsky, however, social class distinctions and other oppressive structures are certainly driving forces in his political activism, explicable from his biography.[7]

12 ORWELLIAN TIMES?

What insights can an Orwellian slant on (the language of) propaganda provide? Are we not living in Orwellian times, some commentators claim? This raises the further question of how long we have already been experiencing such times. As we saw, Noam Chomsky explicitly uses the term "Orwellian". The 'engineering of consent' was being practised in democracies before Orwell fictionalized state propaganda in *1984*. For Chomsky it is "not a very good book, incidentally, a very bad book" (1988a: 672). Nonetheless the British linguists Hodge and Fowler claim that George Orwell's *1984* has affected the general consciousness about language (1979: 25): "Not many books by linguists have been able to alter a whole society's understanding of the role of language in its basic political and social processes", as much as Orwell's writings. A little earlier the same authors speculate on what Orwell's book actually referred to (1979: 7): "Was he really predicting a horrific totalitarian society growing out of the rule of the post-war Labour government ('Ingsoc' from 'English socialism')?"

Perhaps the responses to George Orwell's work can serve as a further rallying point for linguists like Paul Chilton who put their academic work of socially useful linguistics in the service of activist causes and are interested in "the interaction between language and social processes". If this is the case they will have "to take into account the unequal distribution of power in institutionalised communication settings" as Chilton (1988: 99) puts it. So the issue of freedom of expression and speech *is* right at the centre of attention in the case of "public discourse [. . .] mediated by television, radio, newspapers, official publications." Here we must consider "limitations on rights to take turns, rights to issue information, express attitudes, challenge assertions, and so on" Chilton (1988: 99). (Cf. also Herman's (1992) Power Laws mentioned above.)

The book these quotations are taken from is entitled *Orwellian Language and the Media*. Indeed, it is striking how a number of academics from various disciplines have taken Orwell's writings on propaganda and language as an impetus to adopt a critical stance on the phenomena and actions he highlighted (in his novels). This includes culture theorists (like Raymond Williams), social psychologists (Alex Carey) and linguists (Paul Chilton). In particular, British linguists who have been inspired by the functional theories of language of Michael Halliday can be adduced. Fowler et al. claimed that Halliday's work meshed in well with their "aims in insisting that the functions of linguistic structures are based on social structure" (1979: 3).

13   ON FREEDOM OF SPEECH AND LANGUAGE CONTROL: ORWELL'S VIEW

Williams' chapter on Orwell in *Culture and Society* identifies him as a figure of paradox, essentially trying to live humanely in an inhumane society (1958). For Williams "[t]he total effect of Orwell's work is an effect of paradox." One particular paradox of Orwell he notes is that "[h]e was a socialist, who popularized a severe and damaging criticism of the idea of socialism and of its adherents. He was a believer in equality, and a critic of class, who founded his later work on a deep assumption of inherent inequality, inescapable class difference" (1958: 277). And yet Williams can write of Orwell (1971: 76): "His vision of power politics is also close and convincing. The transposition of official 'allies' and 'enemies' has happened, almost openly, in the generation since he wrote." And, arguably, it continues to this day, as we mentioned above in relation to 'dropped' friendly dictators! Williams found the global division into three blocs "of which two are always at war with the third [. . .] again too close for comfort." Citizens of the 3rd millennium also! Nor can there be little dispute with Williams' judgement on the role of Britain today: "And there are times when one can believe that what 'had been called England or Britain' has become simply Airstrip One" (1971: 76). Despite such projections being generally recognizable, not everything, however, can be taken as being apt.

In particular, Williams sees one of the failures of *1984* in the treatment of the 'proles' as subhuman masses, among other features (1971: 78ff). And certainly we know how this attitude has been used and continues to be used by the reactionary forces in society to exclude people from participating fully in social and political life. The Australian social psychologist Alex Carey has commented very soberly in a paper written in 1987 and tellingly entitled 'The Orwell Diversion': "the danger has always come from the Respectable Right. It has come in the form of a widespread social and political indoctrination, an indoctrination which promotes business interests as everyone's interests and in the process fragments the community and closes off individual and critical thought" (1995: 133–4).

Carey's own work (1995: 138) demonstrated "the growth of propaganda sponsored by industry as a means for managing democracy until it became by 1950 a significant American industry in its own right". He continues by detailing one of the sinister activities these people engaged in: "This

Orwellian industry combined an intensive surveillance of public opinion to detect early signs of ideological drift and the employment of a large corpus of experts from all the social science professions on the refinement and dissemination of corrective persuasion through all media and all parts of the society."

As we shall see, the messages Orwell set out to transmit particularly in his fiction were not always clear. That it could be utilized by some of the very people he wished to attack is a point Carey makes (1995: 139): "Whatever Orwell's intentions, his work has been exploited so as to misdirect and confuse the public into looking in the wrong places for the 'brainwashing' instinctively felt by many. [. . .] Almost forty years after Orwell wrote *1984* no writer has attempted to update it so as to make clear the seriousness of Orwell's misguidance for democratic societies."

Despite the reservations, Raymond Williams' judgement on Orwell's work is of relevance to our thesis. It echoes Carey's. "Soon after his death Orwell became, in effect, a 'symbolic figure'" (Williams 1971: 83). In particular the Right could employ both *Animal Farm* and *1984* to combat the socialist revival in Europe after the Second World War. Orwell himself emphasized his desire to destroy the myth of Soviet society that he felt was common among left intellectuals in the West in the 1940s (Williams 1971: 70). His experiences fighting on the Republican side in the Spanish Civil War had not made him a friend of Stalinism. The ambivalence in Orwell's writings which several commentators detect may allow a more nuanced reading, however. Particularly in the case of *1984*, many elements of which "belong to a more liberating consciousness" in Williams' judgement (1971: 74). Of especial interest for our purposes is Williams' singling out of the Appendix 'The Principles of Newspeak'. For Williams "its central perception of a relation between linguistic and social forms is powerful" (1971: 75). It is worth recalling that in an earlier analysis Williams saw a paradox in Orwell's treatment of propagandistic language. "He was a notable critic of abuse of language, who himself practised certain of its major and typical uses" (1958: 277). A little later Williams, however, demonstrates that Orwell was supporting freedom of speech: "His attacks on the denial of liberty are admirable: we have all, through every loyalty, to defend the basic liberties of association and expression, or we deny man" (1958: 281).

This is to situate Orwell in a long Anglo-Saxon tradition which we do well, in times of near draconian restrictions on civil liberties in so-called Western democracies, to continue to uphold. It is encouraging to see Roy Harris, Oxford emeritus professor of general linguistics, reiterating in a public forum, 'Speaking out for the right to speak evil' (*The Times Higher*) (2005), the main arguments he made in a specialist context (Harris 1990) referred to above. Harris argues that universities have a duty to allow even repugnant racist doctrines to be heard, "because freedom of speech is required by freedom of inquiry". His final thought fits in with Mill's ideas in *On Liberty* (1859). This is a position he shares with Chomsky.[8] "Before we enforce restrictions on freedom of speech as a way of defeating 'extremists', we should ask ourselves whether we wish to join them" (Harris 1990). Again the relevance of the Orwellian position for today's growing self-censorship and intolerance is clear.

Let us return to the Appendix on Newspeak in *1984* and its function. For Hodge and Fowler (1979: 20) it is obvious "that this is a satire on language-planners and experts on language, not a prediction about developments in the English language." Williams would disagree with this assessment, shrewdly spotting in the 1970s that the jargon of "'modernization'—that extraordinary substitute for social democracy which the British Labour Government adopted and propagated in the sixties—is almost wholly Newspeak" (1971: 75). Fairclough's investigation of the language of New Labour (2000) demonstrates the continuity of the insight into this trend, which would have had Raymond Williams' assent (he died in 1988, too soon to personally experience it), I am sure. Fairclough (2000: 157) underlines the fact that "language is a very important part of the action in the social practice of government—much of the action of government *is* language." Fairclough appears to echo Williams when he writes: "it is true [. . .] that New Labour seeks to reconcile in language what cannot be reconciled in reality given their commitment to neo-liberalism—neo-liberal 'enterprise' and 'social justice'—that also enhances the importance of political discourse" (2000: 157–8).[9]

14   A CRITICAL ANALYSIS OF LANGUAGE AS AN INSTRUMENT OF POLITICAL CONTROL IS ORWELLIAN

Fowler et al. (1979: 2–3) acknowledge that "Orwell recognized some of the connections between language, ideas and social structure which are at the centre of our argument, and in his novel *1984* he explored the notion that language-structure could be mobilized to control or limit thought" in their preface. As they say: "His concepts of 'doublethink', 'newspeak' and 'duckspeak' rest on recognizable principles of language-patterning." Perhaps such a linguistic approach would be of direct value in a critical account of contemporary culture. Take Hodge and Fowler's comment on *1984* (1979: 6): "[F]or a novel which has had such an impact on our general consciousness about the language of politics, *1984*'s analysis of this topic is curiously underestimated. It is as if the talismanic words 'Newspeak', 'reality control' and 'doublethink' have passed too quickly into the English language." How would Chomsky's work fit in here? Considering the role of language in propaganda alongside the other devices of Western propaganda systems can be of benefit. Even if the focus is not explicitly on the forms of language for Chomsky, Chilton shows a shared concern and orientation with Chomsky, writing (1988: 79): "The purpose of these propaganda systems is, to quote Noam Chomsky [(1979: 38)], 'to fix the limits of possible thought'." Chomsky's very words themselves are reminiscent of the creatively destructive 'lexicographer', Smythe, who tells Winston in *1984* (Orwell 1949: 45) that "the whole aim of Newspeak is to narrow the range of thought".

Hodge and Fowler (1979: 24) hold that Orwell saw "clearly that the social structure acts on every aspect of personal behaviour, affecting active and passive linguistic experience. He was concerned especially with one aspect of social structure, inequality in the distribution of power." Given two social classes at odds with each other:

> It is the material interests of the [. . .] group [in power] to maintain their authority over the second (and to persuade them that it really is in their best interests not to challenge this authority). The central asymmetry— *society is organized upon a principle of unequal power*—is sustained through a vast repertoire of behavioural convictions which relate role to role, status to status, institution to individual. In linguistic behaviour, Orwell saw this principle realized through forms of public communication. Newspapers, governments, bureaucracies and intellectuals cannot risk telling the truth because doing so might give others access to their power base. (1979: 24)

Hodge and Fowler insist (1979: 25): "In all these beliefs Orwell seems to us to have been essentially correct". Such Orwellian insights have to be repeated today, perhaps more so. It should be the task of linguists to "make a systematic study of the relations Orwell was concerned with". Linguistic analysis can uncover "ideological processes and complex states of mind." Like Orwell, Chilton examines (1988: vii) "language as an instrument of political control" but from a linguistic perspective. In short, an Orwellian linguistics will be a 'critical' linguistics directed at language practices which are instrumental in maintaining social inequality and the concealment of truth. According to Fowler et al. (1979: 2) the control of members of subordinate groups by members of dominant groups is partially facilitated by sociolinguistic mechanisms. They understand their book "as a contribution to the unveiling of linguistic practices which are instruments in social inequality and the concealment of truth" (1979: 2).

Here of course we need to recall that Herman's power laws are first and foremost, sustaining the rich and powerful. Chilton notes (1988: 39) that after all "[t]he ultimate achievement" [for interest groups] would be to have their vocabulary taken over in popular usage. Consider the contemporary case of 'climate change' tending to replace 'global warming', which sounds more threatening (see Poole 2006: 42–9). We are thinking here of "the public use of contemporary English by powerful individuals and organisations" (Cook 2006: 2). It is the task of an Orwellian critical linguistics to subject such public use of language whether by politicians or commercial corporations to close scrutiny.

In previous chapters of this book we, too, have demonstrated some of the mechanisms and the tools used. They include, in the first instance, selection of grammatical constructions, such as nominalization, that exclude explicit reference to causes, agents, time and place. Also we have highlighted the preference for particular words and metaphors helping to conceal certain aspects of reality and directing attention at others. Riding on the surface appearance of such discourse and the assumptions inherent in it, space is thus created for doctrinal messages to be passed on, almost unnoticed.

What Chomsky has referred to as Orwell's problem (see above) comes into play at this point. Chomsky (1986) has illustrated this by discussing concrete examples, such as the so-called debate between the 'hawks' and the 'doves' during the Vietnam War and the US intervention in El Salvador and Nicaragua in the 1980s. As Chomsky shrewdly argues (1986: 281): "The nature of Western systems of indoctrination was not perceived by Orwell and is typically not understood by dictators, who fail to comprehend the utility for propaganda of a critical stance that incorporates the basic assumptions of official doctrine and thereby marginalizes authentic and rational critical discussion, which must be blocked. There is rarely any departure from this pattern." Reading about the selective reporting of massacres in Central America in the 1980s under Reagan, one realizes that disinformation techniques have not changed much in nearly forty years. A recent book by Chomsky demonstrates how persistently successful the system has remained (Chomsky 2006). Perhaps the only hope is that the level of awareness of ordinary citizens in the world about the true purpose of the 'war on terror' is rising. And together with the assistance of new technologies, providing alternative sources of information, this can assist in the build up of internationalist opposition to what is going on. As John Pilger (2006) argues, there are several countries where the people are successfully resisting the powerful, especially in South America.

15 HOW DETERMINISTIC IS LANGUAGE?

To argue as in the previous section is to negate linguistic determinism. Indeed one of the weaknesses of the Orwellian legacy is to suggest that thought control can be definitively implemented and to support those who are proponents of a theory of human malleability. "The basic premise of the Newspeak programme is a very crude form of linguistic determinism, that is, the belief that language completely determines thought. In linguistics, thinkers like Whorf have developed subtle forms of this theory, but the view in the Appendix is not subtle" (Hodge and Fowler 1979: 20–21). There are a number of contradictions in *1984* which Hodge and Fowler notice (1979: 22). The role of Newspeak is not really developed and integrated imaginatively into the novel, after all. If Newspeak can really control thought, why have to manufacture the news? Yet Orwell was presumably glossing his experience of working at the BBC during the Second World War. And for Williams (1971: 75), "the techniques of news management sound [. . .] familiar. The Fiction Department, as an institution, would now hardly even be noticed."

Why bother to work on the Newspeak dictionary, if thought crime can be prevented via language? Although, more correctly, Orwell describes Newspeak as aiming to make "other modes of thought impossible." It is here that we see two features abutting. Firstly, Orwell's wish to chronicle personal, working experience of how propaganda machines (like wartime BBC departments and Soviet institutions) operate overrides his ability to convincingly fictionalize such elements. But, secondly, and more importantly as historical experiences of resistance have shown and, as stated, continue to show, totalitarian and authoritarian regimes can be overthrown. This is the hope and the anthropological insight which some of Habermas' (1971) writing on communication,[10] in particular his concept of communicative competence and the ideal speech situation, underlines. Chilton (1988: 26) has usefully and very lucidly paraphrased this as having "two key components: it is posited as an explanation of human ability to engage in any speech encounter, and it is posited as an explanation of the ability of humans to recognize distortion, deceptions and oppression." Hence this ability of humans 'to recognize distortion, deceptions and oppression' is presumably in a complementary relationship with the human potential for freedom of speech. And it is this which leads many linguists to question a strongly Whorfian deterministic position despite its seemingly explanatory value in other circumstances. Certainly, a weaker position about language 'influencing' thinking and perceiving seems to be a part of received wisdom which anyone who has struggled to master a foreign language will subscribe to. Thus with Chilton (1988: 47) we can agree "it would be rash to jettison Orwell's original insight—that language can be used in some way to control thought (particularly where ideology is concerned)." We need to explicate what the phrase 'in some way to control thought' can mean, however.

One feature linguists have accented are presuppositions. Even journalists like Poole are aware of this, observing how all words and phrases carry some unexpressed presuppositions or 'unspoken' arguments (2006: 3). Certain choices, such as the anti-abortionist groups' 'pro-life' self-naming, seem to be aiming to avoid having to justify certain positions. Poole goes on to describe what is a commonplace of systemic functional theory, namely: "Every word arrives at the ear cloaked in a mist of associations and implications; and every choice of a particular word represents a decision not to use another one" (2006: 3). This, fascinatingly, echoes a passage in Kress (1989: 446) in which he discusses significant factors affecting the relationship between language and social structure: "One, which is central to systemic functional linguistics, is the characterization of meaning as choice from sets of systems in specific contexts. This makes all linguistic form the effect of (deliberate) choice." The systemic insight into the role that grammatical form plays in constraining choices, such that "every choice of a particular word represents a decision not to use another one", is important. But once we extend it to the Hallidayan notions of 'meaning potential' and 'social semiotic' (Halliday 1978) it becomes evident that the social semiotic is not a prison; grammatical form does not tell us what to say. It may provide a range of possibilities of what we can mean, can say and thus can do. And in Edward Sapir's memorable and ambivalent phrasing (1921: 38): "Unfortunately, or luckily, no language is tyrannically consistent. All grammars leak." It is impossible to exclude human actions, intentions and interests finding their expression in the final analysis.

Chilton doubts the validity of the 'consensus' view of people's communicative ability "that languages are tacit conventions between members of the speech community as a whole" (1988: 52). Bolinger can be cited as a representative of this school of thought (1980: 22): "The words we use are the words that are *there*; we can only choose from them, rarely invent them." Although, interestingly, a sentence later he does allow that "we can put them together more or less as we please." The phrase, "more or less as we please" suggests that a conflictive or contestational view, in Chilton's terms, "a dynamic jostling for competing forms of language", appears more appropriate.

Support for this position can be adduced from several quarters, firstly, George Lakoff's framing position derived from cognitive linguistics (1996, 2005). Secondly, of course, it can be adduced from the sociological factor of power, particularly as highlighted by the Foucauldian turn in discourse analysis (see Fairclough 1992). Here we can mention the language of sexual differences and sexual dominance which feminists like Deborah Cameron (2006) have made us aware of. Also Van Dijk (1995) adopts a differential view of speakers and consumers' abilities to interpret texts. In other words, it is by now a truism that different groups nominally speaking the 'same' language can be shown to be speaking 'differently'. This slippage or 'drift', to use Sapir's word, allows us to focus on the dynamics of change and to question static, 'harmonious' models of language use. Sapir's comments on diachronic language change are worth revisiting. Although Sapir's focus was mostly on sound change, his remarks can be seen to apply both to social change more generally and synchronic language variation, when he speaks (1921: 171) of "the invisible and impersonal drift that is the life of language."

16   THE SOCIAL SEMIOTIC IS NOT A PRISON: AWARENESS PROVIDES THE EXIT

The interim conclusion that language influences thought and action makes us speculate as to what extent this can occur. Chilton does allow that "it *is possible* to think your way round received words" (1988: 79). However, he surmises that "most people don't or won't think round or beyond the language they consume, or maybe have not acquired the skill to do so. So they use whatever words and phrases they are given and endlessly exchange the concepts attached to them." From a Hallidayan perspective it is a truism that language, through the lexico-grammar, partially encodes a view of the world. So, dialectically speaking, when one activates the language one knows, specific attitudes and beliefs may well be channelled or bolstered. This still leaves room for freedom of speech and expression. Other cognitive powers and mental capacities alongside language play a role. Chomsky would doubtless argue that people just need to use their common sense in order to see through "interest-laden concepts".

Even Winston in *1984* is capable of doing this. In a canteen scene (Orwell 1949: 44) Winston hears a "harsh gabble almost like the quacking of a duck." 'Duckspeak' is the language of party hacks, Hodge and Fowler (1979: 18) note. Its manifestations are by no means restricted to political language however. As Hodge and Fowler (1979: 8) indicate, "political and commercial language is often mendacious, pretending to deliver the goods" but like Duckspeak "just giving vent to noise." Language-aware people make use of the Orwellian yardstick to critique and contest the discourse engineering that they experience in their working lives in society. But citizens' capabilities clearly vary in their power to reduce or prevent it. Otherwise how else can we explain the apparently institutionalized persistence of such features in political life, business and the media in general? At the same time, contemporary appreciation of this set of behaviours and processes, in the English-speaking world, is fairly widespread in certain circles. The frequent appearance of publications highlighting and mostly satirizing these tendencies in the modern world—even by philosophers, like Harry G. Frankfurt (2005), *On Bullshit*—is testimony to the ubiquitous nature of the phenomenon (see Beckwith 2006, Busch 2005, Newbrook 2005 and Poole 2006). Busch (2005: 32), for example, claims that "business-speak is running amok".

Such awareness is not new.[11] In the USA the National Council of Teachers of English and especially its Committee on Public Doublespeak, founded in 1971, are among "many signs of growing irritation and alarm at the spread of obscure language", as Dwight Bolinger (1980: 125) commented. Later Bolinger appears, however, to underplay the power and control element involved in "jargon—gobbledegook—doubletalk—doublespeak" on the part of officials. To be sure, he provides very many juicy examples of such duckspeak or bullshit—although his terms are far more restrained—but his assessment of the phenomenon is singularly elitist. This becomes visible, for example, when he states (1980: 134): "Jargon at its worst is partly a product of unfinished education, and if we have more of it today, one reason is that we have more half-educated people in a position to afflict the public with their words—and, as often as not, a wish to hide something."

The next chapter (11) will focus more closely on the military ramifications of that wish to hide something.

11 Concluding Obfuscation and Disinformation

1 THE MILITARIZATION OF RHETORIC: THE 'PERMANENT WAR ECONOMY'

At this point we can turn to an area where, on the part of the powerful, the wish to hide something is very forceful. This is the case where language control is employed in the service of the military powers and for war purposes. Orwell's work for the BBC during the Second World War clearly sensitized him to this usage and informs his late fiction. Hodge and Fowler (1979: 22) see the work on the Newspeak dictionary as corresponding "to the use of war as an economic strategy. The 'war' guarantees full employment to the Proles, by generating endless useless tasks, such as the building of successive floating fortresses, each one scrapped as obsolete before it is used (ibid.: 155). Outer Party members are similarly engaged in totally futile enterprises. Winston's own job is a case in point. He rewrites past copies of *The Times*."

For many of us the persistent use of war as an economic strategy by countries like the USA and UK has accompanied most of our lives, often unbeknown, much as it did the citizens of Eurasia. Given the lexicalization of 'cold' and 'war' and hence the corresponding shift in meaning of 'peace', practically reducing it to a null-term, whole populations were prepared for the ideology of cold war and deterrence. Several linguists, like Chilton, directed their work in the 1980s at the debate about nuclear weapons and deterrence and what Chilton termed 'nukespeak'. Chilton claims (1988: 50), "It is [. . .] above all on the level of phrases that the existing language can be remotivated to yield categorisations of reality that are in the interests of specific ideologies." Nearly twenty years after the protests against the stationing of Pershing rockets, the propagandistic pronouncements of politicians like Reagan and Thatcher appear remarkably close to the rhetoric of the 'War on Terror.' Recall that Reagan declared a 'war on terrorism' in 1985 (Chomsky 1988b and 2001: 68). The result of this is that, as Chilton put it (1988: 53), "[e]xisting language is processed, subjected to numerous semantic readjustments, and fed back to the population predominantly via the media." Lakoff's notion of framing again comes to mind here. See especially his study (Lakoff 2005) 'War on Terror: Rest In Peace'.

The ongoing real world, material basis for this ideological smokescreen is the permanent war economy. The American historian Chalmers Johnson has this to say on disinformation and the US Pentagon system (2004: 119): "The military's extreme fetish for secrecy and disinformation—the dissemination of plausible but false data—makes a farce of congressional oversight." He subjects the continuous growth of militarism to very detailed scrutiny and historical documentation. Johnson's analysis leaves us in no doubt concerning both the contemporary scope and objectives of the US military. In 1995 we could have read this for ourselves in the National Military Strategy of the United States of America, if we had seen fit to (see Joint Chiefs of Staff 1995). The Strategy "emphasizes worldwide *engagement* and *enlargement* of the community of free market democracies" (ibid.: i). (See also the White House 1996.)

For Chilton the fact that media rhetoric has become militarized (1988: 72) "is part of the general militarisation of our economic and social life in the age of the military-industrial complex."[1] The British role in this permanent war economy is worth looking at.[2] Chilton (1988: 41–2) discusses the Falklands war of 1982. He shows how the Thatcher government, "with the support of the media, effectively ruled criticism of that war off-side, together with any perception of the links between that war and the economic and political situation at home." As he states, "The war itself was not necessary; it was a symbol in political discourse." He shows how war was conceptualized metaphorically in terms of the world of work, 'war-as-business', during the Falklands War. Fighting was undertaken by a 'Task Force', while soldiers became resources and were 'poured in' or 'pulled out'.

This is where Orwell can be brought in again. In *1984* Winston gets hold of a heretical text, 'The Theory and Practice of Oligarchical Collectivism' (a term used by Borkenau) written by Emmanuel Goldstein (a not very thinly disguised allusion to Trotsky). Here we find passages that capture remarkably accurately developments we are experiencing in our own times. The passages on continuous war ring especially eerie. Take this quote from Goldstein's book for example (Orwell 1949: 160):

> The war, [. . .] though it is unreal it is not meaningless. It eats up the surplus of consumable goods, and it helps to preserve the special mental atmosphere that a hierarchical society needs. [. . .] [T]he object of the war is not to make or prevent conquests of territory, but to keep the structure of society intact.

In view of Johnson's (2004) book, Blum's chapter 17 (2003: 125–67) 'A Concise History of United States Global Interventions, 1945 to the Present' and Curtis' list of British military activities since 1945 (2003b: 441–5), another passage still reverberates most virulently today (Orwell 1949: 160): "The very word 'war', therefore, has become misleading. It would probably be accurate to say that by becoming continuous war has ceased to exist."

In a talk during the London 'Stop the War conference' at the School of Oriental and African Studies, in 2002, the British writer on international affairs Mark Curtis (2002) explicitly demonstrated how propaganda carried out by the British government is supported by the media. It is interesting how standard features of disinformation, silence and avoidance strategies associated with Orwellian mechanisms are employed. In particular his use of the term 'framing' shows the family resemblance with Lakoff's cognitive view (1996: 372–3) and what he has unearthed in his many 'political interventions' (Lakoff 1991, 2005, Chilton and Lakoff 1995 and Lakoff, Ferguson and Ettlinger 2006):

> There are various ways the media distorts the reality of Britain's foreign policy:
> by framing discussion within narrow parameters
> by ignoring and not explaining relevant history
> by parroting government statements and offering no counter to them
> by not mentioning some issues at all. (Curtis 2002)

The media do not openly discuss available statements from government sources, to take the last point. Curtis quotes from a government document called 'The future strategic context for defence'. The authors state that "we need to be aware of the ways in which public attitudes might shape and constrain military activity". The strangely undemocratic presupposition that citizens' ('public') opinions 'constrain' unnaturally what military practices a government engages in can only surprise someone who is not aware that in the British constitution there is no need to ask Parliament for 'permission' to go to war. It just looks better if British governments do so! But the considerable evidence of often not doing so has been amassed by Curtis (2003b) himself. Of course, in the context of actively canvassing support for opposition to the Iraq war, which was in the offing at the time of his talk, Curtis optimistically expects his unearthing of propagandistic machinations to help prevent war. Unfortunately, we know that one clear analysis such as we quote below can hardly withstand the combined effort of not only the Murdoch-owned press and TV. Let us quote Curtis citing from and commenting on the document already mentioned (2002):

> It says that: 'A public desire to see the UK act as a force for good, is likely to lead to public support, and possibly public demand, for operations prompted by humanitarian motives'. Therefore, 'public support will be vital to the conduct of military interventions'. In future, 'more effort will be required to ensure that such public debate is properly informed'. The meaning of this is clear: government propaganda will tell us that the government is acting from humanitarian motives because this is the way of securing public support. It is interesting to see a government openly commit itself to lying.

Contemporary political élites appear to be following a closely studied Orwellian template, we might surmise. 'Uncertainty' and its accomplice 'fear' are being sown almost daily with the complicit aid of most of the mainstream media. As we know from history (and Orwell), uncertainty and its creation are part of everyday political practice. History teaches us that all tyrants were (are?) concerned only with deploying tyranny's favourite weapons: uncertainty and terror. Under these circumstances Goldstein's analysis (Orwell 1949: 155) does more than hit the nail on the head, we might claim: "the consciousness of being at war, and therefore in danger, makes the handing-over of all power to a small caste seem the natural, unavoidable condition of survival." And we are now witnessing the almost daily restrictions on our civil liberties following this pattern as a consequence.

While Orwell's projections in *1984* about the worldviews now sound very outdated, the general scenario appealing to 'morality and common sense' and how to deal with enemies closely matches present day tendencies (1949: 158–9):

> In Oceania the prevailing philosophy is called Ingsoc, in Eurasia it is called Neo-Bolshevism, and in Eastasia it is called by a Chinese name usually translated as Death-Worship, but perhaps better rendered as Obliteration of the Self. The citizen of Oceania is not allowed to know anything of the tenets of the other two philosophies, but he is taught to execrate them as barbarous outrages upon morality and common sense.

Today's ruling élites in Western democracies committed to imperial hegemony in the world also know that it is necessary that the war should continue everlastingly and without victory.

> And, as usual, the ruling groups of all three powers are simultaneously aware and unaware of what they are doing. Their lives are dedicated to world conquest, but they also know that it is necessary that the war should continue everlastingly and without victory. Meanwhile the fact that there *is* no danger of conquest makes possible the denial of reality which is the special feature of Ingsoc and its rival systems of thought. Here it is necessary to repeat what has been said earlier, that by becoming continuous war has fundamentally changed its character.

Lakoff (2005) has noted that the "war frame is all-consuming". As in *1984* it "takes away focus from other problems, from everyday troubles, from jobs, education, health care, a failing economy." Once the frame is in place it justifies "the spending of huge sums, [. . .] the deaths of tens of thousands of innocent civilians, [. . .] torture, military tribunals, and no due process." And it "justifies scaring people, with yellow, orange, and red alerts." Then he argues "the war frame never fit the reality of terrorism. It was successful at consolidating power, but counterproductive in dealing with the real threat."

Again this is pure *1984*! Where Lakoff's analysis differs, or so he claims, "the war frame includes an end to the war—winning the war, mission accomplished!" It is a worthwhile political argument and as an academic turned activist with the foundation of the Rockridge Institute[3] praiseworthy indeed. But he may well be overestimating the power of retention and memory on the part of media consumers today. Who remembers what happened (or was deliberately falsely reported, via disinformation, more likely) three days ago, let alone over a year ago? Lakoff wishes to make the point that "The 'War on Terror' is no more. It has been replaced by the 'global struggle against violent extremism.'" This coincided with the July 7, 2005 bombings in London, and was perhaps the reason for Bush invoking it in the first place. Here we see Orwellian semantic engineering in full flight at any rate.

There are also British academics intervening with their scholarly work in current political debates. David Keen, a London School of Economics (LSE) lecturer, provides an analysis which soberly reflects and gives credence to the Orwellian scenario laid out above (2006b: 16):

> My research suggests that prolonging a war—whether civil or global— can be more important than winning it. In terms of the War on Terror, the military-industrial complexes of the Cold War are neatly maintained while political opposition in the US and its allies can be stigmatised for having 'sympathy with the devil'. [. . .] Those who sell us the War on Terror must first sell us the fear. Their failure to make us safer, paradoxically, increases our demand for their bogus solutions. Thus, failure magically transforms into success. Just as consumerism has not been defeated by its inability to fulfil the promises of advertising, so it is with the War on Terror. If skilfully manipulated, frustrated desires can be encouraged to focus on some new product, some new pledge that is also unlikely to be fulfilled. It all hinges on forgetting. [. . .] In this endless (but not aimless) war, we must always be seen to be winning. But we can never be seen to have won.

Many points of contact between ongoing analysis and commentary on contemporary events and those of the past forty years or so come to mind (Keen 2006a). Our needing to remain with the background to the military and war issues seems set to persist, whether we want it or not.

2 WHO OR WHAT IS WAR 'GOOD' FOR? HISTORICAL GROUNDING OF THE 'MILITARY-INDUSTRIAL COMPLEX' AND 'THE PERMANENT WAR ECONOMY'

The reasons for war being of such pivotal importance in contemporary life and business are actually not hard to discover once one begins to search. The strange situation in which most people are (or were?) unaware of the persistence of its significance for Western states today is related to 'Orwell's problem' again. Indeed Chomsky (1999b: 139) quotes Randolph Bourne to the effect that war is "the health of the State". But Chomsky shrewdly adds that "we have to understand 'state' in terms far broader than mere governmental functions." And, moreover, he has demonstrated frequently how particular ruling groups have claimed to be acting in the 'national interest' (Chomsky 1985), while furthering the vested interests of selected industrial and other sectors. The hierarchically organized nature of US society is at the root of such practices (Chomsky 1994c). The control over the apparatus of state is nominally, according to the constitution, in the hands of the people. Yet more than 50% of the voters are regularly excluded from the electoral process. Moreover the constitutional framework means that only the election for the House of Representatives every two years stands a chance of being partially 'democratic'. And even the voters' will in these congressional elections is drastically limited by gerrymandering of Congressional districts to the advantage of certain parties. Chomsky (1999a: 46) has explained the origins of this set-up: "The reigning doctrine was expressed clearly by the President of the Continental Congress and first Chief Justice of the Supreme Court, John Jay: 'The people who own the country ought to govern it'." The 'people' today are the private corporations and the legislative and juridical structures devised to protect and uphold them. This is the background we need to bear in mind in considering the role of the MIC (which we discussed above). As Chomsky (1999b: 138) puts it:

> Military spending has been a primary cover for the huge state sector of the high-tech economy, the basis for U.S. preeminence in computers and electronics generally, automation, telecommunications and the internet, and indeed most dynamic components of the economy. The story goes back to the origins of the U.S. system of mass production in the early days of industrial development, though it only took on enormous proportions after World War II.

The American historian Howard Zinn has underlined the boost the Second World War provided for this sector (1995: 416): "The war rejuvenated American capitalism." Between 1940 and 1944 there was an increase in corporations' profits from \$6.4bn to \$10.8bn. As he goes on to comment:

> It was an old lesson learned by governments: that war solves problems of control. Charles E. Wilson, the president of General Electric Corporation, was so happy about the wartime situation that he suggested a continuing alliance between business and the military for 'a permanent war economy'.[4]

The continuity in the utilization of the military force this system has built up escapes the awareness of many citizens of the countries whose rulers and traders are and, more importantly, have long been involved in sustaining such industrial and institutional structures. One used to have to search long and frustratingly for scholarly treatments of, for example, the British Empire and its significant military 'wing'. Noam Chomsky seems to have been ploughing a lone furrow for several decades. But even he is dependent on the specialist work of historians and scholars of various disciplines, many of whom have been marginalized and treated as 'renegades', or stamped as 'anti-American' in the USA and as 'leftist troublemakers' in the UK. Nowhere is this more obvious than in the toned down, if not openly 'triumphalist' writing on the history of the British Empire. Some scholars do not approve of using the word 'imperialism', two British historians, Cain and Hopkins (1993: 42) note. Pussy-footing around the area themselves to a certain extent, they try to show the connection between trade expansion and imperialism. Knocking on the door of a person and waiting for him or her to open it and invite you in is different from kicking it down and entering shooting, of course. If states sponsor or permit pacific expansion beyond their own borders this is not necessarily imperialism, they say. For them "imperialism is used [. . .] to refer to a species of the genus expansion." This might strike people on the receiving end of the expansion as a far too benign interpretation. We see in contemporary 'international relations' that English-speaking nations, in particular, are finding it hard to get out of this mind-set. Cain and Hopkins (1993: 42–3) helpfully 'define' 'imperialism':

> The distinguishing feature of imperialism is not that it takes a specific economic, cultural or political form, but that it involves an incursion, or an attempted incursion, into the sovereignty of another state. [. . .] What matters for purposes of definition is that one power has the will, and, if it is to succeed, the capacity to shape the affairs of another by imposing upon it. The relations established by imperialism are therefore based upon inequality and not upon mutual compromises of the kind which characterise states of interdependence.

Certainly, it is consoling to see how some historians try to put the record straight by demonstrating how British imperialism has had a downside as well as successes. But somehow the idea that acquiring an Empire can and did take place by accident in an almost absent-minded fashion came to be established. This is a rather 'friendly' and making-it-seem-harmless-and-kind-of-everyday-you-know-we-are-all-little-sinners procedure, essentially cementing the social structures as they are. The prime objective of the British, the author was taught in his schooldays, was to selflessly spread their specific version of Christianity, the wonders of Shakespeare (culture), cricket and their (awful) cooking habits in the name of 'civilization' (the four or five 'C's' of the Empire). To be sure, it is not a story that large parts of the world (and not just Africa) can stomach or swallow.

Cain and Hopkins (1993: 44) do, fairly, grant that the imperialist thrust, the stimulus associated with it, must have had a source of energy. They do not actually refer to the Second Law of Thermodynamics at this point. But it is evident that people acquiring territory, goods, mineral and petroleum resources, slaves, indentured servants, dependent indigenous peoples and all the other accompaniments of Empire do not leave entropy to do it for them, which it would not anyway!

Yet there is still the inevitable issue of how much force (aka military violence) is needed to build up an Empire with outposts on every continent of the globe. Trade preceded violence and military takeover, a lot of imperialist chroniclers claim, despite singing the praises of merchant adventurers such as 'Clive of India'. Gentlemanly capitalists wanted a return on their investment, in commerce. Later on the captains of manufacturing industry were looking for extended markets to export to. So "there was a tendency for expansionist impulses to become imperialist, especially where they came up against societies which needed reforming or restructuring before expansionist ambitions could be realised, and which also seemed to be either amenable to change or incapable of resisting it", Cain and Hopkins (1993: 45) write.

There is perhaps no region more damaged by and currently destabilized by the unintended consequences or sorrowful aftermath of such activities than the Middle East, which for some amnesiacs is the current source and sole cause of contemporary barbarism, rather than the effect. The imperialist heritage simply gets written out of history and practically all major media and press reporting, as the death toll is daily rung up in Iraq, Lebanon, the Occupied Territories or Afghanistan.

3   FAÇADE: A METAPHOR FOR OBFUSCATION IN DISCOURSE

Perhaps the operative metaphor for obfuscation in imperialist discourse has always been and will continue to be the creation of a 'façade'. Language scholars might prefer to assume that we are really dealing with metaphors here. But a brief glance at the history of Iraq shows that the British were deadly earnest in their 'literal' reading of the term. Chomsky shows what happened in the 1920s. Lord Curzon, the British Foreign Secretary described the activities the British engaged in Iraq after the First World War as proceeding behind an "Arab façade". Chomsky ironically (2005: 45) notes[5]:

> Lord Curzon was very honest in those days [1920s]. Iraq would be an Arab façade. Britain's rule should be 'veiled' behind such 'constitutional fictions as a protectorate, a sphere of influence, a buffer State, and so on'. And that's the way Britain ran the whole region—in fact, the whole empire. The idea is to have independent states, but with weak governments that must rely on the imperial power for their survival.

Tariq Ali employs a similar metaphor, that of 'an Arab smokescreen' in describing the way in which total British control was erected in Iraq. He recounts what happened (2003: 46–7):

> The League of Nations Mandate had not specified how Britain should administer the state. The British Indian government wanted the new state to be run just like India and preferably under the tutelage of Delhi. To their surprise, Curzon, who presided over the committee making the decisions, vetoed the project, opting instead for Gertrude Ball's plan of total British control behind an Arab smokescreen. This was regarded as a more subtle form of domination. It was also more convenient. [. . .] If carefully nurtured and protected, Arab dynasties could in due course become the trusted custodians of the new imperial possessions.

Curtis (2003b: 2) has highlighted the gap between words and deeds in British foreign policy since the Second World War: "Former Foreign Office minister Peter Hain has written of 'our mission to conquer world poverty and build international peace and a world based upon justice, equality and human rights'." The British have a long post-Second World War experience of this sort of thing. Once the British are involved or have intervened somewhere, the reporting and the choice of language tend to avoid telling the public truth. We might quote long lists of isolated examples of language abuse, as this gem by a British general demonstrates. He was heard to utter it on 'The World at One', BBC Radio 4, on June 10, 1999, in the war zone at the time Tony Blair had involved the British forces in. "If our troops are faced by life-threatening behaviour in any form they will respond in a robust and decisive fashion." This is a military euphemism which maybe highlights the British penchant for understatement. (Translation into ordinary English: "They will kill anyone who they consider to be acting aggressively.") Chilton (1988: 80) gives examples of military manipulation from the Vietnam War, such as 'pacification', a term used by Orwell too. Below we will return to some further occurrences.

At the same time, it is important to keep matters in proportion. The examination of military euphemisms and the 'militarization' of language should not be used to suggest that language is somehow primary or 'significant'. Indeed it is one of the main contentions of this and the previous chapter that language or discourse is merely an epiphenomenon. After all, there is perhaps no area of human activity other than war, military violence and force which could demonstrate as compellingly and definitively how insubstantial language is when people are confronted with violently socialized (and brutalized) groups of human beings (aka soldiers) directing bombs and missiles at them.

Notwithstanding, the fact is that warfare and aggression-practising groups and nations have always set out to 'spin' their activities and present themselves in the best possible light. One consistent European tradition has been to give military violence a religiose or 'sacral' coating, as Chomsky (2000: 156–9) shows in a chapter entitled 'The Legacy of War'. The role of the Church aims to deflect or distance the primacy of violence and to erect a façade of righteousness and hence 'acceptability'. It is our task as analysts of effective reality to show how this hegemonic discourse functions by naturalizing such tropes. It hinders the visibility of the permanent war economy. And it has been so successful that the vast majority of the North American and Western European populations simply fail to acknowledge what has been carried on 'in their name' for the past sixty years. To be sure, the fact of geographical remoteness, for the most part, and its affecting 'unpeople' (Curtis 2004) has aided this amnesia.

4   MILITARISM: THE MATERIAL BASIS FOR MILITARIZATION OF LANGUAGE

We have already referred to Chalmers Johnson's (2004) volume *Sorrows of Empire*. The procedure he adopts in this book parallels that of Noam Chomsky (2005). Both writers seem to peel the onion. The public face presented by government and official political actors in the USA is subjected to sustained deconstruction. Johnson sets the scene:

> As distinct from other peoples on this earth, most Americans do not recognize—or do not want to recognize—that the United States dominates the world through its military power. Due to government secrecy, they are often ignorant of the fact that their government garrisons the globe. They do not realize that a vast network of American military bases on every continent except Antarctica actually constitutes a new form of empire. (Johnson 2004: 1)

His book sets out to document the scope of this 'militarily based empire'. It is significant that Johnson pays close attention to the use of language. As a historian and analyst of American militarism his exact and clear analytical procedure in demonstrating how language is used to present what the rich and powerful want their audience to see and hear is a boon to critical scholarship. In the course of his convincing study Johnson underlines how the concealing of what goes on is aided by the use of language. He comments on the phrase 'collateral damage' (2004: 28): "Such obfuscation is intrinsic to the world of imperialism and its handmaiden, militarism." He continues: "Imperialism is hard to define but easily recognized." Johnson speaks explicitly of "a long-standing American urge to find euphemisms for imperialism that soften and disguise the U.S. version of it, at least from other Americans" (2004: 29).

This section will provide some background to illustrate how militarist the United States has been ever since its violent military beginnings. After all, the fact is often overlooked or underplayed that the state is the result of a revolutionary war against England in the 18th century. The violence employed in colonizing and settling the territory of the USA scarcely gets mentioned in public or in the nation's schools, universities and school textbooks. But there are outstanding exceptions. As James W. Loewen, professor of sociology at the University of Vermont (1996: 14), clearly puts it: "Why are history textbooks so bad? Nationalism is one of the culprits. Textbooks are often muddled by the conflicting desires to promote inquiry and to indoctrinate blind patriotism." His book puts the record straight, as too does Howard Zinn (1995), *A People's History of the United States: 1492 to Present*. He documents the extermination of the indigenous people. The losses of life caused by the slave trade are put on the record. And yet the myths propagated by Hollywood and 'official history' still join forces to play down this side of North American history.

Authors like Johnson (2000, 2004) and especially Blum (2000, 2003) have been 'blowing the whistle' on the ideology of the peaceful Americans. Others have bravely questioned their own personal roles, often as CIA agents, in intervening violently in other people's countries. Philip Agee (1975), for example, worked for the CIA for twelve years, in three different countries. He began by accepting the 'Company's' views and aims, but as time went by he came to see it as a bureaucracy designed not to help those in whose countries it works, but simply as an arm of American interests. Chomsky has brought these positions together in many of his publications.

The work of writers like Gore Vidal (2002, 2003, 2004) and Kurt Vonnegut (1973, 1982) provides further critical descriptions of this institutionalized framework. They have provided often sardonic, but serious and well-documented commentaries on this heavily militarist history. It is worth noting that, together with Howard Zinn, all these men were in the US armed forces during the Second World War. This is where Johnson's sensitivity to the 'bullshit' of military jargon derives from. Zinn was a major protester during the Vietnam War. Here are men who participated in the Second World War and know what war really means, unlike the warmongers of today—namely Blair and Bush!

The title of one of Vidal's essay collections, *Perpetual War for Perpetual Peace* (2002), concisely paraphrases the way such activities are cynically and Orwellianly rationalized. And it is interesting to see manipulative parallels at work in justifying the modern form of imperialism. In this connection it is worth quoting what Johnson has to say about how a form of 'inevitability discourse' is used in connexion with corporate globalisation. He aptly comments (2004: 260):

> Perhaps the most deceptive aspect of globalization was its claim to embody fundamental and inevitable technological developments rather than the conscious policies of Anglo-American political élites trying to advance the interests of their own countries at the expense of others.

5   MILITARISM, EMPIRE, GLOBALISATION AND ITS 'HANGERS ON'

An important commentator on the militarist beginnings of, motivation for and representation of the American empire is Edward Said. He has written (1993: 348–9):

> Enough work has been done by American cultural historians for us to understand the sources of the drive to domination on a world scale as well as the way that drive is represented and made acceptable. Richard Slotkin argues, in *Regeneration Through Violence*, that the shaping experience of American history was the extended wars with the native American Indians; this in turn produced an image of Americans not as plain killers (as D. H. Lawrence said of them) but as 'a new race of people, independent of the sin-darkened heritage of man, seeking a totally new and original relationship to pure nature as hunters, explorers, pioneers and seekers.'

The role of the American 'Empire' has, like its British predecessor, been presented to Americans as a beneficent accomplishment. The American historian, Howard Zinn, in his essay 'Aggressive Liberalism' (1990) has analyzed the reality of US expansionism within the nation, for example 'removing' the Cherokees from the East along the 'Trail of Tears', on which 4,000 of the 14,000 died. The expansion that then took place into the Caribbean and the Pacific proceeded outside the borders of continental America, until "with World War II we spread military bases onto every land mass, every ocean in the world, intervened openly or stealthily in Greece, Lebanon, Guatemala, Cuba, the Dominican Republic, Korea, Vietnam" (1990: 206–7). The essay was first published in 1970. As we know, there are many other places and bases that now need adding, especially since 1989 and 2001.

Johnson (2004: 26) notes how established this military system is: "There are so many interests other than those of the military officials who live off the empire that its existence is distinctly overdetermined—so much so that it is hard to imagine the United States ever voluntarily getting out of the empire business." Clearly, once such a system is in place it develops its own 'logic' and sense of momentum. More importantly, the need for countless 'vested interests' to maintain the militarized empire (with the military and their families) is bound to grow.

Johnson provides a long list of 'hangers on'. It threatens to run off the end of the page (2004: 26):

> the military-industrial complex, university research and development centers, petroleum refiners and distributors, innumerable foreign officer corps whom it has trained, manufacturers of sport utility vehicles and small-arms ammunition, multinational corporations and the cheap

labor they use to make their products, investment banks, hedge funds and speculators of all varieties, and advocates of 'globalization,' meaning theorists who want to force all nations to open themselves up to American exploitation and American-style capitalism.

Johnson's mention of 'theorists' underlines how much 'ideological work' is required, in addition to the hardware, for the absurd construct to persist. The fact that Johnson is a former naval man permits him to demonstrate how this absurdness is reflected in military and diplomatic language usage. For example, Johnson describes a military installation in Qatar "that the air force calls Camp Andy, after Master Sergeant Evander Andrews, the first U.S. casualty of the Afghanistan operation, who died as a result of a forklift accident. It is hard to know whether the officials who supply these names are being intentionally saccharine or are running out of genuine heroes." A further example is of a permanent housing complex for the soldiers "rechristened Expeditionary Village" (2004: 248).

Johnson's language sensitivity is reflected further in his analysis of the 'privatization' of the US military (2004: 247). One of the disturbing developments Johnson draws our attention to is the growing influence which private military companies are coming to have within the armed forces. "The top thirty-five of these private military companies are among the most profitable businesses in the country today" (2004: 140). He sardonically refers to them as "private rent-a-trainer, rent-a-mercenary, and rent-a-cop companies whose leaders and employees, mostly retired high-ranking officers and members of the Special Forces, hire themselves out to the government and its foreign allies to perform any number of military tasks, including troop training" (2004: 135). The operations they engage in are mostly taboo in the public domain. The company names themselves take on a euphemistically surreal quality. A Virginia firm, with 700 full-time staff members and a roster of 10,000 retired military personnel it can call on, is MPRI, Military Professional Resources, Inc., which trained and equipped the armies of Croatia and Bosnia in 1995 (2004: 140–41). And to cap it all, "[t]he companies even have their own industry trade group, the International Peace Operations Association—a name George Orwell would have cherished" (Johnson 2004: 141). Agencies like the CIA use cynical, Orwellian euphemisms too as Blum (2003: 100) documents: "[A]t one time, those at the CIA who were concerned with possible assassinations and appropriate methods were known internally as the 'Health Alteration Committee'."

But these distancing and distracting tactics are especially virulent when the disbursement of large sums of taxpayers' money has to be concealed. Johnson notes that the "official name for the black budget is 'Special Access Programs' (SAPs), which are classified well above 'top secret'". He sardonically and parenthetically adds: "('SAP' may be a subtle or unintentional bureaucratic reference to the taxpayer)" (2004: 118). There is no clear informing of Congress on these programmes. At least 185 black programs are known to exist and an estimated $30 to $35 billion are spent per year on secret military and intelligence activities.

Johnson is a shrewd observer of the naming practices of the military. "[A] series of fanciful names" are given to 'weapons and operations' officially listed in the published Pentagon budget. 'Grass Blade,' 'Chalk Eagle,' 'Dark Eyes,' 'Guardian Bear,' 'Senior Citizen,' 'Tractor Rose,' 'Have Blue,' 'Sea Nymph,' and many more. Independent analysts of the defense budgets have noticed that in these unclassified nicknames, 'Have,' 'Senior,' and 'Constant' are frequently used as the first word in air force programs, 'Tractor' in army programs, and 'Chalk' in navy ones" (2004: 118). As we will see below, this is reminiscent of the items Vidal has published.

6   MILITARY EUPHEMISMS, DECEPTION, DISPLACEMENT AND DISTRACTING ASSOCIATIONS

To see the relevance, but also the partiality, of Orwell's perspective in *1984*, we might take examples from language used in the Vietnam War. It is reported that the American B-52 pilots who flew bombing missions in Southeast Asia during the Vietnam War invariably described them as 'protective reactions' in their flight reports. Chilton (1988: 80) provides examples of military manipulation from the Vietnam War: 'pacification' a term used by Orwell too, 'protective reactions' (bombing raids) and 'urbanization' (the destruction of peasant villages). "The whole terminology of the war—'pacification', 'defoliation', 'resources control program', 'strategic hamlet', etc.—was a shockingly exact fulfilment of Orwell's vision", Fowler et al. (1979: 23) argue. It became routinized. Bolinger (1980: 131) provides the examples 'ambient noncombatant personnel' for refugees and 'waterborne logistic craft' for sampans, "both from the rich harvest of jargon from Vietnam." Chilton (1988: 80) argues that "the men who plan and perform the killing apparently have a need to be linguistically anaesthetised." And additionally, "[m]ilitary jargon [. . .] constitutes a misleading smoke-screen for the general public." The whole point is to desensitize populations at home to the reality of what their armed forces are engaged in by means of distracting associations. As we know, this process is still with us. Contemporary military conflagrations are spawning plenty more examples, as if to underline the 'same procedure as every year'. In chapter 10 we have already cited Fisk (2001), who wrote "We are engaging—an Orwellian cracker this, from the Pentagon on Friday night—in 'protective retaliation' ". Compare 'protective reactions' from the Vietnam War, above! US forces no longer employ 'torture' when dealing with prisoners, but 'coercive interrogation' (Kennedy 2006).

Some patterning is bound to show up where military war game planning is involved, as this colourful pair of phrases illustrates: 'blue on blue' is the accidental death of allied soldiers. In war games allies are blue and enemies red (Thorne 2006: 22). Also 'green on green' refers to 'abuses' not committed by the USA or British forces, but considered as internal Afghan affairs, as the policy of 'peacekeeping' shifted onto the annihilation of the Taliban (Clark 2006).

7   US CODE NAMES OF MILITARY OPERATIONS

An interesting source provides examples of this obfuscation. Vidal (2002: 22–41) provides a list of US military operations since the Second World War. Vidal comments (2002: 21): "We are given, under 'Name,' many fanciful Defense Department titles like *Urgent Fury*, which was Reagan's attack on the island of Grenada, a month-long caper that General Haig disloyally said could have been handled more efficiently by the Provincetown police department."

The list is useful for two purposes. The primary one is historical: as a partial record of the US interventions around the world since 1947. A secondary purpose allows us to reflect on the calculated means employed by the Pentagon to systematically obscure or ideologically euphemize many of these operations. If we subject the total number of code names in the list to a quantitative and qualitative analysis we come up with a number of interesting insights. They show the semantic or metaphorical engineering that goes on at the Pentagon, as well as the military kind.

A brief perusal shows that most of the operational names consist of two words, such as 'Joint Guardian' (Kosovo 11 Jun 1999–200?) or 'Deliberate Forge' (Bosnia-Herzegovina 20 Jun 1998–present). Some have the appendage 'Operation' before the code name. The military operations during the Vietnam War are thus named. The 'harmless' cowboy or sports allusions hide vicious actions which not only broke international law but also included gross crimes against humanity, like dropping napalm on civilians. 'Operation Ranch Hand' was a series of US Air Force herbicide spray operations in Vietnam between 1961 and 1971 (using Agent Orange, namely dioxin solutions). 'Operation Rolling Thunder' (Vietnam 24 Feb 1965–Oct 1968, also known as the 'Rolling Thunder Program', in the terminology of the McNamara Department of Defense) was the first of three sustained bombing campaigns against North Vietnam, followed in 1972 by 'Operation Linebacker I' (North Vietnam 10 May 1972–23 Oct 1972) and 'Operation Linebacker II' (18 Dec 1972–29 Dec 1972).

Further code names given by the Pentagon to its largely bombing operations during this period are 'Operation Arc Light' (Southeast Asia 18 Jun 1965–Apr 1970), 'Operation Freedom Train' (North Vietnam 6 Apr 1972–10 May 1972), 'Operation Pocket Money', (North Vietnam 9 May 1972–23 Oct 1972), 'Operation Endsweep' (North Vietnam, 27 Jan 1972–27 Jul 1973), 'Operation Ivory Coast/Kingpin' (North Vietnam, 21 Nov 1970–21 Nov 1970), 'Operation Tailwind' (Laos 1970–1970) and finally 'Frequent

Wind' (29 Apr 1975–30 Apr 1975), for the evacuation of personnel from Saigon as it fell.

'Powerpack' (Dominican Republic 28 Apr 1965–21 Sep 1966) was the name for the sending of 23,000 troops to ensure that a US-friendly group of generals defeated the 'rebels' in 1966. Some more recent names employ either verbs or adjectives followed by mostly abstract nouns: 'Provide Hope I–V' (Former Soviet Union 1992–9), 'Provide Relief' (Somalia 14 Aug 1992–08 Dec 1992), 'Restore Hope' (Somalia 4 Dec 1992–4 May 1993) and 'Continue Hope' (Somalia 4 May 1993–Dec 1993), with the last three operations supporting the brutal dictator Siad Barre. Then there were 'Decisive Endeavor/Decisive Edge' (Bosnia-Herzegovina Jan 1996–Dec 1996) and 'Decisive Guard/Deliberate Guard' (Bosnia-Herzegovina Dec 1996–20 Jun 1998), both self-proclaimed 'humanitarian interventions' (Johnson 2004: 62).

Sometimes one has the impression that these naming procedures provide the occasion for black or sick humour on the part of Pentagon officials. This rather cynical use is to be seen in the Vietnam War names. What the phrases are expected to convey in some other cases when the two words meld is perhaps simply an everyday, homely 'set phrase', like 'Early Call', 'Just Cause', 'Classic Resolve', 'Ernest Will', 'Silent Promise', 'Fundamental Response', 'Open Arms'. Other instances, like the use of the adjectives 'decisive' and 'deliberate' in the two examples above, conjure up no-nonsense manly actions and are supposed to trigger positive, even virtuous associations. Perhaps they imply virile, masculine qualities, even moral strength, goodness and righteousness, in any case 'heroic and generous endeavour'. One is reminded of what Chomsky (2000: 156) said about the sacralization of war, mentioned above, whereby the butchering of 'savages' is sanctified in the name of 'God'.

Table 11.1 shows the automatic count of some frequent adjectives used.

What processes, participants or circumstances do the nouns metaphorically refer to? What is being highlighted? We might ask what sort of associations these names are supposed to conjure up. How affirmative are they?

Table 11.1 Adjectives in US Military Operation Names

Determined (4)	Joint (4)	Red (4)
Sharp (2)	Shining (2)	Silver (2)
Vigilant (2)	Noble (2)	Ivory (2)
United (1)	Blue (1)	Bright (1)
Central (1)	Infinite (1)	Intense (1)
Intrinsic (1)	Fiery (1)	

What is a 'typically' positive and military association? The metaphors from the 'hard' world of the ironsmith: anvil (2), forge (2), steel (1)?

We might consider what categories or ways of classifying military actions and violence their authors create by choosing abstract nouns in so many cases. Table 11.2 displays some items and their frequency. Abstractly speaking, four areas predominate: that of precursory conditions and operations ('guard', 'guardian'), corporate activities ('joint'), positive affections ('hope') and general volition or determination (as represented by the adjective 'determined'), judging by the groupings in Tables 11.3–11.6.

Apart from names which clearly are informative or merely indicate geographical locations, e.g. Suez Crisis, Taiwan Straits, Korean War, Berlin Airlift, Achille Lauro, Gulf of Sidra, Six Day War, Central America and Cuban Missile Crisis, the disinformation functions are uppermost. Most Americans had no idea what their armed forces were actually doing in these and other places. Often they began and remained covert. A projection of probity, justice and, essentially, assistance, kindness, even, appears to be aimed for. To be sure, the heroic characteristics of military, fighting ability are suggested by several adjectives and nouns. And a final listing of animal names used (Table 11.7) demonstrates that, for all their exaggerated willingness to help and succour its allies (cf. 'joint' for many NATO operations in recent years), the US armed forces are no 'pussy cat' or teddy bear.

8 ON THE CONTINUING POWER OF SEMANTIC ENGINEERING

The ideological function is evident. Justify the unjustifiable. This is the propaganda function. Consider, for example, the Kosovo War in 1998–9. This was a NATO action for which there was no justification under international law. However, the media saturation so softened public opinion that there was practically no opposition to the bombing of civilian targets in Yugoslavia. The large numbers of Kosovaran Albanian refugees only started fleeing as a result of Serbian violence *after* the NATO bombing started. This was anticipated by NATO military authorities (Chomsky 1999b: 21). By

Table 11.2 Nouns in US Military Operation Names

Hope (10)	Guard (6)	Strike (5)	Force (4)
Guardian (3)	Vigil (3)	Edge (3)	Eagle (3)
Sentry (2)	Forge (2)	Anvil (2)	Endeavor (2)
Haven (2)	Fox (2)	Shield (2)	Venture (1)
Victor (1)	Warrior (1)	Provide (1)	

Table 11.3 List of Precursory Conditions and Operations and Their 'Theatres'

Determined Guard (Adriatic Sea 1996–Present)	*Joint Guard* (Bosnia-Herzegovina Dec 1996–20 Jun 1998)
Decisive Guard (Bosnia-Herzegovina Dec 1996–20 Jun 1998)	*Deliberate Guard* (Bosnia-Herzegovina Dec 1996–20 Jun 1998)
Maritime Guard (Adriatic Sea 22 Nov 1992–15 Jun 1993)	*Sharp Guard* (Adriatic Sea 1993–Dec 1995)
Guardian Retrieval (Congo (formerly Zaire) Mar 1997–June 1997)	*Guardian Assistance* (Zaire/Rwanda/Uganda 15 Nov 1996–27 Dec 1996)

Table 11.4 List of Corporate Activities and Their 'Theatres'

Joint Guardian (Kosovo 11 Jun 1999–TDB 200?)	*Joint Endeavor* (Bosnia-Herzegovina Dec 1995–Dec 1996)
Joint Guard (Bosnia-Herzegovina Dec 1996–20 Jun 1998)	*Joint Forge* (Bosnia-Herzegovina 20 June 1998–Present)

Table 11.5 List of 'Hope'-Bringing Operations

Shining Hope (Kosovo)	*Sustain Hope* (Kosovo)
Provide Hope I (Former Soviet Union 10 Feb 1992–26 Feb 1992)	*Provide Hope II* (Former Soviet Union 15 Apr 1992–29 Jul 1992)
Provide Hope III (Former Soviet Union 1993–1993)	*Provide Hope IV* (Former Soviet Union 10 Jan 1994–19 Dec 1994)
Provide Hope V (Former Soviet Union 6 Nov 1998–10 May 1999)	*Quiet Resolve/Support Hope* (Rwanda 22 Jul 1994–30 Sep 1994)
Restore Hope (Somalia 4 Dec 1992–4 May 1993)	*Continue Hope* (Somalia 4 May 1993–Dec 1993)

Table 11.6 List of Operations Demonstrating Determination

Determined Force (Kosovo 8 Oct 1998–23 Mar 1999)	*Determined Falcon* (Kosovo and Albania 15 Jun 1998–16 Jun 1998)
Determined Effort (Bosnia-Herzegovina Jul 1995–Dec 1995)	*Determined Guard* (Adriatic Sea 1996–present)

Table 11.7 Animal Names of US Military Operations

Eagle Eye	Determined Falcon	Blue Bat	Desert Fox
Phoenix Scorpion I–IV	Desert Falcon	Golden Pheasant	Coronet Nighthawk
Grizzly	Golden Python	Hawkeye	Praying Mantis
Eagle Claw	Eagle Pull	Red Fox [Pueblo incident]	Red Dragon

contrast, few questions are asked when repression of minorities, like the Kurds, in a NATO country, Turkey, does not lead to similar bombings, if, as claimed, 'interventions' are driven by universal humanitarian principles. The partiality and careful choice of, usually, weaker countries against whom to employ force and military violence is seldom if ever discussed in the mainstream media.

In this connection it is interesting to note what Edward Herman in an essay entitled 'The Banality of Evil' (1995: 97) states: "Doing terrible things in an organized and systematic way rests on 'normalization'." There is a long historical record during the twentieth century of how this has functioned. Herman again: "There is usually a division of labor in doing and rationalizing the unthinkable, with the direct brutalizing and killing done by one set of individuals; [. . .] others working on improving technology (a better crematory gas, a longer burning and more adhesive Napalm, bomb fragments that penetrate flesh in hard-to-trace patterns)." This sounds very close to what is still happening, often under the rubric of 'advanced technological research' (recall the November 2004 attack on the Iraq city of Fallujah by US forces employing phosphor). The real engineering and its application in military operations are then legitimated ideologically by means of semantic or discourse engineering: "It is the function of the defense experts, and the mainstream media, to normalize the unthinkable for the general public" (Herman 1995: 97).

9   TWO OR THREE WAYS OF SEEING THE THREATS OF WAR AND ENVIRONMENTAL DISASTER

It is almost as if what counts as the 'normal' in contemporary societies are features which can only be 'understood' by thinking people if we invoke the phenomenon of acting in 'mauvaise foi'. Lynas (2004: 24) has noted how President Bush and his vice-president, Dick Cheney, deny that global warming is taking place. They have behaved as if under the influence of cognitive dissonance, passing a series of anti-environmental laws.[6] Also many powerful US senators—including James Inhofe (Republican, Oklahoma, and chair of the Senate committee on environment and public works), Larry Craig (Republican, Idaho) and Craig Thomas (Republican, Wyoming)—are actively combating environmentalist policies. They are supported in this by academic studies produced by far-right think tanks such as the Competitive Enterprise Institute and the George C Marshall Institute. These are largely financed by multinationals, especially oil companies.

Fortunately, the history of the world proves that things can be changed. Actions have resulted in the reduction of repression and the diminution of autocratic activities. The establishment of relatively democratic societies was achieved by groups of people refusing to accept what autocrats and powerful forces imposed on subject populations. In our times colonial oppression was overthrown in many former imperialistically exploited countries. How can we account for history and the dynamics of change? It is not such a wild leap to suggest that such oppositional practices often are accompanied by developing forms similar to what Halliday (1978) calls 'anti-language'. This literally stands 'normal' language on its head. Accordingly, language comes to negate the ruling norms of society. Certainly, the language of the powerful becomes hegemonically projected so much so that the Orwellian scenarios we discussed in chapter 10 appear to rule. However language use is not just a case of the reproduction of social practices (Kress 1989). Social contestation and oppositional stances *are* possible.

Having said this, we need to recall that there are a number of ways in which contemporary developments are being analyzed in pluralistic societies. Consider what the British professor of social thought John Gray has to say on what he calls 'climate change'. He correctly analyzes the interconnections between phenomena that, at first sight, not every citizen in the West is likely to link (2006: 34): "The resource war being fought for oil in the Gulf is likely to be one of many in the coming century, and will be accompanied by conflicts over fresh water. Population growth, resource war and climate change are intertwined."

Gray sketches a pessimistic scenario for today: "It may be that the shift in habits of thinking that is needed is beyond human powers." He emphasizes the role that "our capacity for denial" has played in the course of human evolution. In the past this may have worked. But now, to deny "the dangers we face has itself become dangerous". His blunt conclusion is (2006: 37): "Abrupt climate change seems an apocalyptic prospect, and rather than face up to it and do what can be done to mitigate its effects, humanity may well opt to let it run its course." What is missing from this analysis is a full acknowledgement of how powerful groups in the world, not 'humanity' in the abstract, are propping up, if not cementing, such scenarios by means of the construction of false consciousness. After all, we need to ask who is responsible for both activities leading to environmental degradation and potential ecological disaster and, at the same time, the kinds of semantic engineering we have been talking about.

There are clearly 'backroom boys and girls' whose job it is to propose both what critical linguists call 'relexicalizations' and also discourse semantic patterns and rhetorical ploys in order to structure arguments and thus persuade listeners. Luntz, Maslansky Strategic Research is such an organization. This is a polling company advising the US Republican Party on which 'words work' (as their documents say), when speaking to the voters and trying to influence media presentations of issues. Consider the phrase 'climate change'. "'Climate change' is less frightening than 'global warming'." This is what Fred Luntz suggests the Republicans employ to keep the population on side (quoted in Poole 2006: 42). Poole details the role lobby groups from US corporations played in semantically engineering the shift in usage mentioned above. As he notes, US corporate lobbies from the oil-producing sector were very successful in the early 1990s in persuading the United Nations to shift from 'global warming' to 'climate change' in their official diction. (See Poole (2006: 42–9) for a well-documented history of this exercise in semantic engineering by certain agents of false consciousness.) [7]

One component of the environmental issue we might also briefly mention is the conflict over genetically modified (GM) plants and crops. We have discussed this in chapters 8 and especially 9. It is interesting to see a British linguist investigating the discourse employed by the various actors involved in the controversy (Cook 2004). In his introduction Cook hints at broader contestations (2004: 6): "GM is part of a much larger debate in which themes, issues and ideological differences recur and intertwine." Yet Cook's desire to remain rather abstract grates or is slightly puzzling. After all, it is important to know whose interests or benefits are furthered by the dominant discourses he looks at. Who is involved in "the polarisation of opinion and understanding"? And surely we need to formulate more pointedly which "individuals, [. . .] cultures and [. . .] nations" are participating, as a neo-imperialist world takes on an ever more evident shape and affects "so much of contemporary life." Cook does mention some names in the course of the book, but fails to relate them explicitly to the corporate globalisation being pursued by certain multinationals which constitute the major centres of power, like the energy corporations, high-tech industry, arms producers and so on.

Against this background the "four critical issues" distinguished by Chomsky (2006b) take on a new dimension. Firstly, there is the possibility of nuclear war, and secondly the likely environmental disaster, which is in the making. The third issue is most significant, namely, the global superpower's government role in enhancing these threats. And the fourth issue he isolates is what he terms a growing democratic deficit. This is "the gap between public will and public policy, a sign of the increasing failure of formal democratic institutions to function as they would in a democratic culture with vitality and substance."

In view of this imperial world order, we may query whether uncovering disinformation and deceit on the part of political, military and corporate élites really can help to 'overcome' what Chomsky calls a "growing democratic deficit" (2006a: 251, 2006b). The activist viewpoint that Chomsky takes up is that, optimistically, on all of these critical issues something can be done. It is a hopeful situation because it can be overcome, and again, "practical ways to proceed are well understood, and have often been implemented under far more difficult circumstances than those faced in the industrial societies today" (2006b).

10 CONCLUSIONS

Given the mass of evidence showing how systematically much of the discourse of both anti-environmentalism and militarization is being engineered, many people may find it difficult to be as hopeful as Chomsky that much can be done. At this point we can refer back to the impression the fictional treatment in Orwell's work provides. Hodge and Fowler (1979: 23) developed a similar position. "Orwell's pessimism in *1984* poses the challenge: can anything be done? His understanding of a form of false consciousness is totally convincing as far as it goes. In fact, it is too convincing, because it is unable to contemplate any alternative to its own impotence and despair."

Orwell's problem is strictly speaking not a 'problem' in the course of the mundane daily activities which citizens or consumers engage in. It is an academic rhetorical figure employed to pinpoint a more deeply seated phenomenon. The discussions of disinformation, circumlocution, euphemisms which we have presented are certainly not aimed at providing solutions to the communication problems of corporate and government bodies. It would be jejune or naïve to reduce the lies employed by these bodies to a communication or a linguistic or language problem. It should have become clear that this author does not see his task as improving semantic and discourse engineering processes on behalf of the rich and powerful. There are, unfortunately, sufficient willing volunteers to help those institutions already, manifesting, in Hodge and Fowler's phrase, 'a form of false consciousness'! Nor is it realistic to imagine that it would suffice for people to put pressure on governments and the like to engage in 'plain English'. The 'verbal hygiene' campaigns which periodically attack linguistic processes of 'jargonization' may well have additional (hidden?) agendas. These sometimes appear to be of a rather authoritarian nature relating to concerns about a more desirable moral or ethical order (Cameron 2000: viii). But such campaigns aiming at the linguistic surface of society are likely to guarantee that nothing will change.

11 IF WE CAN TELL THE TRUTH ABOUT THE PAST, THEN MAYBE WE CAN TELL THE TRUTH ABOUT THE PRESENT

There are many inspiring examples of writers, artists, scholars, journalists and film makers who remain optimistic that something can be done. For example, in the UK the re-writing of the self-serving, establishment based history of British imperialism is an area of contestation. Take the Irish Civil War in the 1920s. Ken Loach's film 'The Wind That Shakes the Barley' takes a dim view of British imperialism. Loach says: "Our little film is about a step, a very little step, in the British confronting their imperialist history. And if we can tell the truth about the past, then maybe we can tell the truth about the present. . . . I don't need to [talk about] where the British now illegally have an army of occupation, and the damage in casualties and brutality that is emerging from that" (quoted in Brooks 2006: 46). The scriptwriter of Loach's film, Paul Laverty, writes about the way the film was conceived and made. He refers to how present day politicians continue to make vacuous and ideological claims about British history (2006: 46–7). Laverty quotes from a speech by then Chancellor Gordon Brown which reflects a revisionist, triumphalist, imperialistic history in progress (2006: 47):

> We should celebrate much of our past rather than apologise for it. And we should talk, and rightly so, about British values that are enduring, because they stand for some of the greatest ideas in history—tolerance, liberty, civic duty—that grew in Britain and influenced the rest of the world. Our strong traditions of fair play, of openness, of internationalism, these are great British values.

This is not only dismissive of the facts—exonerating Britain from slavery, corrupt systems of indentured labour in the colonies and illegal invasions of numerous countries. It is also arrogant. What is astounding is to hear such imperialistic preaching from a nominal representative of the Left, a British Labour Chancellor of the Exchequer. But clearly the 'office of state' has a levelling effect on such views. There are clear echoes of "Mrs Thatcher called yesterday for a return to traditional values", as reported in the *Guardian* 1978. Stuart Hall quotes this passage in 1982 at the time of the Falklands War, when Thatcher was populistically underlining the myth of British greatness. Hall summarizes the use of this vocabulary of imperial greatness, in an essay called 'The Empire Strikes Back' (1988: 68):

> Empires come and go. But the imagery of the British Empire seems destined to go on forever. The imperial flag has been hauled down in a hundred different corners of the globe. But it is still flying in the collective unconscious.

In short, "[t]he culture of an old empire is an imperialist culture" (Hall 1988: 73). As Laverty comments, such 'history' always serves a contemporary purpose: "It is one thing to forget, quite another to invent selectively. Brown is not alone among the British establishment in trying to romanticize colonial days. [. . .] Perhaps it is much easier to lie about the present and future if we lie about the past" (2006: 47). What we see here is a politician playing the imperialist and authority card—features which go hand in hand in Britain. As we know a general tactic of all power élites or hierarchically ordered groups and organizations is to appeal to or to awaken authoritarian and deferential attitudinal structures.

The objective of the bulk of Ken Loach's film work over the years (Hayward 2004) has been to critically interrogate the imperialist and deferential values of societies like Britain with their implicit appeal for the 'obedience' and 'loyalty' features of the authoritarian character structure (Adorno et al. 1950). Loach's films aim to encourage solidarity feelings with and among the oppressed and lower classes. In connection with the film 'The Wind That Shakes the Barley' Ken Loach is quoted as saying: "I'd encourage people to see their loyalties horizontally, across national boundaries. [. . .] People have much more in common with people in the same social position in other countries than they do with, say, those at the top of their own society" (Brooks 2006: 47).

A parallel figure in the USA is the documentary film maker Michael Moore. His stand against governmental lies and corporate corruption has resulted in a number of outstanding documentaries. 'Fahrenheit 9/11' can be cited as an excellent example of investigative journalism. It uncovers with humour and emotion the deceit of a political class which manipulates public opinion for private gain (see Moore (2004) for the screenplay). The film ends with Moore, the narrator, drawing a direct parallel between the US invasion and occupation of Iraq and Orwell's *1984* (2004: 130): "George Orwell once wrote that it's not a matter of whether the war is not real or if it is. Victory is not possible. The war is not meant to be won, it is meant to be continuous. A hierarchical society is only possible on the basis of poverty and ignorance. This new version is the past and no different past can ever have existed. In principle, the war effort is always planned to keep society on the brink of starvation. The war is waged by the ruling group against its own subjects and its object is not the victory over either Eurasia or East Asia, but to keep the very structure of society intact."

12   CHOMSKY'S INTELLECTUAL SELF-DEFENCE KIT

Ordinary people are not stupid. They can see through the lies and deception. During the War in Vietnam in the 1970s the Black American comedian Dick Gregory included the following routine in his act: "What we're doing in Vietnam is using the black man to kill the yellow man so the white man can keep the land he took from the red man." Élite groups fear the response of the population, so they "construct a world of fable and fantasy" (Chomsky 1985: 170). Chomsky wrote this during the 1980s when US intervention in Central America (Nicaragua, El Salvador and Guatemala) was frequent and supported violent dictators and their death squads. Reagan and other leaders told the voters fairy tales about what the US forces and agents were engaged in. Chomsky captured succinctly what was involved: "If the people they [the leaders] address were to learn the truth about the actions they support or passively tolerate, they would not permit them to proceed. Therefore, we must live in a world of lies and fantasies, under the Orwellian principle that Ignorance is Strength" (1985: 170).

"No different past can ever have existed." Who makes this possible? Chomsky demonstrated in his Massey Lectures (1989: 197–261) in Appendix IV "The craft of 'Historical Engineering'" how the interventions of the 1980s, already mentioned, were written out of history and the role the media and scholarship played in this "more effectively than the productions of any Ministry of Truth" (1989: 260). Two decades later at least Michael Moore and Ken Loach are making films that unearth what is going on and Chomsky is still analyzing the current contributions to this historical amnesia. Is this a sign of 'progress' or 'stagnation' or the proof that the Orwellian world is well and truly now upon us?

What I have set out to ascertain and to underline in this chapter is that disinformation techniques are a feature of inegalitarian and hierarchically class-ordered societies (perhaps more pronounced in (ex-)imperialist ones). These linguistic and discourse strategies are in the service of the maintenance of the hegemonic order. They are instruments of coercion and accordingly the only solution to the problem outlined is their destruction and removal. That this is unlikely to be an easy activity to ensure is obvious. But there are first necessary steps that can be taken towards that end. A preliminary one is enlightenment and education and making people more actively aware of what is going on. After all, as Kress and Hodge (1979: 150) bluntly put it: "Inability to interpret doublethink is a form of social incompetence, a severe handicap if doublethink is endemic to that society."

Overcoming this social incompetence will involve developing "a more critical cultural consciousness". In Chomsky's opinion no scientific expertise is required for this. The Chomskyan insight into human nature makes this much clear. As we have seen, everyone has the equipment needed to discuss and understand political matters and political issues. In his discussion of Chomsky's political interventions, McGilvray (1999: 25) has summarized the link with the cognitive psychological bases of humans, "because political discussions rely on the resources of common sense understanding, and common sense understanding depends heavily on the largely innate conceptual resources of natural languages."

When faced with questioners who do not quite know what to make of his analyses of political and social developments, Chomsky calmly suggests that they should discover for themselves, through rational inquiry, whether his description of the world is accurate. He argues, "I believe in Cartesian common sense. I think people have the capacities to see through the deceit in which they are ensnared, but they've got to make the effort" (in Achbar 1994: 20). What his critics call a conspiracy theory, Chomsky calls 'institutional analysis'. There are no mysteries involved. Sceptical and clinical attitudes, dialectical and forensic analysis are basically all one needs as a concerned citizen. Although some of the long words in the previous sentence sound complicated, there is no hocus pocus involved.

As stated everybody is capable of finding out for themselves by employing their intellectual self-defence kit. The tools can be employed to deal with propaganda, mendacity and deceit in the public sphere. The broad types of tools included are those of scepticism, the cognitive power of scrutiny and critical faculties in general. What are you supposed to do with them? The gist of the matter consists in engaging in a number of process such as unearthing 'evidence', gathering arguments, 'thinking', questioning, investigating, seeing through arguments, finding weaknesses in arguments, taking issue with positions, uncovering bias, acknowledging value positions and in sum 'reasoning'. Basically one need simply put oneself in the shoes of the small child in Hans Christian Andersen's story of the Emperor's New Clothes. What the next step then could be, is to put the results to some more practical use. But that would be the topic of a further book.

Appendices

APPENDIX 1: LIST OF DISTORTION TERMS IN ENGLISH

Processes

BAMBOOZLE—BEFOOL—BEGUILE—BLUFF—CANT—CHEAT—
CHICANERY—CONFUSE—COZENAGE—DECEPTION—DECEIT—
DEFRAUD—DELUDE—DELUSION—DIDDLE—DISSEMBLE—
DISTORT—DISTORTION—DOUBLE DEALING—DO OUT OF—
DUPE—DUPLICITY—EQUIVOCATE—EQUIVOCATION—
FABRICATE—FABRICATION—FAKE—FIB—FIDDLE—FRAUD—
GUILE—HOAX—HOODWINK—HYPE—ILLUDE—ILLUSION—
IMPOSTURE—KID—KIDDING—LIE—LYING—MISINTERPRET—
MISINTERPRETATION—MISLEAD—MISREPRESENT—
MISREPRESENTATION—MYSTIFICATION—MYSTIFY—
OBFUSCATE—OBFUSCATION—OUTSMART—OUTWIT—
PULL THE WOOL OVER S.O.'S EYES—RACKET—SCAM—SHAM—
SHARP PRACTICE—SHENANIGAN—SIMULATE—SIMULATION—
SKULDUGGERY—SLEIGHT—SWINDLE—SWIZ—SWIZZLE—
TERGIVERSATE—TERGIVERSATION—TRICK—TRICKERY—
TWISTS—WANGLE—WHITEWASH

Agents

CON-MEN—CONFIDENCE TRICKSTERS—COZENERS—
DISSEMBLERS—DOUBLE DEALERS—FABULISTS—FIBBERS—
HOAXERS—HYPESTERS—HYPOCRITES—ILLUSIONISTS—
IMPOSTERS—LIARS—MANIPULATORS—PEDDLERS—
PROPAGANDISTS—PUBLIC RELATIONS OFFICERS—SCAMMERS—
SHAMMERS—SHUCKSTERS—SHYSTERS—SPIN DOCTORS—
STORY-TELLERS—SWINDLERS—SYCOPHANTS—
TERGIVERSATORS—TRICKSTERS—YES-MEN

APPENDIX 2: THE DYNAMICS OF ECOLOGICAL CRISIS (AFTER BATESON 1972: 467)

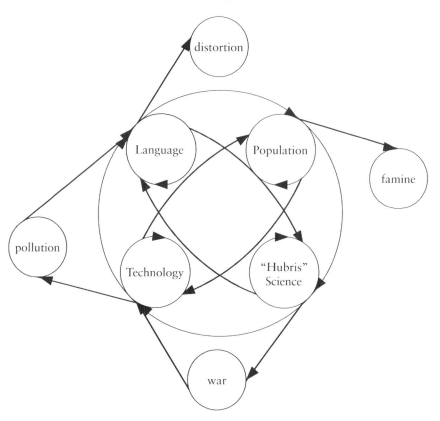

Notes

NOTES TO CHAPTER 2

1. Chapter 10 takes up this approach and develops it further.
2. See the chapter in Fowler (1991) "Analytic tools: critical linguistics" (p. 66ff).
3. As referred to by Cohen and Rogers (1991).
4. See Lele and Singh (1991) and Smith (2004) on the two sides to Chomsky's work.
5. See also the work by Andrew Goatly (1996).
6. It is worth stressing that any statement that is acceptable to nearly everybody means almost nothing. We are thinking of platitudinous and contentless claims such as appear daily in corporate advertizing by multis like Exxon or Mobil or Canon. The bland uncontentiousness of such statements is the mark of their vacuity and emptiness. In connection with political statements or "political declarations" a useful corrective can be to negate the statement. If the opposite of what people are proposing sounds stupid or ludicrous, the odds on the positive having substance sink.
7. See Alexander (1986) for an early analysis of this aspect of the journal. I looked at article headlines in *The Economist* and the role puns, allusions and metaphors play in them.
8. Note the frippery which alludes to a song lyric—"In our mountain greenery, where God paints the scenery."
9. See Roland Howard (1995) on The Ethical Trading World.
10. In Austria too, as was evident at a "Shopping for a Better World", ethical products fair, in Vienna, September 24, 1995.
11. See *The Economist* (1993) A Green Account, September 4th.
12. See Halliday (1985: 202–27), who discusses the mechanisms serving to functionally relate clauses.
13. See Bolinger (1980) for more on these techniques.
14. See Chomsky's early essays on the War in Vietnam in Chomsky (1969).
15. Chomsky (1994a: 89) refers to the distinctive contribution of business propaganda. On this he quotes the work of Alex Carey on 20th century developments.
16. See also Chomsky (1989: 197–261).
17. Chomsky has repeatedly discussed terminological choices like 'pacification', 'terrorism', 'defense', 'conservative' etc. C. P. Otero in Chomsky (1981: 58) draws attention to Chomsky's careful textual analysis, remarking: "For Chomsky, this sort of conceptual analysis has little to do with the study of the structure of language. But for other linguists, it does."
18. See Edwards (1995) which is a sustained précis of Chomsky's work on media, propaganda and corporate consumerism and what one can do against it; it is useful in focussing some of the themes we are discussing here.

19. See the Seabrook article "Vested disinterests" *New Statesman and Society* 20 May 1994.

20. For after all there are limits to what we can do. Otero (in the Introduction to Chomsky 1981: 13) sees this in his presentation of Chomsky and his political work: "The vast majority of our contemporaries do not have the time to do all alone what it takes to extricate oneself and help others extricate themselves from the maze of ideological deception and official mythology." Moreover we might query whether 'Orwell's problem' does not need slightly more that just common sense to crack it. See Chapters 10 and 11 for further discussion of this issue.

21. As Trevor Pateman (1980: 183) writes: "Human facts, unlike things and events in the world of nature, depend for their existence on what human beings *do*." Reification is the name given to those situations where human beings treat human activities and the institutions, like wage bargaining procedures or commercial contracts, etc., maintained by those activities *as if* they were like things in the natural world. Pateman continues (1980: 184): "For example, economists tend to view economic life in terms of an interaction between *commodities* in the market, and see the fate of man as hingeing on price fluctuations. They speak of men being thrown out of work *by* a fall on the gold market." Certainly it is a widespread form of control indulged in by powerful vested or interested knowledge holders (i.e. academics and administrators of dominant institutions) to present the matter thus. We can see elsewhere—in the discussion of deforestation and the connection to debt (George 1992: 1–33), how directly and rapidly the reification process operates in our networked global economy today.

22. Through all of this a discourse-based view of language will best serve us, as represented in McCarthy and Carter (1994: 38): "A discourse-based view of language [. . .] involves examining how bits of language contribute to the making of complete texts. It involves exploring the relationship between the linguistic patterns of complete texts and the social contexts in which they function. It involves considering the higher-order operations of language at the interface of cultural and ideological meanings and returning to the lower-order forms of language which are often crucial to the patterning of such meanings."

23. Chomsky has also said (1987: 81): "What I want to do is identify problems that are first of all important and morally significant, that is there are human consequences to what we do or don't do about them, and that are badly misunderstood and misinterpreted."

24. See Alexander Cockburn (1995: 10–11) on the sad history despite Clinton's early claims to being green.

25. See Edwards (1995: 189), where he stresses that we need to see that "modern environmental problems are deeply rooted in the logic of the economic system."

26. 'Distort' comes from distorquere—to twist apart or asunder. One important connotation is "dismembering, destroying, breaking up" something once whole. The contrast underlying the use of such words containing the cluster of semantic features [+ straight][+ good] versus [– straight, i.e. + crooked] [– good] is frequently activated. The lexical field of *spin, bias, twist, bend* etc. when used metaphorically in English has this negative connotation or actually denotes the semantic features [– straight, i.e. + crooked] [– good].

27. It is worth referring to Hymes and to his discussion of linguistic inequality in relation to Chomsky. I have no space here to go into what some see as the bifurcation of Chomsky and his academic and political writing. There is a tie-in to Hymes' (1973) early work on the issue of linguistic inequality. In Hymes

we find an emphasis on the context in which competence realizes itself. The real world, as opposed to an idealized or reductionist model, provides the starting point for a realistic assessment of linguistic resources in speech communities. Our (earlier) mention of the ecology of language and the upgrading of linguistic diversity is here addressed. Indeed I find Hymes' (1973: 81) characterization of Chomskyan linguistics still as potent and apt today and hence worth repeating here: "Chomskyan theory holds out the liberation of mankind as an inspiration, but its practice can contribute only conceptually at least, if it does not in fact stand as an obstacle to the kind of work that is actually needed." I think it is fair to say that much of the work of colleagues working in the area of language and ecology is testimony to the fact that language in a social context, the ecology of language approach has not allowed itself to be prevented by the obstacle of Chomskyan linguistics. And in combination and cooperation with other disciplinary approaches—the social sciences, life sciences, biology, ecology, and economics—we can begin to untwist the *knot* of distortion which is contributing to the ecological crisis.

28. See Herman and Chomsky (1988) for more on the political economy of the media, and also see also chapters 7 and 10 on Herman's power laws in relation to the media.

NOTES TO CHAPTER 3

1. Using a computer-held corpus of texts with a simple concordancing program, we can automatically ascertain a number of facts. We can know the total number of words (running words) and the total number of different words (word-forms) in a text. On the basis of these two measures we can ascertain the degree of *lexical diversity* manifested in the individual texts. Browne's speech is a short text—396 word forms, 826 total words. This says nothing about the number of lemmata. The type-token-ratio is calculated by dividing the total number of different words (word-forms) by the total number of words (i.e. of running words). Maximum diversity, i.e. every other word being different equals unity (1). The more repetitive the text the closer to zero (0) the ratio will be. (This gives rise to *less* diversity.) The type-token-ratio (TTR) is 0.48. There may be situations in which comparisons of texts with regard to lexical diversity might tell us something about the values coded in the texts. For instance, there may well be a relationship between repetitiveness and accustoming readers or listeners to certain notions. One of the most basic techniques of language data-processing is the production of alphabetical frequency lists. Such lists may be helpful; but they tell us little by themselves. "A frequency list of word-forms is never more than a set of hints or clues to the nature of a text" (Sinclair 1991: 31).

2. The programme used is called Conc., version of July 2, 1992. It is shareware developed by Evan Antworth, Academic Computing Department, Summer Institute of Linguistics, 7500 W. Camp Wisdom Road, Dallas, TX 75236.

3. The numbers in the first column of the concordance tables indicate the lines in the text generated by the software. They are retained for recognition purposes.

NOTES TO CHAPTER 7

1. Such an anthropocentric view should not surprise us if we view language as species-specific to humans and hence as evolutionarily necessary for survival

so far. For Chomsky, in the rationalist and Platonist tradition of philosophy (following the work of Ralph Cudworth), it is evident that the human mind predisposes humans to focus on what leads to human survival. The deepest level of language is universal to all humans. Language concepts such as 'persuade' are central to his conception of the mind, as we know. Chomsky (1975: 6) writes: "Cudworth argued at length that the mind has an 'innate cognoscitive power' that provides the principles and conceptions that constitute our knowledge, when provoked by sense to do so." See McGilvray (1999: 168–76) for a lucid discussion of this aspect of Chomsky's work. The question of whether epistemologically founded anthropocentrism is sufficient to deal with the prevention of environmental destruction is another matter. It is one which is taken up and cogently argued by Goatly (1996).

NOTES TO CHAPTER 10

1. "Orwell's problem is to explain why we know and understand so little, even though the evidence available to us is so rich. Like many other twentieth-century intellectuals, Orwell was impressed by the ability of totalitarian systems to instill beliefs that are firmly held and widely accepted although they are completely without foundation and often plainly at variance with obvious facts about the world around us. The problem is far broader, as the history of religious dogma suffices to show. To solve Orwell's problem we must discover the institutional and other factors that block insight and understanding in crucial areas of our life and ask why they are effective. [. . .] I think it has been amply demonstrated that in democratic societies where violence is rarely used to ensure obedience, Orwell's problem nevertheless arises" (Chomsky 1986: xxvii). Chomsky then contrasts Orwell's problem with Plato's problem, which is amenable to scientific probing. "The study of Orwell's problem is quite different. The patterns that lie behind the most important phenomena of political, economic, and social life are not very difficult to discern, although much effort is devoted to obscuring the fact: and the explanation for what will be observed by those who can free themselves from the doctrines of the faith is hardly profound or difficult to discover or comprehend. [. . .] The context of an inquiry into the nature of language is perhaps not the appropriate place, despite the widespread belief, which I personally share only in part, that misuse or control of language is a central feature of the problem" (Chomsky 1986: xxviii).
2. This is a subscription-accessible part of a very large corpus of 330 million words known as the Bank of English held by the University of Birmingham. Roughly 80% of these are written and 20% are spoken language. There are seventeen separate sub-corpora covering newspapers (42%), books (23%), magazines (15%), television, radio and ephemera (posters, advertising, bus tickets etc.).
3. J. R. Firth's position can be seen in this extract (1937: 19): "Let us begin by regarding man as inseparable from the world in which he lives. He is just part of it. He is not here primarily to think about it but to act suitably, which must be taken to include the ability to refrain from acting when the situation requires it." As the final clause makes clear, men or, as we would say today, persons are not creatures of reflexes to be triggered by the situation. At the same time, there is a tension immanent in the Firthian approach. Human beings operate or 'act', as Firth puts it, in a domain which entails both *constraints* and *choices*. The language system provides the language user with a set of

choices between which she can/may select. But such is the porous nature of the language system and the indeterminate nature of most situations that no inevitable 'choice' is forced upon the language user. Halliday (1978: 51) has argued for this position by referring to language as "a form of human semiotic"; as he says with regard to language, "I want to characterize it in terms of the part it plays in the life of social man."

4. A biographical aside may help to contextualize the highlighting of this approach. I was reading linguistics as well as German and French at Cambridge in the early nineteen-sixties. I had the good fortune to be supervised by John Trim. He impressed upon me the importance of the London School (Firth and Malinowski and of course Daniel Jones) and their approach to the analysis of language. I had a personal skirmish with TG—who didn't?—during which I was forced to plough through Emmon Bach's (1964) *An Introduction to Transformational Grammars*, I recall. But more significant, in retrospect, for my own work, was the fact that we were lectured to by R. H. Robins, a former pupil of Firth's, for a term; he stood in while John Trim was on sabbatical. Here were laid the bases for an implicitly Firthian view of language which has informed my work and has persisted till today, with TG having gone out the window, where it perhaps best belongs. See Alexander (1978).

5. George Steiner argues polemically for this when he quotes Hymes: "Most of language begins where abstract universals leave off" (1975: 472).

6. Chomsky calls his thinking on connecting language and freedom 'speculations'. But he does make a pertinent point (1973: 174): "Language in its essential properties and the manner of its use, provides the basic criterion for determining that another organism is a being with a human mind and the human capacity for free thought and self-expression, and with the essential human need for freedom from the external constraints of repressive authority."

7. In *Keeping the Rabble in Line. Interviews with David Barsamian* (1994b: 108–9), we find the following passage: "The only reason I don't use the word 'class' is that the terminology of political discourse is so debased it's hard to find any words at all. That's part of the point, to make it impossible to talk. For one thing, 'class' has various associations. [. . .] But you can't get away from the fact that there are sharp differences in power which in fact are ultimately rooted in the economic system. You can talk about the masters, if you like. It's Adam Smith's word, you might as well go back to that. They are the masters, and they follow what he called their 'vile maxim,' namely 'all for ourselves and nothing for other people.' That's a good first approximation to it, since Adam Smith is now in fashion."

8. Cf. the furore which Chomsky's "support for the right of Robert Faurisson to express his sharply contrary views, irrespective of the character or the quality of his views" (1981: 15–16) in France created among the self-appointed commissars and censors who clearly still walk the corridors of European universities in many countries! See Carlos P. Otero's introduction to Chomsky (1981: 15–16) and his notes for more documentation.

9. I encountered Raymond Williams, the academic, before I encountered linguistics, so to speak. In this respect my experience is not perhaps especially unique. At my grammar school in Britain we had an English teacher who regaled us with both Richard Hoggart's *The Uses of Literacy* (1957) and Raymond Williams' *Communications* (1962 edition). Williams, in person, I met as an undergraduate at Jesus College, Cambridge, in the early sixties. In politics, in the form of the Jesus College Labour Club, was the first personal context in which I got to know Williams. Later in May 1967 I remember being at the launch of the May Day Manifesto in a Bloomsbury pub at which Raymond

Williams, Edward Thompson and Stuart Hall held forth on the weaknesses of the Labour Party and its analysis of the British Crisis and called for a new orientation of the Left.

10. See 'Vorbereitende Bemerkungen zu einer Theorie der kommunikativen Kompetenz,' in Jürgen Habermas and Niklas Luhmann (1971) *Theorie der Gesellschaft oder Sozialtechnologie? Was leistet die Systemtheorie?* Frankfurt: Suhrkamp, 101–41.

11. See Dickens' satirizing of the government Circumlocution Office in chapter 10 of *Little Dorrit*.

NOTES TO CHAPTER 11

1. Herman (1992: 23) describes the phenomenon: "As the weapons culture grew, the industrial interests producing weapons and their Pentagon and congressional allies—a so-called 'iron triangle' or 'military-industrial complex' (MIC)—of enormous and partially independent power, gradually emerged. The MIC's ability to command resources rested on its service to the transnational corporate system, as well as its own extraordinary institutional power. [. . .] The MIC is a closed self-protective, feedback system, loaded with conflicts of interest, but now built into the political economy."

2. For more on the comparable, if smaller-scale, developments in Britain see Edgerton (2006) and Curtis (1995, 2003a and 2004) and on (West) Germany see Biermann and Klönne (2005: 174–88).

3. See 'Linguistics professor George Lakoff dissects the 'war on terror' and other conservative catchphrases', in an interview in UC Berkeley News. "In 2000 Lakoff and seven other faculty members from Berkeley and UC Davis joined together to found the Rockridge Institute, one of the few progressive think tanks in existence in the U.S. The institute offers its expertise and research on a nonpartisan basis to help progressives understand how best to get their messages across." <http://www.berkeley.edu/news/media/releases/2004/08/25_lakoff.shtml> (Accessed 18 August 2006).

4. Consider also Chomsky (1994a: 100–106) and (2002: 70–6) for a very well documented description of the 'military-industrial complex' and 'the permanent war economy'. See also Galbraith (1992: 133–43), Kidron (1968), Kidron and Smith (1983) and Smith (2003) for facts on the extent of war and its role in international relations for the past sixty years.

5. Based on The Research Unit for Political Economy, *Monthly Review* 55, No. 1 (May 2003).

6. One is reminded of the situation Saul Landau discusses in connection with logic (2001). He says he is planning "courses in the new logic so that students can compare the words officials use against what they see, hear and read." To illustrate the situation he quotes a famous comedian's quip. "If anyone doubts the veracity of our leaders, recall Richard Pryor's wife when she discovers him in bed naked with a naked woman":

"Hey, sugar, it's not what you think," says Pryor.

"What do you mean? Are you nuts? I'm seeing this scene with my own eyes," she says.

"Hey, honey," says Pryor, "who you gonna believe, me or your lying eyes?"

7. The work of Frank Luntz has been made available by some public-spirited bloggers in the USA. See Tom Ball 'Frank Luntz "Straight Talk" The Environment: A Cleaner, Safer, Healthier America' <http://www.politicalstrategy.

org/archives/001330.php> (accessed 30 September 2006). See also the conscious use of 'relexicalization' or re-classification as illustrated by a document 'The Principles and Language of Immigration Reform October, 2005' on the issue of immigration into the USA. <http://images.dailykos.com/images/user/3/Luntz_frames_immigration.pdf> (source accessed 1 October 2006). This provides a summary of six policies and their language to appeal to a majority of Republicans and moderate Democrats. Lakoff refers to this document also on the Rockridge Institute website. See also the recent book by Luntz himself (2007).

Bibliography

Achbar, Mark (ed.) (1994) *Manufacturing Consent. Noam Chomsky and the Media*. New York: Black Rose Books.

Adorno, Theodor W., Frenkel-Brunswick, E., Levinson, D. J. and Sandford, R. W. (1950) *The Authoritarian Personality*. New York: Harper and Row.

Agee, Philip (1975) *Inside the Company. CIA Diary*. Harmondworth: Penguin.

Alexander, Richard J. (1978) What use is a theory of language which excludes a theory of language use? *Linguistische Berichte*, 57/78: 1–13.

Alexander, Richard J. (1986) Article headlines in *The Economist*. An analysis of puns, allusions and metaphors. *Arbeiten aus Anglistik und Amerikanistik*, 11(2): 159–177.

Alexander, Richard J. (1993) Introduction to the Aims of the Symposium, Work So Far and Some Ecolinguistic Principles to Pursue. In R. J. Alexander, J. C. Bang and J. Døør (eds.), *Papers for the symposium "Ecolinguistics. Problems, theories and methods" AILA 1993*, 21–30. Odense: Odense University.

Alexander, Richard J. (1996) Introduction to the Symposium 'Language and Ecology': Past, Present and Future. In J. C. Bang, J. Døør, R. J. Alexander, A. Fill and F. Verhagen (eds.), *Language and Ecology: Eco-Linguistics. Problems, theories and methods. Essays for the AILA 1996 Symposium*, 17–25. Odense: Odense University.

Ali, Tariq (2003) *Bush in Babylon. The Recolonisation of Iraq*. London: Verso Books.

Amidon, Stephen (2000) On Herbert Marcuse's *One Dimensional Man*. *New Statesman* 27 November 2000, 55–57.

Athanasiou, Tom (1996) *Divided Planet. The Ecology of Rich and Poor*. Athens, Georgia: University of Georgia Press.

Austria. Facts and Figures (1994) Vienna: Federal Press Service.

Ayto, John (1993) *Dictionary of Euphemisms* (2000 2nd edition). London: Bloomsbury.

Bach, Emmon (1964) *An Introduction to Transformational Grammars*. New York: Holt, Rinehart and Winston, Inc.

Bang, Jørg Chr., and Døør, Jørg (1993) Eco-Linguistics: A Framework. In R. J. Alexander, J. C. Bang and J. Døør (eds.), *Papers for the symposium "Ecolinguistics. Problems, theories and methods" AILA 1993*, 31–60. Odense: Odense University.

Bateson, Gregory (1972) *Steps to an Ecology of Mind*. Frogmore, St. Albans: Paladin.

Beckwith, Lois (2006) *The Dictionary of Corporate Bullshit*. New York: Broadway Books.

Beder, Sharon (1997) *Global Spin. The Corporate Assault on Environmentalism.* Foxhole, Dartington: Green Books.

Beingessner, Paul (2003) Monsanto sues and sues and sues and . . . . *Cropchoice. An alternative news source for American farmers.* <http://www.cropchoice.com/ pf_lead.asp?recid=1855> (Last accessed 27 December, 2003)

Berger, John (2003) Où sommes-nous? *Le Monde diplomatique* Février 2003, 15.

Biermann, Werner and Klönne, Arno (2005) *Kapital-Verbrechen. Zur Kriminalge- schichte des Kapitalismus.* Köln: PapyRossa Verlag.

Biewen, John (2000) Engineering Crops in a Needy World. American RadioWorks, Minnesota Public Radio. <http://www.americanradioworks.org/features/gmos_ india/index.html> (Last accessed 12 September, 2003)

Blum, William (2000) *Rogue State. A Guide to the World's Only Superpower.* Lon- don and New York: Zed Books.

Blum, William (2003) *Killing Hope. US Military & CIA Interventions Since World War II.* London and New York: Zed Books.

Bolinger, Dwight (1980) *Language. The Loaded Weapon.* London: Longman.

Brooks, Richard (2006) A man of the people. *New Statesman* 19 June 2006, 46–7.

Browne, John (1997) Our common journey. *New Statesman* 20 June 1997, 19.

Busch, Simon (2005) Can you incent? Passionately? *New Statesman* 21 November 2005, 32.

Cain, Peter J. and Hopkins, Anthony G. (1993) *British Imperialism. Innovation and Expansion. 1688–1914.* Harlow, Essex: Longman.

Cameron, Deborah (2000) *Good to Talk?* London, Thousand Oaks, CA, and New Delhi: Sage.

Cameron, Deborah (2006) *On Language and Sexual Politics.* Abingdon and New York: Routledge.

Carey, Alex (1995) *Taking the risk out of democracy. Corporate propaganda ver- sus freedom and liberty.* New York, Sydney, Australia: University of New South Wales Press, Ltd./Urbana and Chicago: University of Illinois Press. (ed. by Andrew Lohrey, with a foreword by Noam Chomsky.)

Carroll, Lewis (1970) *The Annotated Alice. Alice's Adventures in Wonderland & Through the Looking Glass.* (ed. Martin Gardner.) Harmondsworth: Penguin Books.

Carson, Rachel (1962/1999) *Silent Spring.* Harmondsworth: Penguin Books.

Cavanagh, John, Wysham, Daphne and Arruda, Marcos (eds.) (1994) *Beyond Bret- ton Woods. Alternatives to the Global Economic Order.* London: Pluto Press.

Chilton, Paul (1988) *Orwellian Language and the Media.* London: Pluto Press.

Chilton, Paul and Lakoff, George (1995) Foreign policy by metaphor. In C. Schäff- ner and A. Wenden (eds.), *Language and Peace*, 37–59. Aldershot: Dartmouth Books.

Chomsky, Noam (1966) The Responsibility of the Intellectuals. Reprinted in N. Chomsky, *American Power and the New Mandarins*, 256–90. New York: Pan- theon/Harmondsworth: Penguin.

Chomsky, Noam (1969) *American Power and the New Mandarins.* New York: Pan- theon/Harmondsworth: Penguin.

Chomsky, Noam (1973) *For Reasons of State.* London: Fontana.

Chomsky, Noam (1975) *Reflections on Language.* London: Temple Smith.

Chomsky, Noam (1979) *Language and Responsibility. Based on Conversations with Mitsou Ronat.* Hassocks, Sussex: The Harvester Press. (1977 published in France.)

Chomsky, Noam (1981) *Radical Priorities.* (ed. Otero, Carlos P.) Montreal: Black Rose Books.

Chomsky, Noam (1985) *Turning the Tide. US Intervention in Central America and the Struggle for Peace.* Boston: South End Press/London: Pluto Press.

Chomsky, Noam (1986) *Knowledge of Language*. New York: Praeger.

Chomsky, Noam (1987) The New Cold War. In Bourne, Bill, Eichler, Udi and Herman, David (eds.), *Voices, from the Channel 4 Television Series. Writers and Politics*, 65–84. Nottingham: Spokesman.

Chomsky, Noam (1988a) *Language and Politics*. (ed. Otero, Carlos P.) New York: Black Rose Books.

Chomsky, Noam (1988b) *The Culture of Terrorism*. London: Pluto Press.

Chomsky, Noam (1989) *Necessary Illusions: Thought Control in Democratic Societies*. London: Pluto Press.

Chomsky, Noam (1991) *Deterring Democracy*. London: Verso.

Chomsky, Noam (1993) *Year 501. The Conquest Continues*. London: Verso.

Chomsky, Noam (1994a) *World Orders, Old and New*. London: Pluto Press.

Chomsky, Noam (1994b) *Keeping the Rabble in Line. Interviews with David Barsamian*. Monroe, Maine: Common Courage Press.

Chomsky, Noam (1994c) *Secrets, Lies and Democracy*. Berkeley, CA: Odonian Press.

Chomsky, Noam (1999a) *Profit over People: Neoliberalism and Global Order*. (Introduction by Robert W. McChesney.) New York: Seven Stories Press.

Chomsky, Noam (1999b) *The New Military Humanism. Lessons from Kosovo*. London: Pluto Press.

Chomsky, Noam (2000) *Rogue States. The Rule of Force in World Affairs*. London: Pluto Press.

Chomsky, Noam (2001) *9/11*. New York: Seven Stories Press.

Chomsky, Noam (2002) *Understanding Power: The Indispensable Chomsky*. (eds. Mitchell, Peter R. and Schoeffel, John.) New York: New Press.

Chomsky, Noam (2003) *Hegemony or Survival. America's Quest for Global Dominance*. London: Hamish Hamilton.

Chomsky, Noam (2005) *Imperial Ambitions. Conversations with Noam Chomsky on the post 9/11 World. Interviews with David Barsamian*. London: Hamish Hamilton.

Chomsky, Noam (2006a) *Failed States. The Abuse of Power and the Assault on Democracy*. London: Hamish Hamilton.

Chomsky, Noam (2006b) Afterword: Failed States (An expanded version of the afterword to 2006a). *ZNet Commentary* April 26, 2006.

Choudry, Aziz (2002) The Asian Development Bank—'Governing' the Pacific? *ZNet Commentary* June 9, 2002.

Clark, Kate (2006) Talking to the Taliban. *New Statesman* 17 July 2006, 13.

Cockburn, Alexander (1995) Letter from: America. *New Statesman and Society* 28 July 1995, 10–11.

Cohen, Joshua and Rogers, Joel (1991) Knowledge, Morality and Hope: The Social Thought of Noam Chomsky. *New Left Review*, 187: 5–27.

Cook, Guy (2004) *Genetically Modified Language*. London: Routledge.

CorporateWatch (2003) GM Crops Family Tree 2003. <http://www.corporatewatch. org.uk/genetics/familytree.htm> (Last accessed 27 December, 2003)

Curtis, Mark (1995) *The Ambiguities of Power. British Foreign Policy since 1945*. London and Atlantic Highlands, NJ: Zed Books.

Curtis, Mark (2002) Iraq, the Media and the Reality of British Foreign Policy. Talk at the Stop the War conference, School of Oriental and African Studies, London, 12 October 2002 (no pagination). <http://www.cmyk.info/markcurtis/articles.html> (Last accessed 20 October 2003)

Curtis, Mark (2003a) Partners in Imperialism—Britain's support for US intervention. *Frontline Magazine*, India April 26 2003.

Curtis, Mark (2003b) *Web of Deceit. Britain's Real Role in the World*. London: Vintage.

Curtis, Mark (2004) *Unpeople. Britain's Secret Human Rights Abuses*. London: Vintage.

Døør, Jørg and Bang, Jørg Chr. (1996) Language, Ecology & Truth—Dialogue and Dialectics. In A. Fill (ed.), *Sprachökologie und Ökolinguistik*, 17–25. Tübingen: Stauffenburg Verlag.

Dunn, John (2000) *The Cunning of Unreason. Making Sense of Politics*. London: HarperCollins.

Economist (1993) A Green Account. *The Economist* September 4th.

Edgerton, David (2006) *Warfare State: Britain, 1920–1970*. Cambridge: Cambridge University Press.

Edwards, David (1995) *Free to Be Human*. Dartington, Devon: Green Books.

Edwards, David and Cromwell, David (2006) *Guardians of Power. The Myth of the Liberal Media*. London: Pluto Press.

Encarta World English Dictionary (1999) London: Bloomsbury Publishing Plc.

Fairclough, Norman (1989) *Language and Power*. Harlow: Longman.

Fairclough, Norman (1992) *Discourse and Social Change*. Cambridge: Polity Press.

Fairclough, Norman (1995a) *Media Discourse*. London: Edward Arnold.

Fairclough, Norman (1995b) *Critical Discourse Analysis. The Critical Study of Language*. Harlow: Longman.

Fairclough, Norman (2000) *New Labour, New Language?* London: Routledge.

Fill, Alwin (1993) *Ökolinguistik. Eine Einführung*. Tübingen: Günter Narr.

Fill, Alwin (1996) Ökologie der Linguistik—Linguistik der Ökologie. In A. Fill (ed.), *Sprachökologie und Ökolinguistik*, 3–16. Tübingen: Stauffenburg Verlag.

Fill, Alwin (1998) Ecolinguistics—State of the Art 1998. *Arbeiten aus Anglistik und Amerikanistik*, 23/1: 3–16.

Fill, Alwin and Mühlhäusler, Peter (eds.) (2001) *The Ecolinguistics Reader. Language, Ecology and Environment*. London and New York: Continuum Press.

Firth, John Rupert (1937) *The Tongues of Men*. (ed. Strevens, P. D.) London: Oxford University Press.

Firth, John Rupert (1957) *Papers in Linguistics. 1930–1951*. London: Oxford University Press.

Fisk, Robert (2001) Locked in an Orwellian Eternal War. *The Independent* February 19, 2001 and *ZMagazine* 2001. <http://www.zmag.org/crisescurevts/Iraq/fiskiraq.htm> (Last accessed 21 February 2001)

Fowler, Roger (1991) *Language in the Media. Discourse and Ideology in the Press*. London: Routledge.

Fowler, Roger, Hodge, Robert, Kress, Gunther and Trew, Anthony (1979) *Language and Control*. London: Routledge and Kegan Paul.

Frankfurt, Harry G. (2005) *On Bullshit*. Princeton, NJ: Princeton University Press.

Galbraith, John Kenneth (1992) *The Culture of Contentment*. Harmondsworth: Penguin.

Galeano, Eduardo (1998) *Patas Arriba. La escuela del mundo al revés*. Madrid: Siglo XXI de España Editores, S.A. (Translated by Mark Fried (2000) *Upside Down. A Primer for the Looking-Glass World*. New York: Metropolitan Books.)

Genske, Dieter D. (2006) Umwelt begreifen. Transdisziplinäre Umweltkommunikation im Feld. In E. W. B. Hess-Lüttich (ed.), *Eco-Semiotics. Umwelt-Entwicklungskommunikation*, 155–64. Basel/Tübingen: Francke.

George, Susan (1990) *Ill Fares the Land*. Harmondsworth: Penguin.

George, Susan (1992) *The Debt Boomerang*. London: Pluto.

George, Susan (2003) Personne ne veut des OGM, sauf les industriels? *Le Monde Diplomatique* Avril 2003: 4–5.

George, Susan (2004) *Another World Is Possible If . . . .* London and New York: Verso.

Gerbig, Andrea (1993) The representation of agency and control in texts on the environment. In R. J. Alexander, J. C. Bang and J. Døør (eds.), *Papers for the symposium "Ecolinguistics. Problems, theories and methods" AILA 1993*, 61–73. Odense: Odense University.

Gerbig, Andrea (1996) Sprachliche Konstruktion politischer Realität: stilistische Variation in der Ozondebatte. In A. Fill (ed.), *Sprachökologie und Ökolinguistik*, 175–85. Tübingen: Stauffenburg Verlag.

Ghazi, Polly and Hargreaves, Ian (1997) Interview with John Browne. *New Statesman* 4 July 1997, 34–6.

Goatly, Andrew (1996) Green Grammar and Grammatical Metaphors or Language and the Myth of Power or Metaphors We Die By. *Journal of Pragmatics*, 25: 537–60. (Reprinted in A. Fill and P. Mühlhäusler (eds.) (2001), *The Ecolinguistics Reader. Language, Ecology and Environment*, 203–25. London and New York: Continuum Press.)

Gray, John (2006) Rather than Face up to Climate Change, Humanity May Opt to Let it Happen. *New Statesman* 29 May 2006, 34–7.

Greer, Jed and Bruno, Kenny (1996) *Greenwash. The Reality behind Corporate Environmentalism*. New York and Penang: Apex Press and Third World Network.

Habermas, Jürgen (1971) Vorbereitende Bemerkungen zu einer Theorie der kommunikativen Kompetenz. In Habermas, Jürgen and Luhmann, Niklas (eds.), *Theorie der Gesellschaft oder Sozialtechnologie? Was leistet die Systemtheorie?*, 101–41. Frankfurt: Suhrkamp.

Hall, Stuart (1988) *The Hard Road to Renewal. Thatcherism and the Crisis of the Left*. London: Verso.

Halliday, Michael A. K. (1976) Types of process. In Kress, Gunther (ed.) *Halliday: System and Function in Language*, 159–73. London: Oxford University Press.

Halliday, Michael A. K. (1978) *Language as Social Semiotic*. London: Edward Arnold.

Halliday, Michael A. K. (1985) *An Introduction to Functional Grammar*. London: Edward Arnold.

Halliday, Michael A. K. (1990) New ways of meaning. A challenge to applied linguistics. *Journal of Applied Linguistics*, 6: 7–36.

Halliday, Michael A. K. and Hasan, Ruqaia (1976) *Cohesion in English*. London: Longman.

Harré, Rom, Brockmeier, Jens, Mühlhäusler, Peter (1999) *Greenspeak. A Study of Environmental Discourse*. Thousand Oaks, CA: Sage Publications.

Harris, Roy (1990) On Freedom of Speech. In Joseph, John E. and Taylor, Talbot J. (eds.), *Ideologies of Language*, 153–61. London: Routledge.

Harris, Roy (2005) Speaking out for the Right to Speak Evil. *The Times Higher* December 9 2005, 14.

Hayward, Anthony (2001) *In the Name of Justice. The Television Reporting of John Pilger*. London: Bloomsbury.

Hayward, Anthony (2004) *Which Side Are You On? Ken Loach and His Films*. London: Bloomsbury.

Herman, Edward S. (1992) *Beyond Hypocrisy. Decoding the News in an Age of Propaganda. Including the Doublespeak Dictionary*. Boston: South End Press.

Herman, Edward S. (1995) *Triumph of the Market: Essays on Economics, Politics and the Media*. Boston: South End Press.

Herman, Edward S. (1999a) Corporate Sovereignty and (Junk) Science. *Z-Net Magazine* January 1999. <http://www.zmag.org/ScienceWars/corporate_sovereignty.htm> (Last accessed 23 February 1999)

Herman, Edward S. (1999b) Kosovo and doublespeak. *Z-Net Commentary* June 15, 1999.

Herman, Edward and Chomsky, Noam (1988) *Manufacturing Consent: The Political Economy of the Mass Media.* New York: Pantheon.

Hobbes, Thomas (1651) *Leviathan or The Matter, Forme, & Power of a Common-Wealth Ecclesiasticall and Civill.* London: Andrew Crooke. (Macpherson, C. B. (ed.) (1968) Harmondsworth: Penguin Books Ltd.)

Hobsbawm, Eric (1994) *Age of Extremes. The Short Twentieth Century 1914–1991.* London: Michael Joseph.

Hobsbawm, Eric (1997) Barbarism: A User's Guide. In E. Hobsbawm, *On History,* 253–65. London: Weidenfeld and Nicolson.

Hodge, Bob, and Fowler, Roger (1979) Orwellian Linguistics. In R. Fowler, R. Hodge, G. Kress, and A. Trew (eds.), *Language and Control,* 6–25. London: Routledge and Kegan Paul.

Hoggart, Richard (1957) *The Uses of Literacy.* London: Chatto and Windus.

Howard, Roland (1995) Fair Trade Wins. *New Statesman and Society* 27 January 1995, 18–19.

Hymes, Dell (1973) Speech and Language: On the Origins and Foundations of Inequality Among Speakers. *Daedalus,* 102(3): 59–85.

Jameson, Daphne A. (2000) Telling the Investment Story: A Narrative Analysis of Shareholder Reports. *The Journal of Business Communication,* 31/1: 7–38.

Jasanoff, Sheila S. (1987) Contested Boundaries in Policy-Relevant Science. *Social Studies of Science,* 17/2: 195–230.

Johnson, Chalmers (2000) *Blowback: The Costs and Consequences of American Empire.* New York: Henry Holt and Company.

Johnson, Chalmers (2004) *The Sorrows of Empire: Militarism, Secrecy, and the End of the Republic.* London: Verso.

Joint Chiefs of Staff (1995) *National Military Strategy of the United States of America. A Strategy of Flexible and Selective Engagement.* Washington, DC: U.S. Government Printing Office.

Keen, David (2006a) *Endless War? Hidden Functions of the 'War on Terror'.* London and Ann Arbor, MI: Pluto.

Keen, David (2006b) One Down—But There's Always One More to Go. *The Times Higher* June 16 2006, 16.

Kennedy, Helena (2006) Diary. *New Statesman* 20 March 2006, 6.

Kidron, Michael (1968) *Western Capitalism Since the War.* Harmondsworth: Penguin.

Kidron, Michael and Smith, Dan (1983) *The War Atlas. Armed Conflict—Armed Peace.* London: Pluto.

Kidron, Michael and Segal, Ronald (1987) *Book of Business, Money and Power.* London: Pan Books.

Kress, Gunther (1989) History and Language: Towards a Social Account of Linguistic Change. *Journal of Pragmatics,* 13: 445–66.

Kress, Gunther and Hodge, Robert (1979) *Language as Ideology.* London: Routledge.

Lakoff, George (1987) *Women, Fire, and Dangerous Things. What Categories Reveal about the Mind.* Chicago and London: University of Chicago Press.

Lakoff, George (1991) Metaphor and War: The Metaphor System Used to Justify War in the Gulf. (Internet January 1991.) (Reprinted in Pütz, Martin (ed.) (1992) *Thirty Years of Linguistic Evolution,* 463–81. Philadelphia/Amsterdam: John Benjamins Publishing Company.)

Lakoff, George (1996) *Moral Politics. What Conservatives Know That Liberals Don't.* Chicago and London: University of Chicago Press.

Lakoff, George (2005) 'War on Terror,' Rest In Peace. The Rockridge Institute, 2006. <http://www.rockridgeinstitute.org/research/lakoff/incompetent/view> (Accessed August 25 2006)

Lakoff, George and Johnson, Mark (1980) *Metaphors We Live By*. Chicago: Chicago University Press.

Lakoff, George, Ferguson, Sam and Ettlinger, Marc (2006) Bush Is Not Incompetent. The Rockridge Institute, 2006. <http://www.rockridgeinstitute.org/research/lakoff/incompetent/view> (accessed August 25 2006)

Lakoff, Robin Tolmach (2000) *The Language War*. Berkeley: University of California Press.

Landau, Saul (2001) The Logic Of Our Time. *ZNet Commentary* October 10, 2001.

Laverty, Paul (2006) How the personal became political. *New Statesman* 19 June 2006, 47.

Lele, Jayant K. and Singh, Rajendra (1991) And Never the Twain Shall Meet or Language and Politics *chez* Chomsky: A Review of Noam Chomsky's *Language and problems of knowledge* and *On power and ideology*. *Journal of Pragmatics*, 15: 175–94.

Limberger, Eva (2003) *McShrimps. An Analysis of Shrimp Production in Less Developed Countries and Its Effects on the Economy and the Environment in Relation to Sustainable Development*. Vienna University of Economics, Master's Thesis.

Livesey, Sharon M. (2001) Eco-Identity as Discursive Struggle: Royal Dutch/Shell, Brent Spar, and Nigeria. *Journal of Business Communication*, 38(1): 58–91.

Loewen, James W. (1996) *Lies My Teacher Told Me: Everything Your American History Textbook Got Wrong*. New York: Touchstone Books.

Luntz, Frank (2007) *Words That Work. It's Not What You Say, It's What People Hear*. New York: Hyperion.

Lynas, Mark (2004) The sixth mass extinction. *New Statesman* 23 February 2004, 23–5.

McCarthy, Michael and Carter, Ron (1994) *Language as Discourse. Perspectives for Language Teaching*. Harlow: Longman.

McGilvray, James (1999) *Chomsky. Language, Mind, and Politics*. Cambridge: Polity Press.

Makkai, Adam (1973) A Pragmo-Ecological View of Linguistic Structure and Language Universals. *Language Sciences*, 27: 9–23.

Marcuse, Herbert (1964/1968) *One Dimensional Man*. London: Routledge & Kegan Paul/Sphere Books.

Martin, Jim R. (1984) *Factual Writing: Exploring and Challenging Social Reality*. London: Edward Arnold.

Mautner, Gerlinde (1997) *Only Connect*: Critical Discourse Analysis Meets Corpus Linguistics. Paper for ESSE 4, Debrecen, 5–9 September 1997.

Mautner, Gerlinde (2000) *Der britische Europa-Diskurs: Methodenreflexion und Fallstudien zur Berichterstattung in der Tagespresse*. Wien: Passagen-Verlag.

Mead, George H. (1934) *Mind, Self and Society*. Chicago: Chicago University Press.

Mill, John Stuart (1859) *On Liberty*. London: John W. Parker and Son. (Himmelfarb, Gertrude (ed.) (1974) Harmondworth: Penguin.)

Mills, C. Wright (1959) The Cultural Apparatus. *The Listener*, March 29. Reprinted in I. L. Horowitz (ed.), *Power, Politics and People. The Collected Essays of C. Wright Mills*, 405–22. New York: Ballantine Books.

Millstone, Erik and Lang, Tim (2003) *The Atlas of Food and Farming. Who eats what, where and why*. London: Earthscan.

Monsanto Company (2003) "Products & Solutions", "Integrated Businesses", "The Monsanto Pledge 2003". <http://www.monsanto.com/monsanto/images/control/footer_monsantoworldwide.gif>(Last accessed 12 September, 2003)

Mühlhäusler, Peter (1996) Linguistic Adaptation to Changed Environmental Conditions: Some Lessons from the Past. In A. Fill (ed.), *Sprachökologie und Ökolinguistik*, 105–30. Tübingen: Stauffenburg Verlag.

Mühlhäusler, Peter (2003) *Language of Environment, Environment of Language. A Course in Ecolinguistics*. London: Battlebridge Publications.

Nelson, Julie A. (1996) *Feminism, Objectivity and Economics (Economics As Social Theory)*. London: Routledge.

Newbrook, Carl (2005) *Ducks in a Row. A–Z of OFFLISH*. London: Short Books.

New Internationalist (2002) Inside Business. How Corporations Make the Rules. *New Internationalist*, 347: 9–28.

New Internationalist (2003) The Politics of Food and Farming. Peasants' Revolt. *New Internationalist*, 353: 9–35.

O'Neill, John (1972) *Sociology as Skin Trade. Essays towards a Reflexive Sociology*. London: Heinemann.

Orwell, George (1944) Politics and the English Language. Reprinted in Bronwell, Sonia and Angus, Ian (eds.) (1968) *Essays, Journalism and Letters of George Orwell. Volume IV*, 156–70. Harmondsworth: Penguin,

Orwell, George (1949/1967) *1984*. London: Secker and Warburg/Harmondsworth: Penguin Books.

Oxford (2005) *Oxford Advanced Learner's Dictionary of Current English* (7th edition). Oxford: Oxford University Press.

Partington, Alan (1998) *Patterns and Meanings. Using Corpora for English Language Research and Teaching*. Amsterdam/Philadelphia: John Benjamins.

Pateman, Trevor (1980) *Language, Truth and Politics. Towards a Rational Theory for Communication*. Lewes: Jean Stroud.

Petras, James and Veltmeyer, Henry (2002) *Globalization Unmasked: Imperialism in the 21st Century*. London: Zed Books.

Philo, Greg and Berry, Mike (2004) *Bad News from Israel*. London: Pluto Press.

Pilger, John (2004) *Tell Me No Lies. Investigative Journalism and Its Triumphs*. London: Vintage.

Pilger, John (2006) The return of people power. *New Statesman* 4 September 2006, 14–15.

Pioneer (2003) Company Philosophy—The Long Look, The Pioneer Way of Doing business. <http:/www.pioneer.com_info/llook.htm> (Last accessed 12 September, 2003)

Poole, Steven (2006) *Unspeak*. London: Little, Brown.

Ravetz, Jerome (2006) *The No-Nonsense Guide to Science*. Oxford: New Internationalist Publications Ltd.

Read, Herbert (1968) *A Concise History of Modern Painting*. London: Thames and Hudson.

Robinson, Joan (1962) *Economic Philosophy*. Harmondsworth: Penguin Books.

Roddick, Anita (1998) A third way for business, too. *New Statesman* 3 April 1998, 24–25.

Said, Edward (1993) *Culture and Imperialism*. London: Vintage.

Salkie, Raphael (1990) *The Chomsky Update. Linguistics and Politics*. London: Unwin Hyman.

Sapir, Edward (1921) *Language. An Introduction to the Study of Speech*. New York: Harcourt, Brace & World.

Schäffner, Christina and Wenden, Anita (eds.) (1995) *Language and Peace*. Aldershot: Dartmouth Books.

Schleppegrell, Mary J. (1996) Abstraction and agency in middle school environmental education. In J. C. Bang, J. Døør, R. J. Alexander, A. Fill and F. Verhagen (eds.), *Language and Ecology: Eco-Linguistics. Problems, theories and methods. Essays for the AILA 1996 Symposium*, 27–42. Odense: Odense University.

Schumacher, Ernst Friedrich (1973) *Small Is Beautiful. A Study of Economics as if People Mattered*. London: Blond & Briggs Ltd.

Seabrook, Jeremy (1994) Vested Disinterests. *New Statesman and Society* 20 May.

Sekula, Allan (2003) *Performance under Working Conditions.* (ed. Breitwieser, Sabine.) Vienna: Generali Foundation.

Shiva, Vandana (2000a) Poverty & globalisation, 5th Reith Lecture. *British Broadcasting Corporation (BBC) series "Respect for the Earth".* <http://news.bbc.co.uk/hi/english/static/events/reith_2000/lecture5.stm> (Last accessed 12 September, 2003)

Shiva, Vandana (2000b) *Stolen Harvest: The Hijacking of the Global Food Supply.* Cambridge, MA: South End Press.

Shiva, Vandana (2001a) Violence of Globalization. *The Hindu* (New Delhi, India) March 25, 2001 (no pagination).

Shiva, Vandana (2001b) 'The Poor Can Buy Barbie Dolls'. Removal of QRs in India and the Fate of the Poor. *New Renaissance magazine* 10.4 (no pagination). <http://www.ru.org/10-4Shiva.htm>.

Shiva, Vandana (2002a) Terrorism As Cannibalism. *ZNet Commentary* January 23, 2002 (no pagination).

Shiva, Vandana (2002b) On Pests, Weeds And Terrorists: Weaving Harmony Through Diversity. *ZNet Commentary* December 1, 2002 (no pagination).

Shiva, Vandana (2003a) Globalisation And Its Fall Out. *ZNet Commentary* April 5, 2003 (no pagination).

Shiva, Vandana (2003b) The Crisis Of Potato Growers In U. P. *ZNet Commentary* April 24, 2003 (no pagination).

Shiva, Vandana (2003c) Biotech Wars: Food Freedom Vs Food Slavery. *ZNet Commentary* June 24, 2003 (no pagination).

Shiva, Vandana (2003d) W.T.O. Agreement On Agriculture. *ZNet Commentary* September 10, 2003 (no pagination).

Shiva, Vandana (2003e) Coke: Hazardous Even Without Pesticides. *ZNet Commentary* September 25, 2003 (no pagination).

Sinclair, John (1991) *Corpus, concordance, collocation.* Oxford: Oxford University Press.

Singh, Rajnath (2003) Agricultural development in India. Press Information Bureau, Government of India, 8th August 2003 Agriculture, Independence Day feature. <http://pib.nic.in/feature/feyr2003/faug2003/f080820031.html> (Last accessed 27 December, 2003)

Smith, Dan (2003) *The Atlas of War and Peace.* London: Earthscan.

Smith, Neil (2004) *Chomsky. Ideas and Ideals* (2nd edition). Cambridge: Cambridge University Press.

Steiner, George (1975) *After Babel.* Oxford: Oxford University Press.

Stern, Nicholas (2007) *The Economics of Climate Change.* Cambridge: Cambridge University Press.

The Ecologist (1972) *A Blueprint for Survival.* Harmondsworth: Penguin.

Targett, Simon (1994) Brutal New World. *The Times Higher* March 4 1994, 19.

The White House (1996) *A National Security Strategy of Engagement and Enlargement.* Washington, DC: The White House.

Thorne, Steve (2006) *The Language of War.* London: Routledge.

Trampe, Wilhelm (2001) Language and Ecological Crisis. Extracts from a Dictionary of Industrial Agriculture. In A. Fill and P. Mühlhäusler (eds.), *The Ecolinguistics Reader. Language, Ecology and Environment,* 232–40. London and New York: Continuum Press.

Van Dijk, Teun A. (1995) Discourse Analysis as Ideology Analysis. In C. Schäffner and A. Wenden (eds.), *Language and Peace,* 17–33. Aldershot: Dartmouth Books.

Vidal, Gore (2002) *Perpetual War for Perpetual Peace.* Forest Row: Clairview.

Vidal, Gore (2003) *Dreaming War. Blood for Oil and the Cheney–Bush Junta*. Forest Row: Clairview.

Vidal, Gore (2004) *Imperial America. Reflections on the United States of Amnesia*. Forest Row: Clairview.

Vonnegut, Kurt, Jr. (1973) *Breakfast of Champions*. Frogmore, St. Albans: Granada Publishing Ltd.

Vonnegut, Kurt, Jr. (1982) *Fates Worse than Death*. Spokesman Pamphlet No. 80. Nottingham: Bertrand Russell Peace Foundation Ltd.

Waring, Marilyn (1988) *If Women Counted: A New Feminist Economics*. New York: Harper & Row.

Wenden, Anita (1995) Critical Language Education. In C. Schäffner and A. Wenden (eds.), *Language and Peace*, 211–27. Aldershot: Dartmouth Books.

Williams, Raymond (1958) *Culture and Society 1780–1950*. London: Chatto and Windus/Harmondsworth: Penguin.

Williams, Raymond (1962) *Communications*. Harmondsworth: Penguin.

Williams, Raymond (1971) *Orwell*. London: Fontana.

Zinn, Howard (1990) Aggressive Liberalism. In H. Zinn, *The Politics of History* (1970 1st edition), 195–208. Urbana and Chicago: University of Illinois Press.

Zinn, Howard (1995) *A People's History of the United States: 1492 to Present* (revised and updated edition). New York: HarperPerennial.

Index